# 365
## *Daily*
# DEVOTIONS

*by teen girls*
*for teen girls*

*compiled by*
*Patti M. Hummel*

B&H
PUBLISHING GROUP
Nashville, Tennessee

978-1-4336-8782-2


Published by B&H Publishing Group
Nashville, Tennessee


Dewey Decimal Classification: 242.63
Subject Heading: GIRLS \ TEENAGERS \ DEVOTIONAL LITERATURE


All Scripture quotations are taken from the Holman Christian Standard Bible®, Copyright
© 1999, 2000, 2002, 2003, 2009 by Holman Bible Publishers.


Printed in LongGang District, Shenzhen, China, July 2015


1 2 3 4 5 6 7 8 • 19 18 17 16 15

# Introduction

As a teen girl do you find yourself attacked intensively by the onslaught of Hollywood's idea of what you should be and what you should be doing with your life? Do you need help to combat what the world is trying to sell you? Are you finding that the struggle between opposing forces (biblical truth and Satan's fun message) is difficult for you to endure? Do you find that you are clueless about how to ward off the enemy and how to bring glory to God in your life?

From the pages of *Teen-to-Teen: 365 Daily Devotions by Teen Girls for Teen Girls* you will meet girls from many different places in the world who are much like you, experiencing similar pressures and going through similar circumstance. This book provides a glimpse into their lives as they are now able to praise God for His guidance, Grace, and His help in their time of need. You will find between the covers:

Understanding who you are in Christ

Recognizing your need to make room in your life for God and your family

Nuggets of wisdom that will help you in your daily walk as a Christian teen

Precious cordials from God the Father to you, His daughters

Messages of hope

Encouragement for your future

Help in overcoming the attacks Satan throws at teens

B&H Publishing Group is making this powerhouse book available as a ministry tool to build up and bless teen girls the world over. *Teen-to-Teen: 365 Daily Devotions by Teen Girls for Teen Girls* will cause its readers to want to turn to God and His Word for what they need to be mighty women of God in their homes, with their families, in their communities, in their churches, and in every aspect of ministry God calls them to.

*Teen-to-Teen: 365 Daily Devotions by Teen Girls for Teen Girls* should be on the reading list of every teenage girl. This is a gift to Christian families, to the church, and to a world that has for too long discounted God's depth of wisdom and inner beauty that His young daughters possess. It is my prayer that each teen girl who reads this book will be, as 2 Corinthians 2:15 explains, "For to God we are the fragrance of Christ among those who are being saved and among those who are perishing."

Dr. Fred Luter Jr. President, The Southern Baptist Convention
Franklin Avenue Baptist Church, Senior Pastor
Husband, father to a son, and to one of God's precious daughters

# Forging on with Hope

"Be strong and courageous; don't be terrified or afraid of them. For it is the LORD your God who goes with you; He will not leave you or forsake you." —Deuteronomy 31:6

In the drought and the sickness,
There's a piece of hope in my heart.
This hope gives me strength to push through
The pain and suffering.
This hope is peaceful, this hope loves.
This hope is the Lord God Almighty.
It is God who gives me strength and passion
To strive ahead, and have hope,
And to trust in the Lord,
For I know that He will be by my side.

We sometimes feel that we are alone and that we have no one to turn to. God is our comforter at all times, even if no one here on earth is willing to help. Whether you are going through the loss of family or family troubles, God is right by your side, giving you strength. God will always bring us through the pain, we just have to put our faith and trust in Him. Speaking from personal experience, God has put pain in my life for a reason. Those times of trouble taught me to rely on God more, and to trust that His plan for my life was greater than my own. By trusting God, I was able to see the good aspects of my suffering. God gave me strength; He gives it to us all.

Layne Coleman: 14, Little Rock, AR
The Church at Rock Creek and Little Rock Christian Academy, Little Rock, AR

# 2

# Jesus Never Changes!

## "Jesus Christ is the same yesterday, today, and forever."
### —Hebrews 13:8

When I was nine, my sixteen-year-old cousin died in a car accident. Three years later, my papa died from lung cancer. Two years later, a lady very dear to me, my "adopted" grandma, passed away from a heart attack. The summer after ninth grade, my granddaddy got very sick and died, and five months after that my granny died from an aneurism. During those times of loss my faith was tested. I questioned God: *Why, why me, why now, and why do I have to lose so many people that I love?* I wondered if God really loved me all the time. The losses I was going through didn't seem like something you would allow to happen to someone you love. I wondered if God really knew what He was doing at that time, because life felt like a big mess. But then I would open God's Word. I read verses that told me He would never leave me or forsake me. I read that He knows the plans He has for me. I saw a verse that says the Lord is near to the brokenhearted, one that assured me all things work together for the good of those who love the Lord, and another that says Jesus Christ is the same yesterday, today, and forever. These verses reminded me of the character of God. He is the same God yesterday, when the world seemed right; today, when you're going through the toughest trial yet; and forever. Forever, He is love. Forever, He is good. Forever, He is for you and for me. During the hard times in my life I learned to not base what I thought about God on my feelings, but on the truth of His Word. I had to cling to the truth that He is exactly who He says He is, no matter what, always and forever!

McKenzie Sutton: 17, Waverly Hall, GA
Cornerstone Baptist Church, Ellerslie, GA; Homeschooled

# A Greater Vision

"Humble yourselves, therefore, under the mighty hand of God, so that He may exalt you at the proper time, casting all your care on Him, because He cares about you." —1 Peter 5:6–7

If someone offered to buy you a $50,000 Mercedes Benz in one year, or to get you a brand new bicycle right now, which would you choose? Obviously, you'd wait. Yet many times, we do the exact opposite. Instead of waiting patiently and allowing God to work things out for our good, our impatience gets the best of us, and we can't wait. Esau couldn't wait, so he traded his birthright to his twin brother, Jacob, for a bowl of lentil soup. He traded his whole inheritance to feed his craving of the moment. Did you know that the familiar lineage of "Abraham, Isaac, and Jacob" should have read "Abraham, Isaac, and Esau"? It should have been Esau's name in the place where Jacob's name is, but Esau was greedy and had tunnel vision. He could only see what felt good right then, instead of looking at the cost for the long run. We can look at the story and wonder why he would trade something so valuable for something so momentary, but we do the same thing. We sell out and settle for a lesser version of a greater vision. So, what's your "bowl of soup"? Are you thinking of settling on a relationship, your reputation, your popularity, or the trust of your parents? Whatever that is, don't let your "appetite" control you like Esau's did. The devil prowls around like a roaring lion, looking for someone to devour. Jesus offers us short-term pain, with long-term pleasure. I don't know about you, but there is no way that I am going to trade the best God has planned for my life for a bowl of lentil soup!

Hannah McGee: 15, Springdale, AR
Cross Church Springdale Campus, Northwest, AR; Shiloh Christian School, Springdale, AR

# Now That's a Plan!

## "For I know the plans I have for you'-this is the Lord's declaration-plans for your welfare, not for disaster, to give you a future and a hope."

—Jeremiah 29:11

Soccer had always been a major part of my life. Between competitive soccer, high school soccer, and indoor soccer, I played year-round. I had always been an aggressive player, so injuries were nothing new to me. I wasn't too worried when I broke my wrist. It would heal and, in the meantime, I could still play soccer with a cast. When it didn't heal, and I found out I'd have to have a bone graft, I was so upset. I was nervous, angry, and frustrated. I was really upset with God. I didn't understand why my near future had to be ruined with this surgery. My high school soccer team was expected to win the district championship and hopefully have a second chance to go to the state tournament. I'd barely be able to walk (because they would be taking a bone from my hip) let alone play in a championship game. Why *now*? For the longest time I let myself sulk and took my anger out on those around me. I'm sure I wasn't too much fun to be around. After my surgery, I realized that this was all part of God's plan for me. Maybe He put this struggle in my life to show me that He knows what's best for me better than I do. I learned that the plans I have for myself are nothing compared to the plans God has for me. God has a plan for each of us, but the only way for us to know our purpose is by knowing God's Word. Do you know God's Word and, if not, are you willing to learn?

Makenzie Thomas: 16, Sevierville, TN
First Baptist Church and Gatlinburg-Pittman High School, Gatlinburg, TN

# Slow Fade

"When the Spirit of truth comes, He will guide you into all the truth. For He will not speak on His own, but He will speak whatever He hears. He will also declare to you what is to come." —John 16:13

We all know the feeling. It forms in the pit of your stomach when you know what you're doing is wrong. This feeling, better known as the conviction of the Holy Spirit, is given to guide us in our daily lives. When the uneasiness strikes, we have two choices: listen or ignore. Recently, I received a CD from my parents, the latest album by a popular band. I was totally excited and couldn't wait to hear it. On my way to school the next morning, I popped it in and was shocked by what I heard. Right away, the Holy Spirit grabbed me. I knew these songs brought no glory to God, and they praised things He stood against. At first, I told myself I was being overly sensitive and gave the band another chance—big mistake. When the guilt continued, I began to justify listening to it. *My Christian friends love this band, so it's OK for me to listen too,* I thought. I also tried the "I listen to Christian music most of the time" approach. In a final attempt to silence the Holy Spirit, I claimed I was only listening to it because I liked the beat. Slowly the conviction I first felt began to fade. Apparently my justifications worked, or so I thought. For days I listened to it nonstop. Soon I noticed that the songs played through my head constantly, distracting me from my walk with the Lord. When we tell the Holy Spirit "no," He backs off. He does not force Himself on us. As Christians, we are to live a life completely surrendered to Him. We cannot walk in the Spirit and continue playing in the world. Are you trying to silence the Holy Spirit's voice in your life? He will guide you in your daily choices if you let Him.

Carson Gregors: 17, Albany, GA
Sherwood Baptist Church and Sherwood Christian Academy, Albany, GA

# 6

# Worrywart

*"Don't worry about anything, but in everything, through prayer and petition with thanksgiving, let your requests be made known to God."*

—Philippians 4:6

Are you a worrier? I certainly am! I worry about how I look, what people will think about me, and I worry about what my career is going to be. Once I worried that this guy I liked didn't like me. It was during this time that Philippians 4:6 hit me. Don't worry about anything, huh? Yeah, right. Instead of following the advice of this verse, I let my mind wander and worry however much it wanted, which was at least once every day. Over the next few months, I imagined the worst scenarios, and they replayed in my head constantly. Eventually, the worry left me totally miserable. I broke down and wrote my heart out in my journal. And then I prayed. I told God how I was feeling and that I didn't want to feel this way anymore. I asked what He was doing in my life and why I had to go through this uncertainty. Again, I was brought to Philippians 4:6. After that night, every time I felt myself start to worry, I prayed and I asked God to teach me how to trust Him and to let Him do what He wanted with my life. Slowly, I began to not worry so much, and I had even begun coming to God with other situations I was facing. As time went on and I pushed the worry out of my mind, I began to be happier. Then I grew overconfident. I didn't come to God with my worries anymore. I started to think that I could handle life on my own again now that I was past a rough spot. And you know what happened? I was miserable again. I still slip up, but I've come to realize that praying about something is infinitely better than worrying about it.

*Kaylin Calvert:* 18, Medical Lake, WA
Airway Heights Baptist Church, Airway Heights, WA; Homeschooled

# Being a Light

"In the same way, let your light shine before men, so that they
may see your good works and give glory to your Father in heaven."
—Matthew 5:16

People sometimes wonder why I keep an empty root beer bottle on my desk. I must admit, it does look out of place when surrounded by family photos and scribbled verses, but it serves as a reminder that my actions are noticed not only by God but by those around me. Most days we interact with countless people: close friends, family members, and complete strangers. Each of them has an open window to observe us. What do they see? Jesus instructs us to "let your light shine before men" so that God will be glorified. We live in a world that will attempt to ensnare us, that disguises itself in pleasure to attract our sinful hearts. However, Christ has freed us and gives us new desires for Him! Philippians 2:15 tells us to honor God in our actions, "that you may be blameless and pure, children of God who are faultless in a crooked and perverted generation, among whom you shine like stars in the world." This world may be fallen, but we can witness to it about God's grace by acting as living examples of Christ! God has given us the strength to resist sin and has given us a wonderful hope for the future. This hope in us should shine out in our actions, so that people will ask and we can tell them about the gospel (1 Peter 3:15–16). People notice when we refuse to swear, drink alcohol, read popular but degrading magazines, dress immodestly, or watch certain movies. They wonder why. You see, that bottle on my desk was an "award" for showing spirit while abstaining from alcohol. Others may view it as a fun tradition. For me it says we can glorify God in word and deed, and people will take notice. And that is one way God accomplishes His purpose through us!

Kristin Goehl: 18, Princeton, MA
Bethlehem Bible Church, West Boylston, MA; Princeton University, Princeton, MA

# 8

## Too Young?

**"Let no one despise your youth; instead, you should be an example to the believers in speech, in conduct, in love, in faith, in purity."**

—1 Timothy 4:12

Have you ever felt you were too young or too immature to do something? I know the feeling. I'm a thirteen-year-old girl who has been around older people all my life. When I try to socialize with adults or teens they kind of just ignore me. Even at youth group, the older kids just pass me by because "I'm too young." I felt too young to write for this devotional. I prayed, asking God to give me strength. Jeremiah 1:6–7 says, "But I protested, 'Oh no, Lord, God! Look, I don't know how to speak since I am only a youth.' Then the Lord said to me: Do not say, 'I am only a youth,' for you will go to everyone I send you to and speak whatever I tell you." Jeremiah was a prophet that followed God even in his youth. This text gave me the strength to keep serving even in my youth. I remembered all the times I brought light to others through my words and actions, even to people who were older than me. God had opened my eyes and gave me this to share with you. He also gave me the verse 1 Timothy 4:12: "Let no one despise your youth; instead, you should be an example to the believers in speech, in conduct, in love in faith, in purity." This text reminded me not to let others get me down and it built my confidence more than ever. When you start to feel like you're too young, I hope you'll do what I did. I hope you pray that God will give you the strength to remember you are not too young and to remember 1 Timothy 4:12. Don't let your youth get in the way of serving. Remember Jeremiah who, even though he was young, served God with all he had to offer. You are never too young to serve God.

**Deanna N. Davis:** 13, Fairchild Air Force Base, WA
Airway Heights Baptist Church, Airway Heights, WA; Medical Lake Middle School, Medical Lake, WA

# Being a Godly Friend

## "Iron sharpens iron, and one man sharpens another."

—Proverbs 27:17

Most people say that they have friends. These friends consist of the group of people they hang out with, their peers. Would you be comfortable telling every one of your friends your deepest feelings, pains, and struggles? Not likely. I know in my case there are very few of my friends I would share these things with; certainly no more than three. So what separates these special friends from the rest of our group? The people we feel safe being around and sharing our heart with should put God first. It has become important to me to try to think and pray before giving friends advice because, when they confide in me, I should do everything in my power not to lead them astray. Our relationship should be built upon truth and trust. Another thing that makes a relationship really strong is faithfulness. Faithfulness can be seen when a best friend sticks with a friendship even if the other friend doesn't always reciprocate. I don't mean that if you try to be a friend to someone and you grow apart that you should always keep trying. There is a time to move on. But if a relationship is struggling, and you are certain that God still wants you in the friendship, then you should obey Christ despite the situation. When a friendship is strong, it is important that you both share what is going on in your life and not try to be so strong for the other person that you keep your struggles to yourself. We were given friends to grow in Christ together. None of us are called to be the kind of friend that we ought to be alone. We all need Christ to support us and our friends. Are you trying to be the kind of friend God has called us to be? Do you really believe that God will help you if you do choose to try?

Rebekah Byrd: 16, Tulsa, OK
Evergreen Baptist Church, Bixby, OK; Homeschooled

# While We Were Still Sinners

## "But God proves His own love for us in that while we were still sinners, Christ died for us!" —Romans 5:8

While we were still sinners, He died for us. While we were putrid and filthy, Jesus gave His life so that we might live. He loved us so much that He hung on a cross, was buried, and rose again because of His unfailing love. God hates sin; He hates it so much that He can't even look at it. Yet He allowed His Son to be fully covered in the sins of His people. Think of all the people in the world right now. There are over seven billion humans on earth; add to that number the generations before us and to that number the generations after us. Out of that enormous number, how many of us sin? We all do; every one of us. No one is exempt! And we all sin a lot. So multiply a person's sins for his or her entire lifetime by that unthinkable huge number of all the people who will ever walk this earth, then we begin to better understand the number of sins that Christ took upon His shoulders on that horrible day. God couldn't even look upon His own perfect Son because of our sin. And yet, Jesus did this with a willing heart. He loved us so much that He endured the torture and the pain of His death. No one else can ever love us as much as God does. And we can never love others as much as He loves them. But His standards should be our goal. We will never be perfect on this earth as Jesus was, but He died so that we might strive to be more like Him each day. Our duty as Christ followers is to bring glory to our Father. We do that by imitating Him, by being His reflection so others can see His majesty. "Make your own attitude like that of Christ Jesus" (Philippians 2:5).

Sarah LaCognata: 14, Belleview, FL
Church @ The Springs, Ocala, FL; Homeschooled

# Perseverance

**"So we must not get tired of doing good, for we will reap at the proper time if we don't give up."** —Galatians 6:9

In middle school, peers came to me and told me their problems—whether it was a friend issue, boy troubles, or even suicidal thoughts. I would give them advice, encouragement, and enough help to get them through their problem. The first time it happened, I was surprised. The second time, I was flattered, but the more people came to me throughout middle school, the more emotionally and spiritually tired I grew. I was tired because I was trying to help my peers with my own strength instead of God's! In Zechariah 4:6, the Lord says, "Not by strength or by might, but by My Spirit." I learned that the hard way. I became bitter and wondered why I had to help everyone else while nobody seemed to help me. Before I knew it, nobody wanted to be around me, because all I did was complain about my problems. The bitterness, selfishness, complaining, and failure to listen to the Holy Spirit cost me my friends. I was stuck in a self-dug hole of self-pity and I started to let myself believe that nobody cared about me. Then I remembered the verse 1 Peter 5:7: "Cast all your cares on Him, because He cares about you." I started to read my Bible. I learned that I can leave my troubles at the feet of Jesus. I learned that if I do everything by the Holy Spirit's love I won't have to worry. So even through my mistakes God has taught me many things! Galatians 6:9 says, "So we must not get tired of doing good, for we will reap at the proper time if we don't give up." When you go through trials and problems and everyday situations, remember that God cares about you, that you should do everything by the Holy Spirit, and to keep persevering!

Sara E. DuBois: 16, St. Peters, MO
First Baptist of St. Charles, St. Charles, MO; Fort Zumwalt East High School, St. Peters, MO

# Someone

## "There are different ministries, but the same Lord."

—1 Corinthians 12:5

So you're saved, you pray and read your Bible, and you believe wholeheartedly in God, but there's always that someone. Who's "someone," you ask? Someone is that person that prays a little better than you, has more verses memorized than you, and can speak better than you ever will. You feel like the things you do for Christ go unnoticed because people are always paying more attention to someone. But don't worry; you aren't the first person to have a someone. For Miriam and Aaron, it was their brother Moses (Numbers 12). They talked about him behind his back because they were jealous that he was in a higher position of authority. Saul's someone was David (1 Samuel 18:12–16). Saul was jealous of David's successes and responsibilities. First Corinthians 12:12–27 uses the analogy of a human body to demonstrate how the body of Christ works. "For as the body is one and has many parts, and all the parts of that body, though many, are one body—so also is Christ" (v. 12). We, as Christians, are all many parts that create one unit or body in Christ. "But now God has placed each one of the parts in one body just as He wanted" (v. 18). Each member of the body is distinctively important because we all have something to contribute, just as eyes are needed to see and ears are needed to hear. "So if one member suffers, all the members suffer with it; if one member is honored, all the members rejoice with it" (v. 26). We have to work together because we need each other. When you begin to compare yourself to your someone, keep in mind that she may be an arm and you may be a leg. Both are equally important, but serve two completely different purposes in relation to the body. What is your ministry?

Kelsey Roberts: 18, Albany, GA
Sherwood Baptist Church and Sherwood Christian Academy, Albany, GA

# Run with Endurance

"Therefore, since we also have such a large cloud of witnesses surrounding us, let us lay aside every weight and sin that so easily ensnares us. Let us run with endurance the race that lies before us." —Hebrews 12:1

On October 20, 2012, my mom and I ran a half-marathon. It was long and hard, but we had been training for it all summer. We worked on our endurance, our speed, and our form; and we were greatly rewarded for all that hard work when we crossed the finish line. We definitely weren't the fastest or the best, but we did it! The Christian life is like a race. It's hard and takes much work, but at the end it will be so worth it. The Christian race is something you will be running all your life once you are saved, and you will train as you run. You grow as you go. Hebrews 12:1 says to lay aside the sin that ensnares us, so that we are able to run better. To lay aside our sin we must be in the Word daily, so we can know what is righteous and true, and know what sin is. We must also "pray constantly" (1 Thessalonians 5:17). We can ask for strength for our run and for help in laying aside our sin. As we run, we look forward to the end, eternity with Christ. We will all run our race differently and accomplish different things in life. Some may lead thousands to Christ and be known worldwide, while others faithfully serve with the preschoolers at their church. We don't have to be the best in the Christian race, and we aren't the first to finish. We will all be rewarded with eternal life and Jesus welcoming us at the finish line saying, "Well done."

Tyra Ruisinger: 17, Raymore, MO
Summit Woods Baptist Church, Lees Summit, MO; Homeschooled

# Telling Others about God

"Haven't I commanded you: be strong and courageous?
Do not be afraid or discouraged, for the LORD your God
is with you wherever you go." —Joshua 1:9

We all know someone who hasn't accepted Jesus as his or her savior. For some of us, these people are family members or close friends. These are people we care about dearly and wouldn't want anything to happen to. Many times it can be hard to bring Jesus up in a conversation and, when we do, it can get pretty awkward. A lot of people struggle with talking seriously to others about God, including myself. I used to be really shy, but as I've gotten older, I've become a lot more open to others. Still, sometimes I worry about what others will think of me if I bring God up in a conversation. One verse that has helped me is Joshua 1:9. In this verse, God tells us, "Be strong and courageous . . . for the LORD your God is with you wherever you go." This promise gives me confidence in the fact that no matter what happens, and no matter what people think of me, God will always be there with me. God wants us to be strong and courageous. That's how He designed us. So the next time you want to talk to someone about God, be confident and just go with it. God will always be by your side in every situation. You can even shoot up a small prayer for help at any time. Know that nothing can stop you with the presence of God. "I am able to do all things through Him who strengthens me" (Philippians 4:13).

Erin France: 14, Anchorage, AK
First Baptist Church and Eagle River High School, Anchorage, AK

# Hatred

"Lᴏʀᴅ, don't I hate those who hate You, and detest those
who rebel against You? I hate them with extreme hatred;
I consider them my enemies. Search me, God, and know my heart;
test me and know my concerns. See if there is any offensive
way in me; lead me in the everlasting way." —Psalm 139:21–24

There are some people out in this big world of ours that love to make life miserable. A lot of people are just hard-headed and some people just need some common sense. I've had people hurt me, and I've had people to hurt my closest friends. I don't mean the casual hurt feelings that you get over in a day. It was the kind of hurt that pushed me toward hate. I always covered it up by saying, "I don't hate them, I just dislike them with a strong passion," or "They're just hard to love." It took me a while to admit that I actually hated these people. My preacher taught on sins one night and he got on a tangent about hate. Did you know that when you hate someone, you're committing murder with your heart? God sees hatred as murder, and that did not sit well with me. I was mad at these people, but I would never want to kill anyone, no matter how wrong they may have been to me or anyone else. The hardest part of all this was forgiving these people. I was afraid of forgiving, because what if they just did it all again? However, it's not a matter of forgive and forget. Forgive, but don't forget, because if you forget and just let them walk back into your life, they will do it again. They have to regain your trust. Ever since I heard that hatred was equal to murder, I have been able to love more than ever, because I would never want to kill anybody.

Breanna Smith: 17, Sharon, SC
Hillcrest Baptist Church and York Comprehensive High School, York, SC

# The Way God Sees You

**"I will praise you because I have been remarkably and wonderfully made. Your works are wonderful, and I know this very well."** —Psalm 139:14

Being hard on myself comes easily, as I tend to focus on the bad things that have happened and my imperfections. When I compare myself to others, I tend to forget about the way God sees me. God sees me as "perfect" the way He made me, and I need to remember that. This really hit me when my half-brother David was born with only three fingers on his right hand. I was sad and scared for him, because I know how mean people can be and didn't want him to be made fun of. Psalm 139:14 says, "I will praise you because I have been remarkably and wonderfully made. Your works are wonderful, and I know this very well," became David's verse. His song is "Fearfully and Wonderfully Made" by Matt Redman, from Psalm 139:14. This verse and this song remind me that we are wonderful the way God made us, even if the world sees imperfections. Even when there are smaller things, like we think we are dumb or not good enough or not pretty enough, we have to remember that God made us holy and blameless in His sight. As Ephesians 1:4–5 says, "For He chose us in Him, before the foundation of the world, to be holy and blameless in His sight. In love He predestined us to be adopted though Jesus Christ for Himself, according to His favor and will." God loves you no matter what, and He is on your side. No matter what people tell you, you are the best *you* there can be because that is the way God made you, created in His image. When your self-confidence is low, think of these verses to help you remember how God made you in His image. God is amazing and loves us more than we can even imagine.

Allison Fisher: 14, Raleigh, NC
Providence Baptist Church and Leesville Road High School, Raleigh, NC

# Into the End Zone

"Don't you know that the runners in a stadium all race, but only one receives the prize? Run in such a way to win the prize."

—1 Corinthians 9:24

I love football! There's something so exciting about watching two teams battle it out just so they can run the ball into the end zone. Sometimes you wonder why something that seems so simple takes forever. I have my favorite NFL teams and my favorite NCAA teams. I love watching our local public high school play, and any chance I have to participate in a friendly game of two-below or two-hand touch I'll take it. Give me a Madden game and I'll be occupied for hours. We Texans love football. Some of the high school stadiums here could be considered NCAA-sized. Perhaps part of my love for football originates from a comparison. The game of football reminds me of our struggle as Christians. When a wide receiver catches the ball, he is expected to run hard and run fast, gaining as many yards as possible. It's a race against time and the defense. The defense will go to great lengths to ensure that the receiver doesn't reach the end zone. Paul often refers to the Christian lifestyle as a race. If we run our race well, doing our best, when we reach the finish line there's a prize waiting for us. His name is Jesus, and He has a special crown waiting for us. It works the same as if we were a running back or a receiver. We run hard, we run fast, and we give it our all, then the prize in the end zone is completely worth it. It's going to be hard, because the defense we're working against is not limited by penalties or rules. We will be tackled and need our Lord to pick us up and heal our souls and bodies. We may want to give up and forfeit, but we trust in God to see us through to the end zone. Our hope is in Him!

*Hannah Arrington*: 15, Borger, TX
First Baptist Church and Texas Virtual Academy, Borger, TX

# So You Think You Want to Date?

**"My son, keep your father's command, and don't reject your mother's teaching."** —Proverbs 6:20

*Dating!* Just the mention of the word makes fathers itch and mothers twitch, but there comes a time in every teenager's life when we think we are ready to begin dating. Most teens treat dating as if it is no big deal, but the reality is that it's one of the most serious decisions of a young person's life. When I turned fifteen, I just knew I was ready to start dating. Homecoming was coming up, and a friend of mine asked me to the dance. I liked him, but I had never seriously talked to my parents about dating because I was afraid of what they would say. I finally worked up enough courage and, to my surprise, after much thought they both decided I could handle it. I really enjoyed spending time with him, and he eventually became my first boyfriend. Shortly after we started dating, I got so caught up in my relationship with him that I got off track in my walk with God. That strain caused the demise of our relationship, and I was very sad. My parents said that heartbreak will happen throughout the dating process and I must keep my focus on God and let Him direct my dating path. Their advice reminded me of Proverbs 6:20–23 where it says, "My son, keep your father's command, and don't reject your mother's teaching . . . bind them to your heart . . . corrective discipline is the way to life." If you're ready to date, please seek God and your parents' wisdom. The Bible tells us to listen to the advice of our parents even when we think they have no clue about our world. Their wisdom will help us throughout life—especially the teen years.

T'Yanna Janai Jackson: 15, Slidell, LA
Franklin Avenue Baptist Church and Salmen High School, New Orleans, LA

# Missionaries

> "Then He said to them, 'Go into all the world and preach the gospel to the whole creation.'" —Mark 16:15

The term "missionary" reminds us of someone who leaves the country to go share Jesus. I know several long-term missionaries, and you may know some too. God calls us all to be missionaries without ever leaving our hometowns. The mission field is your school, the store; even your own home can be your mission field. You can be a witness for Jesus anywhere. There are many ways to share Jesus with others: you can go on a short-term mission trip with your church or your family, have a conversation about being saved with someone, or just show Jesus' love by helping someone or volunteering with a church or organization. There are many more ways to show Jesus, and you shouldn't limit yourself to a list. You can always be thinking of and finding new ways to be a missionary. To be the most effective in sharing Jesus, you should choose to do things that are comfortable for you. I'm a very quiet and shy person and would choose to volunteer with my church rather than start a conversation about Jesus with someone on my own. We should choose to witness in the most effective ways. Acts 1:8 says, "But you will receive power when the Holy Spirit has come on you, and you will be My witnesses in Jerusalem, in all Judea and Samaria, and to the ends of the earth." Jesus gave this command to His disciples, to start witnessing in their own town and eventually to the whole world. We can do this, too, when we find ways to be missionaries and share Jesus right where we are!

Brenna R. Strain: 15, Spokane, WA
Airway Heights Baptist Church, Airway Heights, WA; Medical Lake High School, Medical Lake, WA

# The "Gracie" of God (Part 1)

"Therefore, confess your sins to one another and pray for one another, so that you may be healed. The urgent request of a righteous person is very powerful in its effect." —James 5:16

Do you truly believe that prayer changes things? Have you ever witnessed a prayer-induced miracle that is simply remarkable? I have had the honor of personally knowing a miracle; a miracle named Dixie Grace "Gracie" Douglass. When Gracie's mother was pregnant with her, everything looked fine until she was twelve weeks into the pregnancy. It was then that the doctors discovered a cystic hygroma, a fluid-filled sac caused by a chromosomal malformation. It was at the back of the baby's right ear and wrapped around to the back of her left ear. The doctors said that the pregnant woman would soon miscarry and she was given the option to abort since there was nothing medically that could be done. But her trust was in God. She said no to the abortion. God had given her this baby and, with His help, they were going to do everything they could to save her. Sixteen weeks into the pregnancy, more bad news from the doctors. Baby Gracie's lungs had collapsed and she had fluid all around her body. The doctors said she had less than six weeks to live because her heart was working too hard and because the fluid was creating multiple problems. At twenty weeks, their church held a prayer service for family, church members, and others to pray for Gracie, the unborn daughter. Gracie's mother prayed and sincerely gave herself over to God. With this prayer, she became calm and accepting. The power of prayer, and corporate prayer, is why this family knew their hope was in Christ. Jesus wants us, even teenagers, to be committed to prayer, trusting Him in the simple things so that we learn how to trust Him with the big things life throws at us.

*Hanna Wilbourn:* 14, Seymour, TN
Seymour First Baptist Church and The King's Academy, Seymour, TN

# The "Gracie" of God (Part 2)

"Therefore, confess your sins to one another and pray for one another, so that you may be healed. The urgent request of a righteous person is very powerful in its effect." —James 5:16

Only God could save Baby Gracie, who was still in the womb, in danger of losing her life. But her parents trusted Him to do His work to save her, which brought peace to them in their darkest hour, even when the doctors delivered more bad news. The doctors said baby Gracie's prognosis was still bad, but she was somehow still alive. Miraculously, the fluid began to dissipate. The doctors told her mother that Gracie would probably not survive even if she was carried full-term because her lungs were collapsed. There was little hope given by the medical professionals. At thirty-seven weeks, on August 11, 2010, Gracie was born. Nine days later, she was released from NICU and breathing fine on her own. Gracie is now a bouncy, talkative two-year-old. She is loving and sweet, and her family fully recognizes God's hand in her miraculous survival. Do you see how prayer can impact not just one life, but many? Scripture says that we should pray for one another, and when we pray, we should truly believe in what we are praying, trusting God for His highest. So do not forget to pray for others and do not be afraid to ask for prayers from others for yourself and your needs. Prayer does make a difference, and so can you.

Hanna Wilbourn: 14, Seymour, TN
Seymour First Baptist Church and The King's Academy, Seymour, TN

# The Box

*"More than that, I also consider everything to be a loss in view of the surpassing value of knowing Christ Jesus my Lord."*

—Philippians 3:8

We all have the desire to live inside the box, to make our home inside the little box, and live nice, comfortable, teen lives as we shrink into the box and remain confined within its walls. The walls of this box are made up of sin such as cursing, sexual immorality, lying, gossip, idolatry, or pride. We build these walls ourselves. Why do we do this? There's one simple reason: acceptance. Teens long to be accepted by our peers, to be popular, to be well liked, so we build up these walls and try to remain inside the boundaries of what is considered cool. We trap ourselves in this box. We believe Satan's lie that if we build this box around ourselves and live inside it, we will be happy. He tells us if we stay inside, like other teens, that our lives will be fulfilling and fun. This is not true. Living inside the box produces an empty life. The friends in your little box will lead you down roads you never intended to go. You will discover that everything you lived for inside your little box was fleeting and held no value. Your popularity led you nowhere. The box is a lie, and it is evil. We do not have to live confined inside the walls of sin. Popularity and being accepted by others holds absolutely no eternal value, but Jesus does. He offers fulfillment, love, and acceptance. He is the answer to everything you are looking for. A relationship with Him surpasses the greatness of any other thing in life. Things like popularity and being considered cool are a complete loss compared to a relationship with Christ. So break out of your little box by turning to Jesus. The two just don't compare.

*Alaina Clem*: 14, Albany, GA
Sherwood Baptist Church and Sherwood Christian Academy, Albany, GA

# Crazy Love, Crazy Quiet, Crazy Life

**"Above all, put on love—the perfect bond of unity."** —Colossians 3:14

Crazy: that's the only way I can describe life as a high school sophomore. Sometimes I want to sit down and cry with papers due, friend problems, tests to study for, church, and about a bajillion other things I think I need to accomplish right this second. However, I'm taking these few moments to stop and think. One of my favorite songs is "Love Like Crazy" by Lee Brice (written by Doug Johnson and Tim James and released by Curb Records, June 2010). The lyrics tell the story of a couple getting married out of high school and still being together fifty-something years later. My favorite part of the song is when he sings, "Never let your prayin' knees get lazy, and love like crazy." Now, it's a little weird walking around saying, *"I love youuu!"* to every person you meet, but the little things we do really express our love toward them. Love others like crazy. I think we are all used to a little craziness in a schedule, but why not go crazy with loving others, too? The verse above says, "Above all, put on love—the perfect bond of unity." Perfect unity in my crazy life sounds pretty great. Also, as I'm thinking through my crazy moments, I think of my crazy quiet moments with God. Psalm 46:10 says, "Stop your fighting—and know that I am God." When I sit still and talk to my Daddy, everything floods into my head. Friends, the stress over school, my cousin being deployed, and me getting braces for a third time, etc. They all just go *bam* in my head. I can't even sort out my thoughts! But, the thing is, God knows. He knew all the craziness before I ever thought it. I encourage you, teen to teen, to stop and do a couple of things. Be crazy in love. Have crazy quiet moments. And keep on living your crazy life. 'Cause He promises us that this is only a season of craziness.

**Hannah Thompson:** 15, Leesburg, GA
Sherwood Baptist Church and Sherwood Christian Academy, Albany, GA

# Handling Hardships

"I will instruct you and show you the way to go; with
My eye on you, I will give counsel." —Psalm 32:8

Growing up in Gatlinburg has allowed me to develop a love for skiing because Ober Gatlinburg Ski Lodge is pretty much in my backyard. No matter how good you are at skiing or snowboarding, there are always tourists who have absolutely no idea how to ski and they can be dangerous. They can hit you from behind, the side, or the front, and usually there is no way to avoid it. Sometimes skiing injuries can be life-threatening or life-altering. Just like there are crazy, out-of-control tourists, there are sin, hardships, and temptations that can hit a good skier from any side and knock them right into the side of the mountain. No matter how much a person studies God's Word or believes and has faith as strong as a mountain, they can be knocked down and beaten up by the waves of life. The Bible helps us to become better at handling whatever life throws at us, just as a skier improves by spending more time on the slopes, developing his or her skills. Skiers soon become more accustomed to sudden movements and are able to avoid disasters with better speed and agility. The Bible is like a guide for life and helps everyone to take on hardships with better wisdom and agility. Proverbs 2:6–9 says, "For the Lord gives wisdom; from His mouth come knowledge and understanding. He stores up success for the upright; He is a shield for those who live with integrity so that He may guard the paths of justice and protect the way of His loyal followers. Then you will understand righteousness, justice, and integrity—every good path."

*Abby Fortner*: 15, Gatlinburg, TN
First Baptist Church and Gatlinburg-Pittman High School, Gatlinburg, TN

# You Are a Masterpiece!

"For we are His creation, created in Christ Jesus for good works, which God prepared ahead of time so that we should walk in them."

—Ephesians 2:10

Ephesians 2:10 has always been one of my favorite verses. It simply makes me feel special. As young adults, we sometimes feel like we are not good enough or not pretty enough. I have, at times, felt ashamed of whom I am or felt like I'm not beautiful. But God says it plainly in His Word that we are His creation, His workmanship, we're His masterpiece! He made us in Christ Jesus who died on the cross to save us from an eternity separated from God. He put thought into it when He created you and me. He took time when He gave us our individual personalities. There is nothing that you or I can do to make Him love us any more or less. When God created you and me, He had a specific plan in mind just for our lives. He had a plan for you and for me even before either of us was born, and He wants us to trust Him with our futures. Always remember that you are a beautiful, wonderful, marvelous, one-of-a-kind masterpiece created by the King of kings and Lord of lords! What could make one feel more special?

Imani McBean: 14, Leesburg, GA
Mt. Zion Baptist Church and Sherwood Christian Academy, Albany, GA

# A Delayed Visit

## "So when He heard that he was sick, He stayed two more days in the place where He was." —John 11:6

Lazarus is sick, and his sisters, Mary and Martha, send word to Jesus letting Him know. (As if He didn't know already, but that's beside the point.) Anyway, when Jesus gets the news, you would think that He would rush to their aid, rent the next donkey He saw, and take off to save the day. But He doesn't. He waits two more days before going. And by the time He gets there, Lazarus is dead. Mary and Martha let Him know their hearts. They are like, "If You had been here, if You hadn't delayed in helping us, our brother would still be here." Jesus heard their cries and wept with them, but He knew what was coming—He was going to raise Lazarus from the dead. His delay, His plan was for the glory of God and for those around that they might believe. I recently experienced something like that. My sister was sick and in the hospital. During that time, I questioned God, wondering why He was delaying healing my sister. Selfishly, I wanted her and my mom home with us. I wanted a normal life again. (She was only in the hospital for a week, but it felt like much longer.) And even though God heard my heart and knew what I wanted, He was waiting for the perfect time to begin to heal my sister so that we would see His hand at work and learn to trust Him more. Sometimes the things God takes us through are hard and they might not always end well. But we have to trust that all the things God does are for His glory and our good. He always has our best interests at heart. And His timing is always perfect.

McKenzie Sutton: 17, Waverly Hall, GA
Cornerstone Baptist Church, Ellerslie, GA; Homeschooled

# Ermahgerd!

"Do not misuse the name of the LORD your God, because the LORD will not leave anyone unpunished who misuses His name." —Exodus 20:7

How many times a day do you say, "Oh my God"? Once or twice, or maybe twenty times each day? In reality, we shouldn't say it at all. That is taking the Lord's name in vain, after all. That is one of the Ten Commandments. It is a sin just like murdering or stealing. Cursing isn't specifically stated in the Bible, but it is just rude and shows a lack of aptitude in proper and appropriate language. I've grown up in a home where using the word *butt* isn't very acceptable, so "Oh my God" is completely off limits. There are many times where I have been around people who curse and take the Lord's name in vain. It isn't hard to find someone who says, "Oh my God," on a regular basis. When you think about it though, what kind of example does that set for the people who aren't Christians? As a Christian, you aren't supposed to be this holy person who never sins. That is impossible because ALL have sinned. However, we are supposed to set the example. And constantly taking the Lord's name in vain is not setting a good one. Think twice before you text "OMG!" Or exclaim, "Oh my God!"

Megan Medford: 14, Bryant, AR
The Church at Rock Creek and Bryant High School, Little Rock, AR

# Enthroned Forever

"The Lord is in His holy temple; the Lord's throne is in heaven. His eyes watch; He examines everyone." —Psalm 11:4

Have you ever felt like there was a moment when God deserted you in your time of need? A time when you were in distress and yet you didn't feel like God was near? Recently, I experienced that feeling. Life was going fine and nothing seemed to be out of the ordinary, until one day my family received a phone call that my uncle had died. I could hardly believe the news, yet it was true. The next days following were awful. *How could God do this to me? Why did He let this happen? Doesn't He see the pain that it caused me and my family?* These were all questions that constantly floated through my mind. Yet, in time, God allowed me to stumble upon this verse in Psalms. God showed me that although it felt like I was deserted, He had never left my side. He was right there with His arms wrapped around me. He still was enthroned and in control. He showed me that He saw what I was going through and was there to comfort me. God is enthroned and sees a bigger picture that we cannot see. He sees how everything fits together, but we just see a small speck in the big scheme of things. Don't lose faith. God does not let anything go unnoticed nor is He shaken by anything. He has ordained your life, and He knows the plans for it. All we have to do is seek Him.

Haley Smith: 16, Tarpon Springs, FL
Calvary Baptist Church and Calvary Christian High School, Tarpon Springs, FL

# 29

## Going Back in Time Is Not an Option!

"For the discerning the path of life leads upward, so that he may avoid going down to Sheol." —Proverbs 15:24

"Not that I have already reached the goal or am already fully mature, but I make every effort to take hold of it because I also have been taken hold of by Christ Jesus. Brothers, I do not consider myself to have taken hold of it. But one thing I do: Forgetting what is behind and reaching forward to what is ahead, I pursue as my goal the prize promised by God's heavenly call in Christ Jesus. Therefore, all who are mature should think this way. And if you think differently about anything, God will reveal this also to you" (Philippians 3:12–15). Have you ever wished that you could go back in a time machine and change a choice you made in life? What you have to keep in mind is that no one is perfect or without sin. But now is the time to repent from sin and turn from the road that leads to destruction. To experience the most joy possible in life, we as Christians need to raise our white flags and surrender our whole lives to serving our Father and making choices that are pleasing to Him. God is forgiveness. God is love. It is sometimes hard to forgive ourselves for choices, but keep in mind that by sending Jesus to die as atonement for our sins on the cross at Calvary, God washes our sins white as snow.

Michi Werner: 16, Gatlinburg, TN
First Baptist Church and Gatlinburg-Pittman High School, Gatlinburg, TN

# Will of God

"By the mercies of God, I urge you to present your bodies as a living sacrifice, holy and pleasing to God; this is your spiritual worship. Do not be conformed to this age, but be transformed by the renewing of your mind, so that you may discern what is the good, pleasing, and perfect will of God." —Romans 12:1–2

I love thinking about the future. I have it all planned out. I could tell you all about my future husband and me, up until the day that we die. I know none of this will work out my way, because I'm not in control, nor do I want to be. I would completely mess everything up. So I ask, "What is God's will for my life?" Romans 12:1–2 is the answer for every person who knows and loves God.

1. "Present your bodies as a living sacrifice, holy and pleasing to God." This shows that God wants every part of us. As Christians, we give our whole lives over to God to be in His control. If we are willing to sacrifice our lives, and live our lives on the edge for God, then we are doing what we should be.

2. "This is your spiritual worship." Worship isn't something that only happens on Sundays and Wednesdays. Living your life for God is a DAILY sacrifice. That's true worship. Not a "just when I feel like it" type of thing. You worship God through your actions and living for Him.

3. "Do not be conformed to this age, but be transformed by the renewing of your mind." Plain and simple, we must live our lives to please God. "Love God, and love people."

"Be in the world, not of the world." This is a quote I hear quite often. It sums up this passage at the beginning quite well. If we, as Christians, will love God and His people daily and do not become part of this world, we will be following God's will.

Hannah Savage: 16, Dodge City, KS
First Southern Baptist Church and Dodge City High School, Dodge City, KS

# Looking Like the World

*"Do not be conformed to this age, but be transformed by the renewing of your mind, so that you may discern what is the good, pleasing, and perfect will of God." —Romans 12:2*

Looking like the world is quite possibly the most prevalent problem that Christians have, especially in school. Romans 12:2 says to "be transformed." That means you change. When you accept Christ, people who don't even know your name should see an obvious, visible difference in you, at school and everywhere you go. That means something different for everyone because God has placed us all in different places. The song "Live Like That," by Sanctus Real, is a very convicting song, especially when it comes to this subject. I encourage you to listen to it after you read this and really focus on the words. We have to be different, or our witness is not as strong. When we present the gospel and talk about how Christ has changed us, it's gonna make a lot more sense if the person has actually seen it with their own eyes. What does this mean? This means that when someone is getting made fun of, you stop it because they are fearfully and wonderfully made (Psalm 139:14). It also means that we don't wound people by gossiping about them (James 4:11). Gossip is one of those things in our lives that we don't easily recognize as wrong. The Bible tells us that God hates gossip. These are only a few ways to not look like the world. When people look at their yearbook thirty years from now and see your picture, let them remember you as "the Jesus freak." That's the biggest compliment you can get. It's not going to be easy to be different. But God does not call us to a life of comfort; He calls us to a life of obstacles. The cause of Christ is worth it.

Christa Morgan: 17, Alabaster, AL
Westwood Baptist Church and Thompson High School, Alabaster, AL

# Important Lessons from Psalms

## "Keep your tongue from evil and your lips from deceitful speech."

—Psalm 34:13

There is a reason why swear words are called bad words. It is wrong to use foul language, which can lead to bad habits, and using them shows a terrible lack of knowledge and good vocabulary! In Psalms, God says to "keep your tongue from evil" or, in other words, don't use curse words—words that Jesus would not want us using. If our ultimate goal in life is to be like Jesus, why would we even consider uttering a curse word? I know as a teenager it is hard to go to school and not hear a swear word every so often. One thing to remember is not to sink to the level of those using bad words. God wants our speech to be something that we will never be ashamed of and that we can use anywhere, even in church or in front of our parents! Pray for God to give you strength to say nice and encouraging words. Also, do not let your lips speak lies. Did Jesus ever lie or deceive people? No. God loves you and wants to hear pleasing words and the truth. Being honest is also the basis for respect and trust. The more you tell the truth, the more liberties and respect you will receive from family members and friends. Keep reaching out and wanting to be like God. It may seem difficult, but nothing is impossible with God.

Hannah Zimmerman: 16, Greencastle, PA
Greencastle Baptist Church and Greencastle-Antrim High School, Greencastle, PA

# Be Different

*"For am I now trying to win the favor of people, or God? Or am I striving to please people? If I were still trying to please people, I would not be a slave of Christ."* —Galatians 1:10

Face it. Teenage girls struggle with being accepted, and I am one of them! From watching as the cool kids were chosen on the elementary playground to all the high school stresses and drama, I have experienced every type of desire to be accepted. God got hold of my life in the ninth grade, but that desire and longing was still there. I got caught up in trying to fit in with two girls who were older than I and had a negative influence on my life. While trying to be like them, I lost who I was. I didn't look, act, or talk like myself anymore. I wanted to make a difference and be a leader for Christ and He showed me that I needed to lay everything down, humble myself before Him, and know His will for my life. This is how I came up with this little phrase I tell myself every day: "Be different!" Let me explain. Who is going to remember the average teenager who made decent grades, dated on and off throughout the years, had the newest and latest things, went to all the parties, and played on the championship team? Maybe somebody, for a few years. However, more people may well remember the weird girl who stood for purity, never dated, had cheap clothing, went home after the championship game, and loved the Lord with all her heart. Not that being remembered is my goal, but rather leaving a legacy of someone who strives to please the Lord. If we are slaves of God, then shouldn't our actions make an impact on the people around us? So be different! Someone who looks like the world is trying to be accepted by it, and that person can't be a slave of God.

*Annalise Clem*: 17, Albany, GA
Sherwood Baptist Church and Sherwood Christian Academy, Albany, GA

# Future

**"'For I know the plans I have for you'-this is the Lord's declaration-'plans for your welfare, not for disaster, to give you a future and a hope.'"** —Jeremiah 29:11

Many times, as teens, we go through difficult things that impact our lives. But God has told us that He holds our lives in His hands. Despite what you go through in your daily life, God is there for you. As for me, I grew up in Africa where everything is different than here in America. I really didn't understand why we were the family that continued to carry their baggage after a family dispute. My dad was a drunkard, and my mother was quick to anger. I always wondered why I had to walk with my brother and sisters one-and-a-half hours to go to church, yet our family was never at peace. I remember the time my parents got divorced when I was in seventh grade. Life was too hard for us in my family. One of my friends knew what we were going through, so she shared Jeremiah 29:11 with me, which helped me remember that God has promised my family a future full of hope. We teens get discouraged very quickly, but we have to be patient and wait for the Lord. God says that He will show us things we have never thought of, so don't be troubled over the hard times you have gone through. Let God take control of your life now. God's promises to us are always true, and He said He came to fulfill them. So as teens we should not let what happened in our past determine our future. In Proverbs 23:18 the Bible says, "For then you will have a future, and your hope will never fade." We should always remember we were born to be witnesses to our generation, so we should live for Christ and serve Him forever.

*Lilian Gatheca*: 16, Nanyuki, Kenya (exchange student living in Albany, GA)
Sherwood Baptist Church and Sherwood Christian Academy, Albany, GA

# Judge Not

"Do not look at his appearance or his stature, because I have rejected him. Man does not see what the Lᴏʀᴅ sees, for man sees what is visible, but the Lᴏʀᴅ sees the heart." —1 Samuel 16:7

Have you ever judged someone before really knowing them? I once made the acquaintance of a girl who is a mutual friend of all of my friends. I'm embarrassed to say it, but I decided right then and there that there was something about her I didn't like. I thought, *Oh well, I can't like everyone, right?* What an awful assumption to make, to decide I don't like someone before I know the first thing about them. One night all of my friends and this girl hung out and we all engaged in small talk. I realized that I had made a snap judgment of her. I had decided that she was proud and thought much of herself. But, when I got to know her, I learned that she is just quiet, and I hadn't tried to know get to know her. I was content to just assume and leave it at that, but I realized how ridiculous I was being. I thought about what my life would be like if God made a snap judgment of me. If God had just taken one look at me and judged me, I would be on my way to hell. How can I judge someone when God doesn't judge me? How can I judge someone by what I see? God Himself says in 1 Samuel 16:7 that while man sees what is visible, He sees the heart. I took one look at this girl and judged her. At the same time, God looks at me, all of me, and STILL He loves me. So, the next time you find yourself making a snap judgment, think of how God sees you and then try to look at others with His eyes.

Gabrielle LaCognata: 19, Belleview, FL
Church @ The Springs and College of Central Florida, Ocala, FL

# Perspective

## "Serve with a good attitude, as to the Lord and not to men."

—Ephesians 6:7

I love the second part of Ephesians 6:7 because it reminds me that my motives for service should be the Lord, just as everything else in my life should be. There's one specific area in which I've always struggled to give God the glory, and that is with the gift of playing piano. Throughout high school I've come to realize all gifts are God-given. Nothing is from me, and I am nothing apart from the Lord. All the talent and skill in the world is worthless without Him. When I'm not thinking about myself and falsely taking the credit for what He's given me, everything is so much simpler. I don't get extremely nervous during recitals anymore, because I'm not worried about impressing the audience or wondering if they think I'm talented or musical. Having the right perspective opens up ministry opportunities as well. Even when others question me or offer compliments about my piano playing, God can use that time to tell them about Him. Our gifts and skills are chances for us to serve at church, in the community (e.g., nursing homes or hospitals), and to bless family and friends. No matter how much acclaim a person gets, the REAL praise will be when we stand before the Lord and He says, "Well done, good and faithful servant." Have you used the gifts God has given you to "serve with a good attitude, as to the Lord and not to men"?

Tara Greene: 16, Fort Belvoir, VA
Guilford Baptist Church, Sterling, VA; Homeschooled

# A True Follower

"In the same way, therefore, every one of you who does not say good-bye to all his possessions cannot be My disciple." —Luke 14:33

When I started high school, I had no idea what was about to hit me. It was a new school, and I started to make new friends. Before I knew it, I was compromising my faith in almost every area of my life. I tried to ignore the Holy Spirit convicting me, and I would always ask for forgiveness, but I was not truly broken over my sin. Before the start of junior year, my youth group went to summer camp and the Lord began to work in me. Something that I heard there still rings in my head today: "He has given you everything. Why can you not give Him everything?" A few weeks later, Eric and Leslie Ludy spoke at a gathering we had for the girls in our youth. One of the subjects they spoke on was surrender. I finally saw where I went wrong. I had made the Lord my Savior, but I had not surrendered my whole life to Him. There were things I was trying to hold on to. Luke 14:33 says, "In the same way, therefore, every one of you who does not say good-bye to all his possessions cannot be My disciple." I could not be a true disciple of Jesus Christ. John 3:30 says, "He must increase, but I must decrease." In order to truly follow Jesus, we must let Him reign in every area of our life. He wants all, not part of you. Is there an area in your life you aren't letting God have? Ask God to search your heart and reveal whatever you may need to surrender. He can do much greater things through you than you can do on your own. Just surrender.

Victoria Davidson: 17, Newton, GA
Sherwood Baptist Church and Sherwood Christian Academy, Albany, GA

# Love between Friends

## "Love your neighbor as yourself. There is no other command greater than these." —Mark 12:31

While in middle school, two of my friends fought to spend time with me. They began to dislike each other, and they started holding grudges. Fighting over things such as sitting with me on the bus or sitting next to me at lunch was hard for me because I love all of my friends, and I wanted to spend time with both of them. One of my friends didn't invite the other to her birthday party, which created real problems. It was a never-ending cycle of grudges and bad attitudes. There were times when I was upset and confused. I wanted unity between my friends and not to feel I had to pick one over another. One of my friends had surgery on her foot and came to school in a wheelchair. It was up to me and other friends to be sure she got around all right. Even though my other friend was genuinely concerned about the other girl, things did not get better. You may have been in a similar situation, or you may be one of those girls. Whether you're a girl or a boy, there will always be times when friendships are difficult, especially between teenagers, but we must remember that the Lord wants us to love one another. If someone is mean to you, you shouldn't make it worse by fighting back. Matthew 5:43–44 says, "You have heard that it was said, Love your neighbor and hate your enemy. But I tell you, love your enemies and pray for those who persecute you." God wants us to love everyone, no matter how badly they treat you or how hard it can be. Remember that God has told us to love our enemies.

Michaela Reed: 15, Albany, GA
Institutional First Baptist Church and Sherwood Christian Academy, Albany, GA

# Take a Walk with Your Friend

"Enter through the narrow gate. 'For the gate is wide and the road is broad that leads to destruction, and there are many who go through it. How narrow is the gate and difficult the road that leads to life, and few find it.'" —Matthew 7:13–14

One of my friends and I like to ride our bikes around our town. It's a great pastime; we get frozen yogurt or ride to the beach. Once we went in to all the stores on the main business street and asked each of them for a business card. There's not really a point to our rides, we're just hanging out and having fun. It's a lot like what I imagine hanging out with Jesus would be like. Of course, I don't forget that God is all-powerful and created the whole universe, but don't we all imagine every once in a while what it would be like if Jesus came for the day and we got to hang out? Can you imagine? Just hanging out with your Savior? I can. I do it all the time. The verse above compares our life and our salvation to taking a walk. I walk with God. I don't kid myself and try to tell myself that my life is a constant and easy walk with Christ, because I am constantly falling away and rebelling against God. But, in the end, I see that all God wants is for me to love Him, and He will bless me in His perfect way. Do the same. Take the narrow gate and travel the hard road to be with God. Talk to Him in prayer and read His Word to see what He's saying back to you. Take Him with you when you get frozen yogurt or go to the beach. Take Him because God wants to give you so much more than His friendship. He can give you life.

Bronte Stallings: 15, Mt. Pleasant, SC
Citadel Square Baptist Church, Charleston, SC; Wando High School, Mt. Pleasant, SC

# Teen Pregnancy

"Don't you know that your body is a sanctuary of the Holy Spirit
who is in you, whom you have from God? You are not your own,
for you were bought at a price. Therefore glorify God in your body."

—1 Corinthians 6:19–20

Teen pregnancy is much more prevalent than it was, say, fifty years ago. It used to be an embarrassment to get pregnant before marriage, but now girls get television shows for being pregnant as teenagers and for being teen mothers. Hollywood would love for you to think that fornication is not a big deal when, in reality, it is a huge deal. Teen pregnancy is also now showing up more in Christian communities. This is where abstinence comes into play. My family has a tradition that on your sixteenth birthday you receive a Promise Ring. The Promise Ring is a physical representation of your promise to remain pure until marriage. Sometimes when you are tempted to do what you know is sin, and could result in your getting pregnant, just glancing at that ring can help you remember that you promised to not give yourself away before marriage. I look at this ring every day and remember not only the promise to my parents, but to my God as well.

Taylor Dillon: 17, Stafford, VA
Grace Life Community Church, Bristow, VA; Emmanuel Christian High School, Manassas, VA

# Sticks and Stones

"No foul language is to come from your mouth, but only what is good for building up someone in need, so that it gives grace to those who hear."

—Ephesians 4:29

We've all heard the saying, "Sticks and stones may break my bones, but words will never hurt me." We also all know it's not true. In fact, words can be even more painful than a broken bone. They can leave a sting that may last for much longer than a cut or bruise. However, knowing how much our words can hurt doesn't tend to stop us from saying hurtful things. I know I'm constantly guilty of saying things that may either intentionally or unintentionally hurt someone. I may regret and feel guilty for saying these things later, but I can't take back the things I've said. Once they're out, there there's no way of removing them. There's no delete button in life. Hurtful and demeaning words can damage relationships and friendships. They can also crush someone's self-esteem. One thing I constantly try to remember is that I don't always know the entire story. Someone could have had a rough day or may not leave school to go to the same home situation I do. I don't want to hurt someone with my words. I don't want to regret things I've said. Not only do I want to be positive and kind, but I also want to be a good influence on others to always use kind and uplifting words. I know that with God this is possible. I'm going to take the time and effort to bite my tongue and say something encouraging instead. Will you?

Makenzie Thomas: 16, Sevierville, TN
First Baptist Church and Gatlinburg-Pittman High School, Gatlinburg, TN

# "Aca-scuse Me?"

**"The joyful tambourines have ceased. The noise of the jubilant has stopped. The joyful lyre has ceased."** —Isaiah 24:8

My current obsession is the movie *Pitch Perfect*. It is the perfect mix of love, friendship, and the impeccable ability to harmonize. I have always wished life was a musical. To be honest, I get jealous when I watch television musicals and the characters get across exactly what they want to say through music. I cannot sing to save my life, let alone get my point across in a way that isn't completely awkward. I watch *Pitch Perfect* and see Jesse and Beca sing so beautifully, and I feel so insignificant. Luckily, God didn't say, "You must praise Me and sing to Me with the voice of an angel!" or, "If your musical talent isn't up to par, I will no longer listen to you!" Thank goodness He doesn't, or I'd have no chance of my praise making its way to God. Instead, He mentions, "the *noise* of the jubilant." Not "the wonderful angelic singing of the happy people." It is "the *noise.*" If it is praise to God coming out of your mouth, God is ecstatic about the noise. Whether you are off pitch, off key, off beat, squeaky, or don't know the words perfectly, God still loves it. There are so many ways to make your musical talent seem worthless. There are endless a cappella groups and shows like *American Idol, The Voice, X-Factor,* and movies like *Pitch Perfect* that highlight the judgmental views people have on those who are less talented vocally. But God doesn't care. To Him it doesn't matter how capable you are of singing, playing an instrument, and clapping along with the music. He just wants you to praise and worship Him. He deserves it and it's time to show Him.

*Hannah Savage*: 16, Tarpon Springs, FL
Calvary Baptist Church and Calvary Christian High School, Tarpon Springs, FL

# Enjoy the Journey

"You reveal the path of life to me; in Your presence is abundant joy; in Your right hand are eternal pleasures." —Psalm 16:11

Life can overwhelm us sometimes; it is messy, confusing, stressful, and sometimes seems hopeless. *Where am I going to go to college? How am I going to buy those new shoes I want? Why doesn't he like me?* These are among the many "problems" thrown at teens every single day. We forget that we have an Almighty Father who laughs at these problems, and He looks at them as bumps in the road of this journey He has created called life. God already has the tiniest details of our lives planned out, so why do we waste our energy worrying when we could be praising and delighting in our Maker? However cheesy and cliché it may seem, instead of shedding sorrow over a problem, try to find the beauty in it. Be thankful for the struggles and hardship that help us to grow. Love God enough to form a relationship with Him. Start with today. Watch the sunrise, dance in the rain, count the stars, or just simply breathe in the fresh air. God created each of these for us to enjoy. We need to know Him as Savior. Now, I am not saying just because you form a relationship with God that you will get everything you have ever wanted in life because, surprisingly, that would be extremely disappointing. If God only gave us what we wanted, life would be pretty boring. Be open to the idea that God has a plan so abundantly overwhelming for you, that no one can ever imagine where it may lead. It's exciting, it's mysterious, it's captivating, and it's one of a kind. So, be patient, be open minded, dig into the world, look for the beauty, endure the hardships, and hang on tight for the crazy, awesome, unknown journey called life. And get ready to enjoy it with the maker Himself, your best friend.

Reagan Bell: 17, Tuscaloosa, AL
Valley View Baptist Church and Hillcrest High School, Tuscaloosa, AL

# Caught Drifting?

"Keeping our eyes on Jesus, the source and perfecter of our faith, who for the joy that lay before Him endured a cross and despised the shame and has sat down at the right hand of God's throne."

—Hebrews 12:2

I don't know about you, but I love going to the beach! I love digging my feet into the sand and splashing about in the water. One time I sat my bag on the shoreline and went into the water and began floating and swimming around. After a short while though, I looked up and couldn't recognize where I was. I searched for my bright blue bag, but to no avail. I began to get nervous. How far had I drifted? But then, I saw it! Way in the distance was my beach bag, and I began slowly but surely swimming against the current to get back to it. Our faith can be a lot like this story, if we aren't careful. Hebrews 12:2 reminds us by saying, "Let us fix our eyes on Jesus," which in this case, can represent my blue beach bag. If I hadn't been so enthralled with the ocean to look up more than once, I probably wouldn't have drifted as far out as I did. In our relationships with Jesus, it's important to remember to keep your eyes on Him, so we won't drift off and lose our way. But because He loves you unconditionally, He will always come back to find you, even if it requires a little work on your part!

Emily Pitts: 16, Palm Harbor, FL
Calvary Baptist Church and Calvary Christian High School, Clearwater, FL

# Being Different

"According to the grace given to us, we have different gifts: If prophecy, use it according to the standard of one's faith; if service, in service; if teaching, in teaching; if exhorting, in exhortation; giving, with generosity; leading, with diligence; showing mercy, with cheerfulness."

—Romans 12:6–8

The Bible tells us that we have different gifts and that we need to use them according to the standard of our faith. We need to know what our gifts are and how to use them according to the Bible. In middle school, one of the major things I struggled with was fitting in. It frustrated me that being normal came so easy to others, and to me it was so hard. I became obsessed with trying to find the right clothes, say the right things, and be friends with the right people. I started to lose sight of who I was, and the struggle between being who I was and who I thought I wanted to be stressed me out. Needless to say, I wasn't too happy with myself, and I lived in constant fear of others' opinions of me. One day God showed me that it was so hard for me to be normal because I wasn't made to be. Everyone is made special and unique because God has different plans and purposes for all of us. If you feel like you're not good enough for society's standards, it's probably because God made you to stand for things that He puts in your heart, to be different and not just normal. So instead of trying to be something you're not, embrace the person God made you to be and enjoy your differences.

Blair Bodnarchuk: 17, Raleigh, NC
Providence Baptist Church and Wakefield High School, Raleigh, NC

# Doubting and Patience

## "And my God will supply all your needs according to His riches in glory in Christ Jesus." —Philippians 4:19

Teenagers and parents worry about college and tuition. As a senior in high school I began to wonder how I was going to pay for college. I was working a part-time job and going to school full-time. My mother is a single parent with little extra spending money. College tuition was due in a couple of days and I was sitting in my room crying, wondering how I was going to pay for school, or even get the money in time. I began to pray and asked God to help me because I really wanted to attend college. I've been a faithful servant, and I just didn't know the path God had for me. Days grew closer, still worrying and doubting that I would even get to attend school that semester. One night at church, I sensed God working to teach me to let go of the stress and worries, giving everything to Him. I knew in my heart that God was telling me to quit worrying and give the situation up to Him. That night I did, and I felt like the weight of the world had been lifted off my chest. I still wasn't sure about the money, but I knew God had great plans for me. I just had to be patient and wait on God's timing. The next day Mom and I received a call that my grandfather wanted to pay the rest of the tuition. I began to cry and thank the Lord because I knew that blessing was from Him and my grandfather was His servant. I thanked God for His blessing. I learned to be patient and to also give my baggage, stress, doubts, and worries to God. God is bigger and can handle anything as long as we submit and surrender it all to Him. Let it go and give it to God. For not my will, but God's will be done.

Brianna Carter: 19, Sharon, SC
Hillcrest Baptist Church and York Technical, York, SC

# Quitters Never Win, and Winners Never Quit

"Therefore we do not give up. Even though our outer person is being destroyed, our inner person is being renewed day by day. For our momentary light affliction is producing for us an absolutely incomparable eternal weight of glory. So we do not focus on what is seen, but on what is unseen. For what is seen is temporary, but what is unseen is eternal."

—2 Corinthians 4:16–18

I am a cross-country runner. People tell me all the time that running is horrible and one of the most painful things in the world, but I don't agree at all. I love the way I feel after running five miles or a good race. One of the things about running, especially cross-country, is the training. It is tough, hard-core work that tires your body very easily. Practice starts in June, and the final race is in November. Six months of hard, tiring training. By the end of the season, with the state championship race approaching, everyone is tired and worn out, ready for the season to be over, but the end is the most important time of the season. You must not give up and endure the pain to achieve your goal—the state title. The more that you train, the more you are prepared to run a good race. I have amazing coaches and, in 2012, both girls and boys teams won the state title. All of our hard, painful work paid off, and we succeeded. Cross-country can relate to our relationship with God in multiple ways. When we are going through hard trials such as divorce, friendship issues, insecurities, death, etc., that is when we should rely on God most. Trusting God renews and grows our spiritual life. God is always by our side. Worldly situations can bring us down, but it is our faith and trust in God that lifts us up.

Layne Coleman: 14, Little Rock, AR
The Church at Rock Creek and Little Rock Christian Academy, Little Rock, AR

# We Are Never Alone

"Be strong and courageous; don't be terrified or afraid of them. For it is the LORD your God who goes with you; He will not leave you or forsake you." —Deuteronomy 31:6

In the summer of 2012, I traveled with my family to Kenya and met some self-less people. One in particular made a lasting impression on me. One night he told us his story. When he was born, his mother abandoned him, leaving him with his grandparents. Years later, she returned but was not well received by her family and was beaten so badly by a family member that she later died. Sometime afterward, my friend was evicted from his home by his grandfather. Now homeless, he wandered the streets sleeping wherever he could find a place. One night while he was praying, the Lord told him to ask the person he saw the next morning to take him to school. The next morning he did exactly that. He soon learned that the man he had asked was a school principal. This man began to help my friend, and his life has never been the same.

My friend's life story taught me so much. When I look at him, I see a young man who is always smiling and so full of joy. I ask myself how this can be. It is because my friend had faith in the Lord and knew that even in his darkest hour, the Lord was still there watching over him and protecting him. It taught me that when I think I'm alone, God is always with me and that He does love me and care for me. I remember these words from Deuteronomy 31:6, "Be strong and courageous; don't be terrified or afraid of them. For it is the LORD your God who goes with you; He will not leave you or forsake you." That message is timeless. It is for you and for me today!

Mallory McClearn: 16, Leesburg, GA
Sherwood Baptist Church and Sherwood Christian Academy, Albany, GA

# Being a Servant

"So if I, your Lord and Teacher, have washed your feet, you also ought to wash one another's feet." —John 13:14

I was sitting in my regular church pew several weeks ago when I happened to glance over at a familiar man sitting several rows ahead of me. He wore a black suit with dark, old tattered shoes, and he had a crooked smile that was consistently present every Sunday morning when he was healthy enough to attend the service. The characteristic I recall most when I think of this respectable man is his dirty, bruised, callused, and poorly kept hands. As I continued to study his coarse hands, I came to the conclusion that these were the hands of one who truly pleased God. The man with dirty hands was always serving others around him while he was still physically able. He truly had the heart of a servant and you could tell simply by looking at his utilized hands.

God calls for us, on many occasions, to serve others by loving them and caring for them. This requires us to sincerely get into the work we are doing for God, just as Jesus did when He humbly washed the feet of His disciples. Likewise, we are called to willingly serve others even though this can often be a challenge. As I watched cancer slowly take the life of the man with dirty hands, I saw clearly and literally that life is not always a walk in the park. This man continuously made serving others a priority, even though his aggressive cancer was constantly a challenge. Nevertheless, he did not make excuses as to why he could not serve. The man with dirty hands replicated Jesus' attitude by obeying the commands of God and selflessly serving others. Today I challenge you to get your hands dirty by putting others before yourself with a servant's heart.

Danielle Quesinberry: 15, Knoxville, TN
Valley Grove Baptist Church Youth Group, Knoxville, TN; The Kings Academy, Seymour, TN

# Betrayed

"She weeps aloud during the night, with tears on her cheeks.
There is no one to offer her comfort, not one from all her lovers.
All her friends have betrayed her; they have become her enemies."

—Lamentations 1:2

Have you ever been betrayed? Maybe your friend told everyone who you have a crush on. Or your sister told your parents about that party last weekend. Feeling betrayed can hurt. *How could I have trusted them? Why would they do that to me?* A lot of times, people want revenge when they are betrayed. In Leviticus 19:18, God says, "Do not take revenge or bear a grudge against members of your community, but love your neighbor as yourself; I am Yahweh." God wants you to forgive those people who betray you. Trust me, I know it's hard, but it will be worth it in the end for you to be the bigger person.

Maybe your best friend is hanging out with the new popular girls and never has time for you. God may be trying to show you that you don't need that person in your life as the one you depend on. He may be telling you that your confidence is in Him. Don't chase after them; they may hurt you worse than they already have. It might be time to think about who you are and what kind of person you want to be. Find some new friends, ones who aren't going to betray and lie, and ones who love Jesus and who will build you up and edify you. God has a plan for everyone, so don't let yourself fall into the traps of others along the way.

Clara Davis: 14, Little Rock, AR
The Church at Rock Creek and LISA Academy, Little Rock, AR

# Social Media

## "Do not love the world or the things that belong to the world. If anyone loves the world, love for the Father is not in him."

### —1 John 2:15

The world has a very big influence on the lives of teenagers, especially girls, and especially when it comes to social media and other outlets. We need to be careful about the music we listen to, the movies we watch, the celebrities we look up to, and how we use social media. The world tells us that things like money, vanity, sex, and self-interest are all fine. God can bring you out of your comfort zone and use you for His will. Are you willing to be used by God in any way possible? Do not let what the world says dictate your future. Vanity affects most teenagers. The Internet, television shows and commercials, and every other form of advertisement tell us how to look and how to behave in a worldly, sinful way. God is not in them and they are often promoting a sinful agenda. Stay yourself, be who God made you to be. Glorify God in everything you do. Stay in His Word and let Him be your guide. The Bible tells us how to live godly lives. God loves you for you, not you trying to be someone else. We can't be so sheltered as to not notice what pops up on our computer screens, or what is thrown at us during television commercials, but we can be so aware of what God's Word says that He will guard our hearts and minds. The devil wants us to see and to listen to the world and accept what the world has for us. He wants to bring us down in any way he can. Keep your guard up, and ask God to help you make the right choices about what the world puts in your path.

Dianah Edwards: 16, West Monroe, LA
First West Monroe Baptist Church and Northeast Baptist School, West Monroe, LA

# Having a Needy Friend

"Dear friends, let us love one another, because love is from God,
and everyone who loves has been born of God and knows God."

—1 John 4:7

There are different types of friends, and we all have at least one of these: the friend with the funny laugh, the friend who eats and never gains weight, the friend who is always a smarty-pants. And most of us have that one friend who needs a bit more attention and is constantly asking for favors. Well I, like many of you, had a needy friend. I considered her my sister and I loved her a lot, but by the end of the day I was emotionally, physically, and mentally exhausted. My grades began to slip because I was always with her and spent less time with my other friends. Our relationship was a constant uphill battle. I was always trying to pull her up, and she was always trying to pull me down. At the end of a two-year friendship, I was so drained that I let the friendship completely fall through.

My advice for friendship is to not pick a person you think you can fix. That's what I did; I thought I could make her life better, but in reality, I couldn't. Ask God to help you to pick your friends and to know how much time you are to give to them. We never want to hurt people, but sometimes we are not ready for certain relationships. The sooner you realize that only God can fix people, the better.

Taylor Dillon: 17, Stafford, VA
Grace Life Community Church, Bristow, VA; Emmanuel Christian High School, Manassas, VA

# Family Love

"Love is patient, love is kind. Love does not envy, is not boastful, is not conceited, does not act improperly, is not selfish, is not provoked, and does not keep a record of wrongs." —1 Corinthians 13:4–5

Family relationships are sort of bipolar. You love your family members because they see you at your worst and put up with you despite it. There are strong physical and emotional ties that connect you to one another, and they are not easily broken. At the same time, they can also make you insanely irritated. Sometimes they're the most incredible people in the world. Other times, they make you want to scream in frustration! How this is possible has always intrigued me. You have to like someone to be able to love them, right? Well, sometimes I don't like my family members. That was how I always thought about my family of two parents, one sister, and three brothers. And I certainly know that they have had the same thought about me. But then I realized that it is the same thing with our relationships with God. He gets upset with us sometimes, but He never stops loving us. The hard part is loving our families when we don't want to—when you and your parents don't agree about the clothes you want to wear, or when your siblings turn the bathroom light off when you're brushing your teeth. It's the little things that make it so difficult because you put up with them on a daily basis, and you get tired of it. But you know you have to overlook the irritations and love them anyway. In our hearts we love them to death, but there are always those moments where we just don't have the strength to love our families at that particular moment in time. But we don't have to. God will thankfully fill our hearts with His love. The same love that He shows us every day.

Sarah King: 18, Gainesville, VA
Emmanuel Baptist Church and Emmanuel Christian School, Manassas, VA

# I Am Lonely

"I waited patiently for the LORD, and He turned to me and heard my cry for help." —Psalm 40:1

Everyone gets lonely. Loneliness does not have an age preference. Why is it that when we are lonely, we do not seek the Lord? We always look for relationships and then wonder why they fail. We should look at loneliness as an opportunity to build a stronger relationship with God and family. I am learning that focusing on what I do not have instead of appreciating what I do have is not the right way to go. Everything takes time. God has a certain order for everything He wants us to have in life. When we rush things and look for new relationships thinking it will make things better, it can actually cause new problems. When we do things on our own terms it delays the great things that God has for us. Some people who suffer from loneliness even resort to drugs and alcohol. Neither of those things will get rid of the problem. You have to seek godly things, or life will become more difficult. Loneliness can also get better when you focus on other people. If you struggle with loneliness, branch out! Reach out to someone else who is lonely. You can help build each other up while deepening your faith in God. You may also need Christian counseling. Pray and ask God to help you understand that His plans for you are better than we can imagine; all we have to do is trust in Him and He will make a way. Nothing can top what God has for us. God can never fail us like people can. Even our most loyal friends will let us down, but God will not!

Reagan Mi'Cole Brashears: 17, New Orleans, LA
Franklin Avenue Baptist Church and Eleanor McMain Secondary School, New Orleans, LA

# Dating

## "Flee from youthful passions, and pursue righteousness, faith, love, and peace, along with those who call on the Lord from a pure heart."

—2 Timothy 2:22

As you get older, you will become more open to the idea of dating and being in a relationship. The most important thing is finding the right guy to date. Second Corinthians 6:14 says, "Do not be mismatched with unbelievers. For what partnership is there between righteousness and lawlessness? Or what fellowship does light have with darkness?" Maybe there's a guy you really like who's doing the wrong things, things God would not want him to do. Maybe he's not even a Christian, and that's where things get rough. You really want to be with him, but he's just not the right kind of man. God wouldn't want you being in a relationship with him because the guy *will* bring you down spiritually, whether you believe it or not. A boyfriend is a very big part of any girl's life. He will affect the way you think, feel, and act. That is why relationships are so dangerous these days. The world's actions are so sinful. Anything could happen, in just the blink of an eye, that would encourage us to move away from God. My challenge to you: Whatever situation you're in, pray to God. You may have someone you want to be with, you may already be with someone, or you may not even be interested in anyone at all. Begin praying about your future regarding dating, because guys will come along that you will want to be with. Pray for the right man, a man God would want you to be with. Pray for the relationship you may already have now, that it will be glorifying to Him and that you will do things that are right in His sight.

Angela Stanley: 17, Woodbridge, VA
Dale City Baptist Church, Woodbridge, VA; Emmanuel Christian School, Manassas, VA

# Broken Cisterns

"For My people have committed a double evil: They have abandoned Me, the fountain of living water, and dug cisterns for themselves, cracked cisterns that cannot hold water." —Jeremiah 2:13

This world has a lot to offer. There is always a new gadget to play with or new places to see and go. This world never sleeps or stops, and is always changing. It is so easy to find ourselves caught up in the worldly pull and forget God. We get busy with other things and, soon enough, those worldly things become more important to us than spending time seeking God. In Jeremiah, God speaks of how His people have left Him to go after the things of this world. The Israelites were worshipping idols and had forgotten about their one true God. God says that they were drinking out of broken cisterns. Back then, cisterns were kind of like wells that were dug into the ground. The cisterns held the water and also caught more water when there was rain. A broken cistern would have been worthless. Rocks and dirt would have been able to fall in and ruin the water inside. Often that was the only supply of water the people had, and to have a broken cistern would have meant their supply of water was gone. God gives a beautiful picture of how, when we chase after the things of this world, we are drinking muddy and dirty water. God is the clean and living water. We must always remember that God's riches are far better than what the world can ever offer us. Seeking and following Him is worth so much more than the muddy satisfactions of this world.

Taylor Glow: 17, Albany, GA
Sherwood Baptist Church and Sherwood Christian Academy, Albany, GA

# Stop Your Grumbling!

"Do everything without grumbling and arguing, so that you may be blameless and pure, children of God who are faultless in a crooked and perverted generation, among whom you shine like stars in the world."

—Philippians 2:14–15

You have probably heard these verses before. I've grown up with them, and I remember a song with the verses too. The song went through the verses and stopped after "children of God," which was fine! The song was in a video for young kids and it served its purpose well. But I think we should look at the rest of the verse! Let's face it: Doing everything without grumbling and arguing is not fun. It's just not. In fact, it feels tedious, annoying, and difficult, especially if you have siblings. Doing everything without grumbling or arguing is one of those actions that doesn't have an immediate payoff. Or does it? The rest of the verse says that we do everything without grumbling or arguing so that we "shine like stars in the world." I know that TV and magazines will tell you, "You're a star! Be you." The Bible does not mean Hollywood when it says stars. It means the stars in the sky! Have you ever looked at the stars at night? It's so amazing to look at all the dots of light holding back the black sky. Believe it or not, these verses are not trying to steal all your fun. They don't end at, "Do everything without grumbling and arguing." No one does anything without a reason. Usually you do things to please someone, whether it's your parents, your friends, or yourself. As Christians, our goal is to please God. God doesn't ask us to do everything without grumbling or arguing just for the fun of it. It's so that we may be blameless and pure, children of God, and so that we may "shine like stars in the world." Ask Jesus to help you shine like a star!

Isabella Bako: 14, Anchorage, AK
First Baptist Church, Anchorage, AK; Homeschooled

# Wrongdoings

## "For all have sinned and fall short of the glory of God."

—Romans 3:23

Sin! It is everywhere and we cannot get out of its reach on our own. Sin is in our flesh. We are born sinners. Everyone has told a lie at some time in their life; I mean, who hasn't? Think about one lie you have told. Every lie is bad. Every lie is a sin! Sin comes with consequences. Romans 3:23 says, "all . . . fall short of the glory of God."

When we sin we need to confess, repent, and ask God for forgiveness. Also, ask the one you sinned against for their forgiveness. We need to think about what the Ten Commandments teach us, "Do not bear false witness." It is vital that we obey the commandments because God gave them as a model for our obedience. If you're not a Christian, pray this now, "Lord, I am a sinner, please come into my life and become my personal Lord and Savior. I am Yours now. Amen." If you are a Christian, even a new Christian pray often and ask, "God, please fill my lamp with oil and help me to be counted worthy to be part of Your bride! Thanks for being a great God, and please help me to have sweet dreams and good thoughts." Pray in your own words, but they should be appropriate to God. Read your Bible every day, pray, and keep your faith. After reading the Bible it's good to keep your notes to help you remember what you learned. Never give up on God! He won't give up on you! Keep your faith, pray, read the Bible daily, and "Love the Lord with all your heart" (Mark 12:30).

Beraiah Benavides: 14, Sevierville, TN
Pathways Baptist Church, Sevierville TN; The King's Academy, Seymour, TN

# I Am Out of Strength!

"The LORD gives His people strength; the LORD blesses His people with peace." —Psalm 29:11

As a junior in high school, schoolwork and life can swallow me up sometimes. Trying to balance my schedule and have time for all that I want to do can be so tiresome. Recently I was running myself ragged, living on my own strength, and trying to accomplish my agenda on my own. God caught my attention by giving me some minor physical problems. I realized that I was living life on my laptop battery and rejecting the power cord.

God promises to help us if we are only willing, but so often we reject His free gift. He says in Isaiah 40:31, "But those who trust in the LORD will renew their strength; they will soar on wings like eagles; they will run and not grow weary; they will walk and not faint." Jesus said, "Don't worry about your life, what you will eat or what you will drink; or about your body, what you will wear" (Matthew 6:25). It is not His design for us to stress about life and what we will do tomorrow. "Those who know Your name trust in You because You have not abandoned those who seek You, Yahweh" (Psalm 9:10). What a wonderful promise! He will not abandon us. The Enemy tells us that if we trust God, our lives will be completely boring. That is very far from the truth, though, because trusting God with your life is the best thing you could ever do for your future! It gives such a feeling of relief and comfort to know that He is in control. Proverbs 16:20 says, "the one who trusts in the LORD will be happy," and it is so true.

*Hannah Cooksey*: 16, McMinnville, OR
Valley Baptist Church, McMinnville, OR; Homeschooled

# Trust the Lord

"When I am afraid, I will trust in You. In God, whose word I praise, in God I trust; I will not fear." —Psalm 56:3–4

When I was younger I heard a lot about trusting the Lord, but it kind of just lost its meaning. I would hear people say things like, "Just trust God about it," "Put your trust in Him," and "Trust in all circumstances." The whole thing about trusting kind of went in one ear and out the other. Finally, I came to a conclusion that I really didn't know exactly what trusting God meant. Although there were tons of lessons about trusting, I never really knew for me what trusting was all about because it just sounded too generic and broad. A devotional book called *Jesus Calling* helped answer my question about trust. Through this great devotional book, that I totally recommend, I learned that trust is actually a pretty simple thing to do. It doesn't even cost us anything. Trusting the Lord means giving everything to Him and believing that He knows better and more than we do. Even that statement is kind of confusing, but then through God's direction I learned that trusting God can be different for every person. The way I trust Him may not be the way that you do. Either way, when we decide to trust God in a little or big thing, we are saying that we are surrendering everything to Him. There is no half-trusting God. You either do or you don't. It's that easy. One thing I've learned through my trusting-God journey is that nothing can go wrong when we do trust Him. God gives us the opportunity to trust Him, but it is truly up to us whether we choose to do so. We can seriously experience great things when we simply put our trust in Him! Just see by trusting Him today!

Amy Meeks: 16, Tulsa, OK
Evergreen Baptist Church, Bixby, OK; Mingo Valley Christian School, Tulsa, OK

# Repentance and Redemption

"We have redemption in Him through His blood, the forgiveness of our trespasses, according to the riches of His grace." —Ephesians 1:7

Teenagers feel like they are invincible. They think that no matter what they choose to do, there will be no consequences. When you are a strong Christian, people don't usually expect you to deal with the same things that the majority of teens do. I lost my best Christian friends due to a nasty rumor and the pressure of a boy that I liked at the time. I got in with the wrong crowd and, after a while I got pregnant at a really young age. I went to church every week, did Bible study, and we were known as a strong Christian family. But I fell into the trap of many of the devil's lies. I needed to be perfect. I needed to be popular. I needed to please people in the wrong ways to get them to think I was cool. I fell behind in school, and after I got pregnant I had to deal with the looks from others and the consequences to my future.

Unfortunately, after things settled down, I went into labor early and, as a result, I lost the baby. I was way too young to deal with all of the emotion involved with sex, relationships, raising a child, and, of course, losing my daughter. I spent weeks and weeks repenting for how I had acted. I know that I have God's forgiveness and also His love, because He never stopped loving me. As I see girls that act the way I did, I just want to hug them and tell them that they are worth the world. It is so easy to give in to the devil and the many tools that he uses, whether you are a Christian or not. Always keep your guard up; trust in Jesus' love.

Leah Harris: 16, Kodiak, AK
Frontier Southern Baptist Church, Kodiak, AK; Homeschooled

# Power Perfected in Weakness

"But He said to me, 'My grace is sufficient for you,
for power is perfected in weakness.'" —2 Corinthians 12:9

Have you ever wondered why God gave you a certain weakness or struggle? Sometimes it seems that my weaknesses have no purpose but to frustrate and discourage me. They have a very specific purpose though, and 2 Corinthians 12:9–10 reminds us of it: "But He said to me, 'My grace is sufficient for you, for power is perfected in weakness.' Therefore, I will most gladly boast all the more about my weaknesses, so that Christ's power may reside in me. So I take pleasure in weaknesses, insults, catastrophes, persecutions, and in pressures, because of Christ. For when I am weak, then I am strong." Christ's power is perfected through our weaknesses, showing His strength to us and others as He works on our behalf. He also uses our trials and the comfort He brings to us in unexpected ways. Second Corinthians 1:4 says, "He comforts us in all our affliction, so that we may be able to comfort those who are in any kind of affliction, through the comfort we ourselves receive from God." He gives comfort so that we may comfort others. When I read this verse it not only assures me but challenges me to minister to others by comforting them. Through our weaknesses we understand that we can't make it without Christ and that we need Him for everything. And not only do we need Him, it becomes a delight to rely upon Him and watch His hand upon our lives. I entreat you to use the experiences and insight you've gained through your weaknesses to minister to others and encourage them in their struggles.

Tara Greene: 16, Fort Belvoir, VA
Guilford Baptist Church, Sterling, VA; Homeschooled

# God's Grace Is Enough

"'My grace is sufficient for you, for power is perfected in weakness.' Therefore, I will most gladly boast all the more about my weaknesses, so that Christ's power may reside in me. So I take pleasure in weaknesses, insults, catastrophes, persecutions, and in pressures, because of Christ. For when I am weak, then I am strong." —2 Corinthians 12:9–10

Think about the toughest times in your life. Maybe a family member or close friend passed away, or you broke up with your boyfriend. Maybe you and your best friend had a big fight. It could be anything that gets you down and makes you feel like you can't go on. But God's grace can get you through it all. Pour your heart out to Him. Tell Him everything that's bothering you. His grace will fill you up and make you feel whole again.

Or maybe it's a weakness. We all have them. One person is good at something that another person is terrible at. It's kind of like the old saying, "one person's trash is another person's treasure." But in your weakness, God is strong. His grace fills you up and gives you the strength to keep going and not give up. And His grace is something you can always count on. When all else fails, God won't ever leave you or forsake you. Paul said that he took pleasure in his weaknesses, the insults he received, the persecution, and in pressure. When we are weak, we need somebody to lean on; in this case, God. God uses our weaknesses to teach us to depend on Him. When we depend on Him, we grow stronger in our faith in Him. So, when we are weak, we are strong because of the strength God's grace gives us. His grace is enough for our needs.

Hannah Abernathie: 15, Tulsa, OK
Evergreen Baptist Church, Bixby, OK; Homeschooled and Cornerstone Tutorial Center, Tulsa, OK

# Corrupted

"Do not be mismatched with unbelievers. For what partnership is there between righteousness and lawlessness? Or what fellowship does light have with darkness?" —2 Corinthians 6:14

School is a place full of corrupted people who are far from God. It isn't easy to go through each school day without being tempted to conform to the ways of the unsaved. No matter what grade you are in, this problem is inescapable. Being surrounded by these types of people is destructive to Christians everywhere. I have six classes per day. The worst is my sixth and last class: Personal Financial Literacy. Despite how difficult it may sound, it is considered by many to be a class people take to avoid having to do serious work. Therefore, it is full of rebels who prefer to do their own thing rather than listen to the teacher. People who act like they aren't Christians, even though some of them claim they are. You know who I'm talking about; they are everywhere. Second Corinthians 6:14 instructs us to avoid getting too close to people like that so that we are not corrupted by them. It tells us that Christians represent light and nonbelievers represent darkness. It then states that it is not right for light and darkness to form a partnership. From going to a public school all these years, I have learned to stand strong in my beliefs and not be ashamed to be a Christian. School doesn't have to be a place where you are intimidated by the pressure others put on you to conform to the ways of the world. God will give you the strength to persevere and stay pure, even in a place full of corruption.

Callie Spencer: 14, Broken Arrow, OK
Evergreen Baptist Church, Bixby, OK; South Intermediate High School, Broken Arrow, OK

# I'm Supposed to Love Them?

"I give you a new command: Love one another. Just as I have loved you, you must also love one another. By this all people will know that you are My disciples, if you have love for one another." —John 13:34–35

If others talk about you behind your back or make fun of you; if others accuse you of things you did not do; if others have betrayed you, then welcome to high school. It is a part of life that will happen to everyone, even the "coolest" people. Even Jesus was betrayed by His closest friends. First the disciples fell asleep, even though He commanded them to stay awake and keep watch while He prayed. Then, Judas came and handed Jesus over to be killed. His close friend betrayed Him— with a kiss! Though He was innocent! Later, Peter denied even knowing Jesus. Not once, but three times. But, you know what? Jesus still loved each and every one of them. He loved them so much that He still gave up His life for their wrongdoings, even though they had hurt Him and let Him down.

Relationships are tough. Nobody is perfect and people are going to make mistakes. However, it is up to you to choose how to handle these situations. Scripture calls us to love our enemies and be kind to them. Psalm 109 records David crying out to the Lord against those who had betrayed and done evil to him. When being faced with these trials, you should look to David as an example. He treated them as a friend would and, most important, prayed for them. You are commanded to do the same. It is fine to hate the sin being committed, but you must love the person. This is impossible, however, to do in your own strength. You must rely completely on God and He will strengthen you and help you to do what is right, even when everyone around you is doing wrong.

Laura Roggenbaum: 17, Palm Harbor, FL
Calvary Baptist Church and Calvary Christian High School, Clearwater, FL

# Healed by His Wounds

"But He was pierced because of our transgressions; crushed because of our iniquities; punishment for our peace was on Him, and we are healed by His wounds." —Isaiah 53:5

Blood is often a sensitive topic for girls. Just the sight of blood has the potential to send some of us spinning. We frequently associate blood with death and suffering. Isn't it ironic that blood actually carries and supports life? Without blood, life as we know it would not be possible. Blood plays a huge role biologically, but it also is largely significant in Scripture. Adrian Rogers once said, "Cut the Bible anywhere, and it will bleed. The blood of Jesus stains every page." It's true. All Scripture reaches its climax at the life, death, and resurrection of Jesus Christ. Why would God put such a focus on perhaps the goriest, most unpleasant part of the Bible, Christ Himself suffering on a cross? Because in order to save His people from the Father's wrath and eternal damnation, in order to secure eternal life and adoption for His beloved, Christ had to spill His precious blood. He lived the perfect life that we (wretched sinners that we are) cannot. Then, He exchanged His robe of righteousness for our sin. He paid the price so that we don't have to. Isn't it ironic that blood, so often used as a symbol of death and suffering, actually carries and supports life? Without the spilling of Christ's blood on our behalf, we could never live in the presence of our God. Christ bled. Christ died. Christ rose again. Praise to God for the gospel of our Lord and Savior, Jesus Christ.

Emily Sherrod: 17, Mobile, AL
Christ Fellowship Baptist Church and Stanford University Online High School, Mobile, AL

# Praising God

"I will praise the LORD at all times; His praise will always be on my lips. I will boast in the LORD; . . . Proclaim Yahweh's greatness with me; let us exalt His name together. . . . Those who look to Him and are radiant with joy; their faces will never be ashamed. This poor man cried, and the LORD heard him and saved him from all his troubles." —Psalm 34:1–6

I'm a runner. It's what I do, and it's my passion. I run through blistering heat, pouring rain, howling winds, and fresh-fallen snow. The Lord Jesus has blessed me continuously through my high school career as a stand-out runner, and I always want to shout and sing, praising Him for all He has done in my life through running. I also run through pain. I have suffered with continuous headaches since 2009. Sometimes, before an important race, I step up to the starting line, heart pounding in my ears so hard it feels like my head will burst, and I just pray. And then, I do what I love. That gun goes off, and so do I. I determine then that I will not just finish with half-hearted effort, but I will finish knowing that the Lord Jesus, the King of the universe, has blessed me, and will allow me to finish strong. For that reason, I give Him all the praise. Through this trial of unrelenting pain, doing what I enjoy more than anything, and finishing the race, I remember that I have a God who is merciful, gracious, and blesses those who don't deserve it. Trials are presented in our lives to help us grow. Please, when you are going through hard times in your life, don't turn to anger. Turn to praise, knowing that the Lord does all things for His will, and that these trials are only to deepen your faith in Him.

Jessie Cardin: 16, Sutton, MA
Bethlehem Bible Church, West Boylston, MA; Sutton Memorial High School, Sutton, MA

# Knowing or Knowing About?

"But from there, you will search for the Lᴏʀᴅ your God, and you will find Him when you seek Him with all your heart and all your soul."

—Deuteronomy 4:29

I've been at church since I was two weeks old. I go every Sunday, I go to small groups every Wednesday, I even volunteer with my church every week. I can recite Bible verses from memory, and I can tell you any Bible story forward and backward. These things mean absolutely nothing. They say that I know *about* God. These things don't say that I know God. See the difference? God doesn't ask for us to know things about Him. He asks for a personal relationship *with* us. There's a huge difference. I heard the example used once of a famous person. An athlete, actor, or musician that you love—well, you know a lot about them. You can probably talk about the things they like to do or things they've done; however, you don't actually know them. You only know about them. To actually get to know God, we can't simply go to small groups and go to church. These things are wonderful, of course, but they are only supplements. The real meat of our relationship with God should be in our personal time with Him. You don't get to know someone by smiling at them in the school hallways. You get to know them by doing things with them, spending time with them, talking to them. Your relationship with God should be no different. To get to know God like He wants us to, we have to spend time praying and in His Word—hanging out with Him, if you will. God desires for us to get to know Him, inside and out, and going to church twice a week isn't the way to do that. God desires nothing more than to have a personal relationship with you. If you seek Him continuously, He will also seek you.

*Sarah Ashley Bryant:* 15, Springdale, AR
Cross Church and Shiloh Christian School, Springdale, AR

# Popularity

**"A friend loves at all times, and a brother is born for a difficult time."**

—Proverbs 17:17

(Hailey) The pressure to be popular starts at a young age. When my family moved to a new location and we began to attend a church, I met Rebekah. We became friends immediately. That summer, some popular girls decided I was cool enough to join their group. Acceptance came at a price. It meant giving up my friendship with Rebekah, my only friend, and I decided to keep Rebekah. I felt more pressure to be popular and I started to give in. The group wanting me involved boys, and it looked more promising than the one real friend I had. I began pushing Rebekah away. When I needed support from my new "friends," I had none! I had to work hard to restore a solid, loving, trusting, and lasting relationship with Rebekah. Teens feel pressured to be popular and accepted. God made us unique and special. We don't have to prove to God that we are good enough to be accepted by Him. He accepts us with all our faults and failures.

(Rebekah) The members of my Sunday school class had been friends with one another for a long time. I felt like the outsider. So, several years ago when Hailey came to my church and everyone was nice and accepted her it hurt, because I was the only one without many good friends. I wondered why I wasn't good enough. Over the years, I have discovered that no matter how many "friends" you have, very few of the people you hang out with will be able to support you in the good and the bad times. When you're struggling you don't need twenty "surfacy" friends. You need those few women of God who will stand by you and help you. You may have lots of friends, but don't forget to cultivate deep relationships. Do you feel alone? Ask God for one or two friends you can trust, and when God gives them to you, in His timing, cherish them.

**Hailey Culberson:** 17, and **Rebekah Byrd:** 16, Tulsa, OK
Evergreen Baptist Church, Bixby, OK; Homeschooled

# God's Perfect Plan

"'For I know the plans I have for you'—this is the LORD's declaration—'plans for your welfare, not for disaster, to give you a future and a hope.'" —Jeremiah 29:11

Ever have something go completely wrong and you're not really sure why it's going that way? You ask God, "Why?" and then you don't really get an answer right away. This is exactly how I felt. Imagine this, you are at the very first basketball game of the season, or maybe you have the big test that will determine what college you get in to, or you have a big piano recital. Then right in the middle of it, something goes wrong like what happened to me—blow out your knee during a basketball game. This injury was going to change my entire life. I knew that basketball wasn't an option this year. When I found out that I would have to have surgery, then a six-month recovery, I was mad at God. I couldn't understand why He had let me get hurt. I later realized that He wasn't going to tell me His plan for me until He was ready and when I was ready. In Jeremiah 29:11, we are told that God has a plan for each of us and He declares that the plan is for our welfare, not for disaster, and that He wants to give us a future hope. Isn't that exciting? We have a hope for all eternity. This verse gave me hope that an injury is part of His plan for me, and I will grow stronger through it.

Anna Sapone: 15, Medical Lake, WA
Airway Heights Baptist Church, Airway Heights, WA; Medical Lake High School, Medical Lake, WA

# Driving Scared!

"Do not fear, for I am with you; do not be afraid, for I am your God. I will strengthen you; I will help you; I will hold on to you with My righteous right hand." —Isaiah 41:10

I am a few months away from being sixteen years old, which for most teenagers brings the excitement of getting to drive. For some reason, I really don't care if I drive or not. I haven't even taken the time to go and get my learner's permit. In the state of Tennessee, you may get your learner's permit by taking and passing a written test as soon as you are fifteen years old. My sister is sixteen, and she takes me everywhere. She takes me to school, the mall, and to hang out with my friends. If my sister is busy my parents take me where I need to go. I guess one of the reasons I don't have the desire to drive is because I am afraid that I will fail the test to get my learner's permit. But the main reason I do not want to go and take the test Is I am scared to drive. There are forty thousand people killed on average each year in car accidents in the US. Every day you hear about teens dying because of drinking and driving. You also hear about other people going out and driving recklessly and killing innocent people. It's not me that I am scared of; it is the other drivers who don't drive responsibly. Even though I am nervous to start driving, I know I can do this with the help of God. He will guide me with the ways of the road and keep me safe from the other careless drivers. The real world can be scary sometimes, but I have to put my faith in God and know that everything is going to be all right.

Madison Thomas: 15, Sevierville, TN
First Baptist Church and Gatlinburg-Pittman High School, Gatlinburg, TN

# I Know You

## "I have called you by your name, you are Mine." —Isaiah 43:1

God knows us; personally, intimately, deeply. He created us in our inmost being. We are because He is. God loves His creation. There is nothing we can hide from Him. He knew us before we were conceived. Before we saw the light of day, He knew our names. He knows what we will say before we say it and what we will do before we think of doing it. We may ask why God puts us through hard situations. "Why would He purposely force such grief upon me?" He must not love me. A father disciplines his child out of love which helps to shape the child to be a better person and a better father or mother to his children and grandchildren. God is our Father, and He will do the same for us that our earthly father does. We should not be afraid of God as our heavenly Father. He loves us more than we can ever understand. When we are broken, God can put the pieces of our hearts back together as they should be. He knows our hearts. He knows our lives. He knows our struggle and our heartache. But we must choose to run to Him in these times of trouble. He has given us free will to choose the direction of our lives. What will you choose? Will you continue to live your life rejecting your Father in heaven, who knows you personally and wants you to come to Him? Or will you give your life to the One who loves you more than you could ever understand? The choice is yours and yours alone. "I know, I know you. I know you know I love you." (Lyrics from Bellarive's "I Know You," from the album "The Heartbeat" released June 19, 2009 by Sparrow Records.)

**Sarah LaCognata:** 14, Belleview, FL
Church @ The Springs, Ocala, FL; Homeschooled

# History

"For as high as the heavens are above the earth, so great is His faithful
love toward those who fear Him. As far as the east is
from the west, so far has He removed our transgressions from us."

—Psalm 103:11–12

God loves us so much, as high as the heavens are above the earth. We can't fully grasp how much that is. We try to describe God's love as unconditional, eternal, and steadfast, but we will never be able to truly understand it. Just like we can't truly understand how high the heavens are above the earth. Even though we may understand the distance in light-years, we can't understand that great of a distance. We also have a hard time understanding how God can forgive us for all the wrong we have done. Maybe we think we did one thing that He just can't forgive. Jesus died so that God could forgive all of our sins and remove them from us. It is only by Jesus' death on the cross that we are able to be forgiven by God. When we accept Jesus as our Savior, His blood covers us and makes us lovable to God. There is nothing He won't forgive if we confess our sins. "If we confess our sins, He is faithful and righteous to forgive us our sins and to cleanse us from all unrighteousness" (1 John 1:9). God not only forgives our sins, He forgets them and removes them from us, as far as the east is from the west. ". . . it is hard to believe . . . history is miles away. So leave it all behind you let it always remind you of the day, the day that love made history" ("History" by Matthew West, Westies Music Publishing/Word Music, LLC). On the day that Jesus made history by dying for us, He made it possible for God to forgive us of all our sins and make them history.

*Tyra Ruisinger*: 17, Raymore, MO
Summit Woods Baptist Church, Lees Summit, MO; Homeschooled

# Singing in the Rain

## "I praise Him with my song." —Psalm 28:7

When we are going through what seem to be storms in our lives, it is hard to find joy. I've gone through life's thunderstorms and I didn't feel like singing or giving praises to God. How could I give praise to God during this time of downpour? In Psalm 28:7, David praises the Lord because the Lord has heard his cry for help. Christians often think that when things in life go dark God is no longer with us. The truth is that God sees that we are in a big storm and He is right besides us, shielding us from the harsh rain. Although this sounds nice and wonderful, it is hard to actually believe it. I was driving home from school one day feeling as if I was in a storm. Life was not all sunny with butterflies fluttering about. It was pouring and hailing and I couldn't see the sun. As I continued on my drive, I entered into a pitch-black sky that frightened me. It seemed to depict what I was going through. After some time battling the rain I made it out of the storm and saw blue skies ahead. There was peace. God used that storm to show me that I could trust Him to guide me to His light. Although my life was difficult, I discovered that God saw where I was and He knew where I was headed. Although we may enter storms in our lives and it takes all the strength we have to keep moving, God has not left our side and He sees the blue skies that are waiting for us. He is walking with us through the storms and is there to be the shield of protection we need. So lift up a song of praise because those blue skies are waiting for us and we have the Lord to guide us there.

Haley Smith: 16, Tarpon Springs, FL
Calvary Baptist Church and Calvary Christian High School, Tarpon Springs, FL

# Forgive Others

"Accepting one another and forgiving one another if anyone has a complaint against another. Just as the Lord has forgiven you, so you must also forgive." —Colossians 3:13

Forgive others! Simple, yet difficult. Forgiving one another is never easy, but it's always the right thing to do. Colossians 3 tells us to "forgive anyone who offends you" because God forgave us. Your sister wears your shirt without asking; forgive her. Your friends forget to text you back; forgive them. Your sister doesn't ask your permission to wear your shirt again; forgive her again. Matthew 18:22 tells us to forgive not seven times, but seventy times seven. Was Jesus telling us to forgive our sister or best friend 490 times? No, He was saying to never stop forgiving. Colossians 3:13 also says, "Just as the Lord has forgiven you, so you must also forgive." We forgive others because He forgave us. God continues to forgive us—for the things we have done in the past, the sins we are currently committing, and those we will commit in the future. He forgives them all. You cannot be prideful and forgive someone at the same time. It is impossible to consider yourself better than others and still genuinely forgive them. You must let go of your pride in order to truly forgive another person. Forgiveness is the key to friendship, and pride is the enemy. Romans 12:17 says, "Do not repay anyone evil for evil." We don't need to get even, but, because of our pride, we feel the need to get revenge. God doesn't take revenge on us for all the ways we have wronged Him. Instead, He gives us grace and has mercy on us. We must strive to imitate Christ; Christ forgave us, so we must forgive others. "Then Peter came to Him and said, 'Lord, how many times could my brother sin against me and I forgive him? As many as seven times?' 'I tell you, not as many as seven,' Jesus said to him, 'but 70 times seven'" (Matthew 18:21–22).

Sarah LaCognata: 14, Belleview, FL
Church @ The Springs, Ocala, FL; Homeschooled

# Illusioned Fake

"Do not be conformed to this age, but be transformed by the renewing of your mind, so that you may discern what is the good, pleasing, and perfect will of God." —Romans 12:2

Have you ever been asked the question: "Tell us a little about yourself," and you didn't know what to say? Everyone has little secrets and fake "truths"; we sometimes change ourselves slightly to try to get people to like us. You do not have to be someone else for people to hang out with you! Change is not bad, it is very good and we all need to be accustomed to it, but pretending to be someone you are not just so someone will like you is not good. They will be disillusioned and love the imaginary person and not who you actually are. If you have a bad attitude or see something in yourself that isn't right, then change is needed. We are called to be transformed by the renewing of our mind, which happens through regular reading of God's Word. Romans 12:2 says, "Do not be conformed to this age, but be transformed by the renewing of your mind, so that you may discern what is the good, pleasing, and perfect will of God." This kind of change is not the same as changing oneself to be accepted in the world's eyes; it is called discipline, and it will shape who you are to become. God made everyone unique. Strive to be more like Christ; your inner beauty will always outshine your outer appearance. We do not have to mask who we are for people to like us. Don't mask who God made you. Shine and love the Lord for everything that makes you you.

Holly Kurtz: 16, Holden, MA
Bethlehem Bible Church and Bethlehem Bible Church Homeschooled Co-op, West Boylston, MA

# Mental Immorality

"For this is God's will, for your sanctification: that you abstain from sexual immorality, so that each of you knows how to control his own body in sanctification and honor, not with lustful desires, like the Gentiles who don't know God." —1 Thessalonians 4:3–5

God's will for the sanctification of His children is that we abstain from sexual immorality. Sanctification means the process of making us holy like Jesus Christ. We are called to be holy, for God is holy (1 Peter 1:16), so according to 1 Thessalonians, part of the process is the complete removal of sexual immorality in our lives. Perhaps you have lived a life of purity, but you want to grow deeper in your faith. You haven't had sex with your boyfriend or, if you have lost your virginity, that was in your past and you now live in forgiveness and redemption. So this verse doesn't apply to us, right? Wrong! Our sanctification is the complete removal of every kind or sexual immorality. Sexual immorality isn't just physical, it's mental as well. We have to learn how to control our minds and not give them over to lustful desires. We have to keep our thoughts pure and holy, and this is much harder to do. We can keep ourselves from physical immorality, but often the mental immorality happens without us even noticing. It can come in many forms. It could be pornography, lingering on the thought of a girl or guy too long, longing for a relationship with the opposite sex, imagining what it will be like when you're married, or watching movies and reading books that are too detailed in the intimate scenes. These things fill our minds with junk that keep us from our intimate relationship with Christ. We must spend time in the Word and diligently guard our minds from sexual immorality, lest we fall into the trap Satan has placed in front of us.

Annalise Clem: 17, Albany, GA
Sherwood Baptist Church and Sherwood Christian Academy, Albany, GA

# Battling Anger

## "A patient person shows great understanding, but a quick-tempered one promotes foolishness." —Proverbs 14:29

The great Mark Twain once said, "Anger is an acid that can do more harm to the vessel in which it is stored than to anything on which it is poured." It is like a dangerous black hole, and it can suck the joy out of everything that makes you happy if you let it. It is common to get angry in certain situations, but we must not allow that anger to consume or destroy us. Having a little brother around the same age as I am can be very challenging at times. It seems as though he knows exactly what to do to push my anger button. Whether it's taking my stuff without asking or pushing me into a heated argument, he knows he can get a rise out of me and cause me to lose my cool. As a growing Christian teenager, I have to keep reminding myself not to let things stir up anger in my heart because it can make me cold and that's not Christlike. Proverbs 14:29 tells us that "A patient person shows great understanding, but a quick-tempered one promotes foolishness." I've learned that there are ways to keep my anger under control, but my first line of defense is usually prayer. It is so relaxing to talk with God and allow Him to help me in the area of self-control and forgiveness. Second, I've learned to search the Scriptures for words of wisdom and grace that cause me to re-evaluate the situation and allow God to handle it. Some of my favorite Scriptures that help me deal with my anger are Job 5:2, Psalm 37:8, and Proverbs 29:11. Anger can wreak havoc on our lives, but we have some very powerful weapons to fight against it. If we learn to let go and let God handle our situations, we will experience a godly healing that pushes away anger.

T'Yanna Janai Jackson: 15, Slidell, LA
Franklin Avenue Baptist Church and Salmen High School, New Orleans, LA

# Stereotyped

**"Let no one despise your youth; instead, you should be an example to believers in speech, in conduct, in love, in faith, in purity."**

—1 Timothy 4:12

Teens are stereotyped. It's something that has always bothered me. Adults just automatically assume that all teens do drugs, get pregnant, and join gangs. But that's not the case. There are some teens out there who do stuff like that, but not every teen. Paul tells Timothy to not let anyone look down on you because you are young, but to be an example for others. When you act differently than the stereotype people have of you, you are showing that not all teens are disorderly and rowdy, and that it is possible for a teen to be mature. Paul tells Timothy to be an example in speech, in conduct, in love, in faith, and in purity. Basically, act the part of a mature teen. This involves not cussing, not using slang, and not speaking in text. Conduct is the way you act. We should act maturely so adults know that we can be trusted with bigger responsibilities. You don't need to put on a show! Don't go around being like, "Oh look at me, I'm being an example to adults." When you are an example in faith, it means that you have a good, steady relationship with God, and it shows through how you live your life. It also means that you trust that God will lead you down the right path. To live a life being an example in purity is to guard your heart until marriage. Girls, don't give your heart away to every guy you meet. Wait and God will give you the right guy. Guys, don't push a girl away from purity. It's something special and to be treasured, given by God. With God's wisdom you can be an example for adults and show that not all teens are what they are stereotyped to be.

*Nellie Otoupalik:* 17, Spokane, WA
Airway Heights Baptist Church, Airway Heights, WA; Homeschooled/Co-op and Spokane Virtual Learning, Spokane, WA

# Serving the Lord

"Better a day in Your courts than a thousand anywhere else.
I would rather be at the door of the house of my God than to live
in the tents of wicked people." —Psalm 84:10

As teens, our focus and prayer should be serving the Lord. In Africa, we all long for someone to encourage us in our walk with Christ. We could only go to church on Sunday mornings, unlike in the U.S., where going to church happens several times each week. Our desire should be to live for Him. We used to say the Lord's Prayer every morning at my school in Africa, but we didn't really understand the meaning because it was routine. Some students didn't know the meaning of salvation. I am excited to be in America because I think there are opportunities to serve Him. I remember I did not know to say a blessing for my food until I was sponsored and went to a boarding school where we prayed. In America, students have parents who love and protect them and read Bible verses before you go to sleep. I did not have that as a child in Africa. So love and thank God for your blessings. I want to speak truth and say that serving God as a teen is the best thing ever. God will always hold you and He will never forsake you. The story of Jesus at age twelve when He went to church with His parents can teach us something. His parents left, thinking that He was in the crowd they later found Him back in the temple seated with the teachers, listening and asking questions, challenging their faith. It's a challenge for teens today to start serving the Lord now, but we must be like Jesus and not wait until we are old.

*Lilian Gatheca*: 16, Nanyuki, Kenya (exchange student living in Albany, GA)
Sherwood Baptist Church and Sherwood Christian Academy, Albany, GA

# Stop Grumbling!

## "Do everything without grumbling or arguing." —Philippians 2:14

I sat at my computer for a good twenty minutes before deciding what to write. As I sat there, staring at the screen of my laptop, I began inwardly complaining about my lot in life. *My situation is so hard, my job isn't fun, I don't like school,* and so on. I ended up stopping and asking myself, *Am I really complaining as I prepare to reflect on who God is?* My heart was anywhere but in the right place. Paul gives us some great words in Philippians 2. He said that what is required of us is that we would "Do everything without grumbling or arguing." God just threw that verse back at me. Do *everything* without complaining. Really, God? When You say everything, do You really mean *everything*? You even mean when I have to do four hours of chemistry homework before bed that I shouldn't complain, and when I have to watch my siblings on a Friday night instead of hanging with my friends, I can't complain? Yes, that is precisely what He is saying! Now, I'm not suggesting God wants us to put on a plastic smile and pretend everything is always good. We do have bad days. Things happen we don't like. But we have to be careful that our being honest with people doesn't become us complaining about our lives. And don't forget, there is a benefit for not complaining and arguing. "So that you may be blameless and pure, children of God who are faultless in a crooked and depraved generation, among whom you shine like stars in the world" (Philippians 2:15). And let's be honest, who doesn't want to shine?

Gabrielle LaCognata: 19, Ocala, FL
Church @ The Springs and College of Central Florida, Ocala, FL

# Tongues of Fire

"And the tongue is a fire. The tongue, a world of unrighteousness, is placed among the parts of our bodies. It pollutes the whole body, sets the course of life on fire, and is set on fire by hell."

—James 3:6

Not being a talker means that I get picked on. I'm a girl of action. Not talking much is often confused with being shy, and so, in the twisted politics of high school, being shy makes you different, which gets you made fun of. I prefer a good book to goofing off with friends, but that isn't a bad thing or something to laugh at. I am often asked, "Hannah, why are you so quiet?" I usually answer with, "Because I just don't want to talk right now." This usually appears to be forced, and I typically have to bite back an exasperated sigh or resist rolling my eyes. I shouldn't have to explain why God made me quiet or why I just don't have anything to say right now. In the Bible there are actually several verses that advise silence, or at least advise thinking through words carefully. The tongue is a weapon and is sharper than a double-edged sword. Perhaps you've been told that if you don't have anything nice to say, don't say anything at all. Sometimes being quiet is better than lashing out with your tongue and saying something you'll regret. Words are very powerful and if we aren't careful with them we can destroy a person, even if we don't mean to. Sometimes silence is golden, other times it's best to speak out. We can pray and ask God to help us to know when to speak. God made the mouth and the tongue, so you can bet He knows exactly what you should do with them. Remember that words can build or break a person, and we need to be aware of exactly what our tongue can do.

*Hannah Arrington:* 15, Borger, TX
First Baptist Church and Texas Virtual Academy, Borger, TX

# Keep Stones

"Each of you lift a stone onto his shoulder, one for each of the Israelite tribes, so that this will be a sign among you. In the future, when your children ask you, 'What do these stones mean to you?' you should tell them, 'The waters of the Jordan were cut off in front of the ark of the Lord's covenant. When it crossed the Jordan, the Jordan's waters were cut off.' Therefore these stones will always be a memorial for the Israelites." —Joshua 4:5–7

It is important to never forget what God does in our lives. We often remember our struggles, but forget the victorious moments when we saw God at work. Going through my journal recently, I was surprised by how much I had forgotten. Remembering what God has done helps us to remember lessons He has taught us, struggles we have overcome, and commitments we have made. I love looking through my journal and finding decisions I made that I can look back on and see results. If we can remember how God sustained us during a time of temptation, those same temptations will hold less power over us. I looked back to when I was ten and had found out my friend wasn't a Christian, and how I prayed for her for years. This summer she accepted Jesus Christ as her Lord and Savior. I praise God for the work He has done in her life and I thank Him because He answered my prayers. Remembering the years of doubting whether my prayers would ever be answered, I can have faith that God does hear and can answer me in the future. I would encourage you to journal as a way to remember God's hand in your life. If that is too much, then write down a sentence or two when something memorable happens and put it in a box to read later. The results may surprise you.

Rebekah Byrd: 16, Tulsa, OK
Evergreen Baptist Church, Bixby, OK; Homeschooled

# Who Do You Say I Am?

**"'But you,' He asked them again, 'who do you say that I am?'
Peter answered Him, 'You are the Messiah!'"** —Mark 8:29

Never forsake what you know to be true! So many times we let the world or others sway our beliefs in a certain way. This is wrong. We must hold to our beliefs, to our Jesus, all the time. We know that even when it's hard to believe He is there. In the Gospels, there is an account of Jesus asking His disciples a question: "Who do people say I am?" They answer a prophet, a good teacher, and other things like that. Then Jesus takes it to the next level saying, "Who do you say I am?" He is more concerned with their belief in Him, where they stand in their faith, than what they know others say of Him. He says, "Yes, you can know what they think about Me; and yes, they may be right. But I want you to focus on who *you* know Me to be. Who I am to you personally is much more important than who they say I am. Know the truth and cling to it." It's like Jesus knew what was coming (which He did, of course), and was like, "OK guys, the next few weeks are going to be hard. They're going to test your faith in Me big time! So you have to know who I am and trust Me. And know that no matter what they say or do to Me, you have seen the truth!" It's time we took a stand for who we know Jesus to be! Read the Bible to learn the truth about Him so that you can be sure of who He is and not let anyone or anything tell you differently. Yes, these next few weeks or years or decades will be hard. They are going to test your faith big-time, but if you know who Jesus is and you are clinging to Him and His truth, you will overcome!

*McKenzie Sutton:* 17, Waverly Hall, GA
Cornerstone Baptist Church, Ellerslie, GA; Homeschooled

# Standing in Awe

## "Take delight in the Lord, and He will give you your heart's desires."
### —Psalm 37:4

Last summer, I was a youth camp counselor for my church's kid's camp. As we were singing songs outside under a pavilion, a huge storm moved in quickly with fierce winds and rains. The wind was terrible, and it was moving the rain under the roof in huge gusts. As kids began to get scared, I remember sensing the Holy Spirit in a gust of wind and rain. It was such an incredible moment between the Lord and me. It made me realize how often I do not stop to enjoy the Lord. He created us to love Him. Psalm 37:4 tells us that we are to "take delight in the Lord." In our culture we get so busy, and we don't take the time to dance in the Lord's glory as David did in 2 Samuel 6:14: "David was dancing with all his might before the Lord wearing a linen ephod." In the moments we enjoy Him, we fall more deeply in love with our Lord. When is the last time you have stopped to experience a moment with Him? There's nothing like the present! He is available, are you?

Victoria Davidson: 17, Newton, GA
Sherwood Baptist Church and Sherwood Christian Academy, Albany, GA

# For The Lord and Not For Men

**"Whatever you do, do it enthusiastically, as something done for the Lord and not for men."** —Colossians 3:23

Don't you just love how verses tend to pop out at you in completely different ways at different times? That happened to me the last time I read this verse. I always used to think about this verse when I was on a mission trip or serving somewhere, or doing some other "noble" thing. But the "whatever" in this verse really means *whatever*. We could rewrite this verse and have it say something like this: "And whenever you do homework, work at it with all your heart, as working for the Lord, not for your teachers." Or how about, "Whenever you are cleaning your room, clean it with all you've got, as cleaning it for the Lord, not for your parents." You see, God doesn't want us to pick and choose what we work hard at. No matter what we do, we are supposed to work at it with all our hearts, just like God was watching. Because deep down, we know He is. So as I finish this post and return to the wonderful world of homework, I hope and pray that you and I will be able to work hard at everything we do, knowing that it is for the Lord. First Corinthians 15:58 says, "Therefore, my dear brothers, be steadfast, immovable, always excelling in the Lord's work, knowing that your labor in the Lord is not in vain."

*Gabrielle LaCognata*: 19, Belleview, FL
Church @ The Springs and College of Central Florida, Ocala, FL

# Speaking Up

**"Then Moses answered, 'What if they won't believe me and will not obey me but say, "The Lᴏʀᴅ did not appear to you"?'"** —Exodus 4:1

I have a friend who *hates* public speaking, and with the first word out of her mouth her face reddens and her voice shakes. The larger the crowd, the worse it gets. She worries about how she will verbalize her ideas and how those listening might respond. Can you relate? God commanded Moses to speak to the Israelites, but he was nervous. Floods of what-ifs rushed to his head. Moses worried that people would not believe him. God told Moses to just trust Him, He would help him. God was going to give him the words to say, but Moses lacked trust. Are you like Moses? Sometimes, not being able to speak in front of crowds is common. Getting nervous when giving a speech in English class is a much smaller problem than speaking up for what is right. We are all faced with plenty of situations that we could speak up against, whether it's that girl getting made fun of on the Internet, your friend doing something you know is wrong, or the boy next to you in history class cutting himself every day. But what do we do more often than not? Ignore it! If God is calling you to speak up against something, do it. Ignoring Him will turn out way worse than the awkwardness you think you'll feel by speaking up. Just look at the story of Jonah. Where did ignoring God get him? Right into the belly of a whale! Place your trust in God, He will speak for you and equip you with more strength and courage than you could possibly imagine. He will never tell you to do something then leave you on your own. God is always going to come through for you as long as you are willing to trust Him.

*Laura Roggenbaum*: 17, Palm Harbor, FL
Calvary Baptist Church and Calvary Christian School, Clearwater, FL

# When You Don't Feel Pretty

"And why do you worry about clothes? Learn how the wildflowers of the field grow; they don't labor or spin thread." —Matthew 6:28

It's a common problem in many teenage girls' lives, including mine: beauty! That one word has been the object of desire for women all over the world. We want it, but we feel we will never obtain it, because in our world to be beautiful is to be perfect. And there was only one perfect human in the world—His name was Jesus. I've been through days where I go above and beyond to make myself look pretty. But what happens when you go through all that trouble and you look pretty, but you don't feel pretty? It's a common thing for me, and I'm sure it is for most girls. I consider my hair my best attribute, mostly because I've been told that I have pretty hair. Most days I just throw my hair up in a bun or ponytail, but on occasions, if I'm going out, I'll spend an hour in the bathroom, curling or straightening every lock, and when I'm done I always manage to find an imperfection. If I don't have time to fix it, sometimes I feel completely terrible for the rest of the day. I'm constantly readjusting it, even asking my friends or family if "my hair looks all right." The Bible tells us that our outside appearance doesn't matter in the long run, because as Christians our inside appearance is being renewed by the Holy Spirit (2 Corinthians 4:16). Those days that we don't feel beautiful even though we try, we can remember that God made us, and He made each of us in His image. The Bible mentions God being beautiful. So if God's beautiful, then we are all beautiful. It's not a bad thing to want to look pretty and presentable, but we need to make sure our insides are as pretty as our outsides.

Hannah Arrington: 15, Borger, TX
First Baptist Church and Texas Virtual Academy, Borger, TX

# Determination

*"Consider it a great joy . . . whenever you experience various trials, knowing that the testing of your faith produces endurance. But endurance must do its complete work, so that you may be mature and complete, lacking nothing."* —James 1:2–4

If there's any book in the Bible that will help you grow spiritually, it's James. It starts out talking about trials, which we all know are a huge part of life. We are not called to an easy life. It says to count it pure joy when you go through rough patches in life. Whenever I fail a math test that I studied for uber hard, or someone dies unexpectedly, joy is not one of my emotions. Being sad is not a bad thing, as long as you see the bigger picture and can find joy in it. It's harder to learn something from God when everything is going the way you want. There's a quote that says, "When life gets too hard to stand, kneel." It's referring to prayer. Persevere, as James 1:2–4 says. Speaking out about our faith can cause others to persecute us. Paul is an amazing example of this, and I can't wait to meet him in heaven one day. He says in Acts 20:24, "But I count my life of no value to myself, so that I may finish my course and the ministry I received from the Lord Jesus, to testify to the gospel of God's grace." Paul was one of the most persecuted Christians to ever live, but he knew that he was put on this earth to tell everyone about Jesus and he persevered through all of the persecution. So next time life gets hard, try to see the positive and be joyous that the Lord can really teach you something through it.

*Christa Morgan*: 17, Alabaster, AL
Westwood Baptist Church and Thompson High School, Alabaster, AL

# Easter

"But He was pierced because of our transgressions, crushed because of our iniquities; punishment for our peace was on Him, and we are healed by His wounds." —Isaiah 53:5

I was thinking the other day just how cruel and evil those Pharisees, Sadducees, and rulers were. You know the ones that put Jesus to death. I was angry at those Roman soldiers who beat and tortured Jesus. But the next thought I had was something very different: "It was me. I am the one who put Jesus on the cross." I wasn't the actual one who nailed Him to the cross, put it was because of my sin that He had to die. He was pierced because of my transgressions. God loved us all so much that He created Easter, even though we didn't deserve it. He sent Jesus to die because of our sins, for us to know Him, and because He loves us. The events that happened during the death of Christ were to become the greatest events in all of history. The very Son of God, hanging on a tree, nail-pierced hands, shed His blood for you and me. But it didn't end there. If it had that would have been the most tragic ending to the greatest love story ever. But three days later He rose from the dead. God raised to life our Savior, and through that He conquered death, sin, and hell forever. How's that for an ending? We have victory through Christ over the very sin that put Him on the cross. It was our sin that put Him there, but He loved us so much that He came. He came, lived, died, and rose again for us. That is Easter; not bunnies and eggs, but a Savior who has healed us through His wounds. Let us be thankful for a Savior who took our place and for the healing that He gives to each of us through the cross, through Easter!

McKenzie Sutton: 17, Waverly Hall, GA
Cornerstone Baptist Church, Ellerslie, GA; Homeschooled

# Choosing Christ

**"'Follow Me,' He told them, 'and I will make you fish for people!'"**

—Matthew 4:19

Having grown up in the church, I have heard people talk about how they feel God wants them to do something or that God called them to do something. So without realizing it, I started to think I was doing something seriously wrong in my walk with God because I didn't feel God. In the summer after my sophomore year of high school, I was dragged to a church camp called "Super Summer." It wasn't the wilderness camping that I was used to. It was a big student conference with a lot of people I didn't know, a lot of rules, and a lot more change than I had wanted to deal with at the time. I hardened my heart, and because of that ,I didn't start to listen 'til halfway through camp. Finally, I did start to listen and I heard the speaker tell us that in a few minutes he wanted everyone that either knew they were going to go into ministry or felt called to go into ministry to follow some camp counselors and talk to them. To my surprise, I got up and went. I'm not exactly sure why or how I got up in front of hundreds of people, but I do know that God called me into ministry that night. I had "felt" God for the first time. The last night of camp, the speaker said three things that really stuck with me. He told us: "When the feelings go away, that's when you offer yourself to Christ," "It's OK if the feeling doesn't last," and "Most the time you will not feel like walking in the Spirit." In other words, it doesn't matter if you don't think you have felt God in some way or not, because it isn't about the feeling. It's about our individual choice to follow God every day!

*Sara E. DuBois*: 16, St. Peters, MO
First Baptist of St. Charles, St. Charles, MO; Fort Zumwalt East High School, St. Peters, MO

# Growing

**"I gave you milk to drink, not solid food, because you were not yet ready for it. In fact, you are still not ready, because you are still fleshly. For since there is envy and strife among you, are you not fleshly and living like unbelievers?"** —1 Corinthians 3:2–3

When I was in seventh grade, I had a desire to learn from one of the older Sunday school classes, so I moved up. Some of my church friends were frustrated with me because I stopped going to the middle school Sunday school class with them. In the older class, I learned things that helped me as a Christian. Even though some people weren't happy with me, I wasn't going to let their opinions stop me. I recalled the Corinthians in 1 Corinthians 3:2–3, "I gave you milk to drink, not solid food, because you were not yet ready for it. In fact, you are still not ready, because you are still fleshly. For since there is envy and strife among you, are you not fleshly and living like unbelievers?" Paul gets onto them, because they still needed the spiritual milk even after he had given the milk to them a while back. If you feel like you're not learning anything or growing, then I encourage you to seriously take steps toward learning more and furthering your walk with God. Whether that is by being discipled by someone, by going to a different class, even if it means just digging into your Bible more often, find a way to continue to grow! In Luke 13:6–8, Jesus tells a parable about a fig tree that didn't bear fruit for three years and the owner told the caretaker to cut it down if it did not bear fruit (grow) in another year. Clearly, God looks at how we grow, and I think we need to take how we grow seriously and continue to strive to get to know more about our Creator!

Sara E. DuBois: 16, St. Peters, MO
First Baptist of St. Charles, St. Charles, MO; Fort Zumwalt East High School, St. Peters, MO

# Idols

"Do not have other gods besides Me. Do not make an idol for yourself, whether in the shape of anything in the heavens above or on the earth below or in the waters under the earth." —Exodus 20:3–4

Idols come in many different forms, and you may have an idol that you didn't even know was an idol. I have discovered that I may have an idol. My idol is video games. I spend hours of my time playing them when I should be spending that time with the Lord. I have learned that I need to work on getting away from that idol. However, that does not mean that I have to give it up completely. I just don't need to treat it as though it is the most important thing in the world. Many teenagers have idols that they never knew they had: a boyfriend or girlfriend, clothes or money. The very first of the Ten Commandments tells us not to have any other gods besides the Lord. The second commandment tells us not to make any graven images. Deuteronomy 5:7–8 says, "Do not have other gods besides Me. Do not make an idol for yourself in the shape of anything in the heavens above or on the earth below or in the waters under the earth." We need to make certain that there are no idols in our lives—accidental idols, or those that are intentionally made—that take our attention away from the Lord. Get rid of that idol because we can only serve the Lord. Matthew 6:24 says, "No one can be a slave of two masters, since either he will hate one and love the other, or be devoted to one and despise the other. You cannot be slaves of God and of money." We have to be careful about the things we do or the things we like to do. We have to make sure that we only serve God, and that we are not making accidental idols.

Michaela Reed: 15, Albany, GA
Institutional First Baptist Church and Sherwood Christian Academy, Albany, GA

# Wanting to Date

"Do not be mismatched with unbelievers. For what partnership is there between righteousness and lawlessness? Or what fellowship does light have with darkness? What agreement does Christ have with Belial? Or what does a believer have in common with an unbeliever?"

—2 Corinthians 6:14–15

Walking to English class, the cutest, most popular couple is in front of you holding hands. *Why can't I have a relationship like theirs?* is a normal thought to have. It's completely OK to yearn for a relationship, especially in high school, as long as you don't find yourself settling. Christians are to date someone who is equally yoked with us. Yes, that means we can't date non-Christians. You may think, *It's no big deal, it's not like I'm going to marry him.* However, dating is practice for marriage. Why would you practice with the soccer team if you were on the football team and had a game Friday? Relationships aren't easy, but a Christ-centered relationship makes the trials and tribulations easier to get through. To ensure this, both need to be on track with God and understand their roles. A godly woman loves Jesus (Matthew 22:34–40), is selfless (Proverbs 31:20), and is a servant (Proverbs 31:15). The guy takes the lead, always (Genesis 1:26 and 2:15, 18). Girls, don't settle for a guy who can't lead you spiritually. I've been there, and while he may make you proud to be with him, satisfying your need for a boyfriend, that won't last like him leading you spiritually will. It's better to have high standards and have to wait a while than to be with guys who don't have the same foundation as you do.

*Christa Morgan:* 17, Alabaster, AL
Westwood Baptist Church and Thompson High School, Alabaster, AL

# The Jesus High

"Imprint these words of mine on your hearts and minds, bind them as a sign on your hands, and let them be a symbol on your foreheads."

—Deuteronomy 11:18

You know that feeling when you get back from a church retreat or camp and you feel on top of the world? You think, *I am going to change my act up! I'm going to read my Bible all the time and pray ten times a day and be nice to everyone!* This is what I call a "Jesus High." I've been in this position many times in my life. The hard part of any "high" is coming back down. You can't stay in that church camp environment all the time. You suddenly enter the real world full of evil and mean girls and rude guys who are hard for you to love like Jesus does. You get busy, too busy to read your Bible, too busy to pray. The thing is, you aren't going to have the same type of "Jesus High" at school that you have at big Christian events. But there are some things you can do to change the way you live in order to stay on top of your walk with Christ. Wake up ten minutes earlier before school to read your Bible and even write a note to self reminding you to pray. It doesn't take long for the "Jesus High" effects to wear off. Applying Christ in the little ways in your life is one way to make sure you are growing, even when you are not at big events.

Megan Medford: 14, Bryant, AR
The Church at Rock Creek and Bryant High School, Little Rock, AR

# Pride and Prejudice

"But they now desire a better place—a heavenly one.
Therefore God is not ashamed to be called their God,
for He has prepared a city for them." —Hebrews 11:16

One of my favorite books is *Pride and Prejudice* by Jane Austen. The last time I read one particular quote, though, I saw it in a different context than I had before. The main character, Elizabeth Bennet, states that "The more I see of the world, the more I am dissatisfied with it." Jane Austen wrote this in regard to adventures and exploration, but this time around I thought about it from the perspective of being a Christian. As a follower of Christ, this earth is not my true home. I should not be satisfied with this world because God has prepared a mansion for me in heaven! And the more I see of this world—the sin and the imperfection—the more I long for my true home. Being the worldly human that I am, I quite honestly have trouble remembering that there is more to life than the things I go through every day. When I am in the middle of a situation I can see it as the ultimate, rather than just the immediate. But if we wrap our minds around this world not being our home, our perspective will change. When we focus on eternal things and not temporal things, it will be easier to have those hard conversations with our coworkers about God. When our focus is right, we see the trials that we are in as temporary situations, even those that last for years. When we see clearly, we will be able to think about our lives in terms of eternity. At the end of the day, isn't that the most important thing? "You don't even know what tomorrow will bring—what your life will be!" (James 4:14). "Set your minds on what is above, not on what is on the earth" (Colossians 3:2).

**Gabrielle LaCognata**: 19, Ocala, FL
Church @ The Springs and College of Central Florida, Ocala FL

# Dare to Be "Uncool"

"Do not be conformed to this age, but be transformed
by the renewing of your mind, so that you may discern
what is the good, pleasing, and perfect will of God." —Romans 12:2

When a boy at school doesn't talk to me, it hurts. But, what if he asked me to attend some function with him, and it is not something that I, as a Christian, should attend? Should I say no, but go on to explain my reasoning? Then, what if he went on to share his views thinking he would change my mind, but his reasons do not jibe with mine at all. Being the loudmouth I am, I would probably make a spectacle of myself by talking about the noble Christian origins of the occasion in question, which is not the way to react! Even if the guy concluded by telling me that he pitied me for deluding myself about my Christianity, I would still remain steadfast. I'm not proud that I sometimes voice my opinion strongly and even argue certain points, because it is not the way to handle a disagreement. But, I am learning. If your faith is strong, your mind is never going to be changed, and people who engage in arguments with Christians are not usually interested in being converted. It is important to take a stand for truth, but we can be kind and share Christ without looking like Satan! I know it's not "cool" to stand up for God. But when we get to heaven, I don't think that God is going to be proud of us for keeping our images popular. He's going to thank us for standing up for His Son. God does not need us to defend Him, but we are to stand up for our beliefs, even if we are standing alone. Don't let everyone around you tell you what is cool or correct. Get all your knowledge from God. Don't let your soul be transformed by anyone but Jesus.

Bronte Stallings: 15, Mt. Pleasant, SC
Citadel Square Baptist Church, Charleston, SC; Wando High, Mt. Pleasant, SC

# Do I Tell or Not?

**"Better an open reprimand than concealed love. The wounds of a friend are trustworthy, but the kisses of an enemy are excessive."**

—Proverbs 27:5–6

I'm a people pleaser. I want people to like me and I don't like to offend or make anyone mad. So, one problem I have is knowing when to tell on a friend. I don't want to be called a snitch, but sometimes friends tell me things they do that are harmful to themselves. In my heart I know I should tell an adult to get them help, but I'm worried they won't want to be my friends anymore. Most of the time, I'll admit, I ignore my conscience and keep their secrets and justify it by saying, "It's not that bad," or "I'm being a good friend by keeping their secret." But I couldn't be more wrong. If you are telling on a friend out of concern for them, because you fear what they're doing is harmful to them or to someone else, then you are being a good friend. A passive friend is not a good friend. I have ignored things that friends have told me in the past. I regret it now because they made decisions that ruined their lives, and I always wonder, *What if I had told someone sooner?* If the reason you want to tell on a friend is to gossip or get them in trouble, then I would say it's better not to tell. The only reason you should tell on a friend is out of love, to help them because you are genuinely worried about them. They may be mad at you, but later on they will appreciate what you did for them.

Blair Bodnarchuk: 17, Raleigh, NC
Providence Baptist Church and Wakefield High School, Raleigh, NC

# Strength in Weakness

## "'My grace is sufficient for you, for my power is made perfect in weakness.' . . . for when I am weak then I am strong."

—2 Corinthians 12:9–10

Have you ever felt worn from the weight of the world? Or that you are too weak to lift your eyes up to the Lord? As a high school student, there is always stress from school, drama, family, and just life. Sometimes life gets to be too overwhelming and we feel weak. In 2 Corinthians, Paul discusses a time in his life when he pleaded with God to relieve him from his suffering. But instead of giving him relief, God responded by simply stating that His grace was enough. If God responded to us that way, I'm pretty sure we would not be pleased. Yet if we take a moment to meditate on the words God spoke to Paul, His answer offered much more than relief. It provided peace and hope. What God did for us on the cross by sending His Son to take on our sin and our punishment is sufficient to relieve us of our weakness. For Christ's power is made *perfect* in our weakness. How incredible is that? We don't have to be strong because God can use us even in our weakness. God sees your weakened heart and He can mend it with His grace. We only have to go before Him, offer up our weakness, and God can do mighty things. I'm sure Paul did not think that in his state of suffering and weakness God could make him strong. Yet Paul would not have told us in the next verse that he delights in his weakness if that had not been true. Sometimes it is a weakened heart that brings us humbled before our Lord, allowing us to trust only in Him who brings us out of our struggle and our weakness strong and empowered by the grace of God.

*Haley Smith*: 16, Tarpon Springs, FL
Calvary Baptist Church and Calvary Christian High School, Tarpon Springs, FL

# Set Apart

"Do not be conformed to this age, but be transformed by the renewing of your mind, so that you may discern what is the good, pleasing, and perfect will of God." —Romans 12:2

Being a teenager is difficult sometimes. Okay, a *lot* of times! Life is a constant battle between wanting to fit in and being accepted, but also making sure that you're doing the right thing. The majority of people in this world will go for what is easy or convenient in life. They will do what is cool to gain popularity and be accepted by those around them, but what they don't know is that every decision they make in life will have consequences. Some will be good, but some will be bad.

This verse is telling us that, as Christians, we need to be set apart for the gospel. There should be something so special and different in our lives that when people look at us, they want what we have. We have to make an extra effort to be different. We weren't created to live like everyone else. God wants His children to be sold-out followers of Him. Total commitment, no compromises! He wants to be the first priority in your life. He wants every single, little part of you, not just your leftovers. He wants you to listen to His calling for you in your life and to not be so focused on your own concerns, wants, or needs. Jesus came so that we can have an abundant life, not only in heaven, but starting right here, right now! He has amazing plans for you. Let go of all of the plans you have for yourself, and let Him take control. He knows what He's doing, and you can trust Him and His ways!

Hannah McGee: 15, Springdale, AR
Cross Church Springdale Campus, Northwest, AR; Shiloh Christian School, Springdale, AR

# Quiet Time

> "But they have no root in themselves; they are short-lived.
> When pressure or persecution comes because of the word,
> they immediately stumble." —Mark 4:17

We are often given resources, such as the Bible, devotion books, prayer, etc., as birthday or Christmas gifts. Do we really know how to use them though? Growing with God will grow your roots deep. Just like a tree, if you have deep roots and a storm comes, it will be easy to withstand. If the roots are shallow, though, the tree will topple over at the first sign of a storm. There are three main things to create an effective quiet time:

1. *Prayer.* Talk to God as if you are talking to your best friend. Tell Him about your day. Tell Him what you're struggling with, and apologize for all the times you've slipped up. Praise Him and thank Him for everything He is and does for you. Colossians 4:2 says, "Devote yourselves to prayer; stay alert in it with thanksgiving." Pray constantly, for everything. God will hear you and will answer as He sees fit.

2. *Scripture.* Psalm 119:105 says, "Your word is a lamp for my feet and a light on my path." Reading the Bible will guide you in making the smallest everyday decisions and some of the toughest decisions you will face. The Word of God is the sword in the passage in Ephesians 6 about the armor of God. The Word of God is what Jesus used to get rid of Satan when He was being tempted in the wilderness. The Word of God will guide you to where you need to go.

3. *Application.* James 1:22 says, "But be doers of the word and not hearers only, deceiving yourselves." Don't just call yourself a Christian, read the Bible a little, then go on living like the world. Dare to be different.

*Hannah Savage:* 16, Dodge City, KS
First Southern Baptist Church and Dodge City High School, Dodge City, KS

# Would You Like Some Fries with That Whine?

### "Do everything without grumbling or arguing." —Philippians 2:14

When you think about what you said during the day, how many times would you say that you complained? "It's too hot," or "It's cold!" "This is boring." "Ugh, I look awful!" We don't think we complain that much until we actually start paying attention to what we are saying. In the seventh grade, our class did a negativity challenge. You had to wear a bracelet, and every time you complained or said something negative, you had to move the bracelet to the other hand. Then you tallied how many complaints you said in a day. I think I had about sixty complaints, or negative comments, in one day! How crazy is that? Philippians 2:14 tells us, "Do everything without grumbling or arguing." That sounds very hard, but it is possible. God does not ask us to do things without providing us with what we need to do that thing. He always provides a way and the stuff we need! Instead of complaining about having to do the dishes, say, "OK, Mom and Dad, I will obey and do the dishes with a positive attitude!" That might shock your parents, but it is a good way to start doing things without grumbling or arguing. Doing this will put us in a better mood and will allow us to be grateful for what we have.

Layne Coleman: 14, Little Rock, AR
The Church at Rock Creek and Little Rock Christian Academy, Little Rock, AR

# A Work in Progress

**"I am sure of this, that He who started a good work in you will carry it on to completion until the day of Christ Jesus."** —Philippians 1:6

Recently I saw an old, rundown house. It was a beautiful house, with a lot of potential. I wanted nothing more than to bring that house back to its former glory. Looking at this house, I realized that, as human beings, we desire to make things better. This desire stems all the way back to our Creator. We desire for others the same thing that God has done for us. When we accept Jesus into our hearts, He changes us forever. He changes us from the inside out. And while we are on earth, our job is to become as much like Jesus as we can, knowing we will never fully achieve that goal. There are times as Christians that we get incredibly discouraged with ourselves and our failures. We get upset when we mess up, thinking to ourselves that, as Christians, we shouldn't have to deal with sin anymore. But Christians are only human. As humans, we will make mistakes. We will continue to make mistakes until we become the very likeness of Jesus Himself. This happens only in heaven. And until we get to heaven, we will mess up. I don't say this to discourage you. On the contrary, this should encourage you. Our God is a very patient God. He looks on us with love and compassion, even when we mess up. He is committed to making us more like His Son. And He will never give up on us. As we go through our day-to-day lives, God is using everything around us to make us more like His Son. So next time you become discouraged with the circumstances surrounding you, remember that God is doing a great work within you, and He will not give up until it is complete.

*Gabrielle LaCognata*: 19, Belleview, FL
Church @ The Springs and College of Central Florida, Ocala, FL

# We Must Endure

"Therefore, since we also have such a large cloud of witnesses surrounding us, let us lay aside every weight and the sin that so easily ensnares us. Let us run with endurance the race that lies before us, keeping our eyes on Jesus, the source and perfecter of our faith, who for the joy that lay before Him endured a cross and despised the same and has sat down at the right hand of God's throne." —Hebrews 12:1–2

These are among my favorite verses in the entire Bible. When I am stressed or feeling tired, I often think of these verses and quote to myself, "Let us run with endurance." This section of Hebrews also encourages us to not allow ourselves to become weary and to always push forward, no matter what or how difficult our circumstances are. This encouragement seems very relevant to me now as a high school student. At times when I want to give up and run away from all my problems, I am reminded of the words from this text and it gives me encouragement and hope. And, because of my confidence in the Word of God, I know I can, through prayer, lay all my worries and all the weight of my sin on the Lord. This allows me to start anew and again resolve to finish the race. Is there a race in your life that His Word can be all you need to get going and running with endurance?

Mallory McClearn: 16, Leesburg, GA
Sherwood Baptist Church and Sherwood Christian Academy, Albany, GA

# Persecution

"If the world hates you, understand that it hated Me before it hated you. If you were of the world, the world would love you as its own. However, because you are not of the world, but I have chosen you out of it, the world hates you." —John 15:18–19

Christ followers will face persecution. Christians have always faced it and always will. During Bible times, they were arrested and served as entertainment for the Romans by fighting lions, bears, and each other. They were hung on crosses and set on fire to light the roads at night. No, we don't have to worry about that type of persecution here in the U.S., but what we do face can be emotionally damaging. Because it is promised that we will be humiliated and torn down by those who don't know the love of God, it's imperative that we know how to respond. First, know the attack isn't your fault. We can't forget what John 15:18–20 says. We are persecuted because of Who we belong to. "If they persecuted Me, they will also persecute you" (v. 20). Second, understand this is likely a test. God wants to see how you will respond. He knows what's going on, and He will help you through it. "My grace is sufficient for you, for power is perfected in weakness" (2 Corinthians 12:9). Our response determines if we pass or fail His test, and the person causing your pain will take note of that response. Be careful to not be angry. "Your speech should always be gracious, seasoned with salt, so that you may know how you should answer each person" (Colossians 4:6). Third, persecution is only temporary. Whatever it may be, don't let it consume your life and steal your joy. "So I take pleasure in weakness, insults, catastrophes, persecution, and in pressures, because of Christ. For when I am weak, then I am strong" (2 Corinthians 12:10).

Carson Gregors: 17, Albany, GA
Sherwood Baptist Church and Sherwood Christian Academy, Albany, GA

# A Call to Arms

**"This good news of the kingdom will be proclaimed in all the world as a testimony to all nations. And then the end will come."**

—Matthew 24:14

You've probably heard testimonies from missionaries. They talk of incredible people, places, and miracles. Perhaps you think, *That's so cool, I wish I could go there,* but wishes are quickly dashed away by a terrible thought: *How on earth could I afford a mission trip?* I've asked myself the same question. First, nothing is impossible with God. If He wants you to go, He will make a way. My mother went on a mission trip to Zimbabwe a few years ago. That trip cost her $1,500. My latest mission trip to Laredo, Texas, was $450. My father took a trip just this past summer and the cost for that one was $2,500. There was no way we could pay for the trips. God made it work, and He used the kind donations that we received from interested people. We all went on our respective trips. Second, God did not command only adults with jobs to go tell the world about Jesus. He commanded Christians. Maybe you're like me and tend to be nervous when trying to tell others about Jesus. That's fine, because one day God will give you the exact words to say, and from then on it'll be easier than talking to your best friend. I had this experience in Laredo when I led someone to Christ for the first time. God doesn't choose His messengers based on age and experience. God's call to arms applies to everyone, and we are expected to obey this call. You may not be called to Asia or Africa to follow God's command; the United States is full of lost people who don't know Christ. You could start small, like at school with your friends. And if God wants you to go bigger, He'll make a way.

*Hannah Arrington:* 15, Borger, TX
First Baptist Church and Texas Virtual Academy, Borger, TX

# Lucky

"A friend loves at all times, and a brother is born for a difficult time."

—Proverbs 17:17

Everyone needs a best friend, and I'm lucky enough to be blessed with some of the best friends anyone could ask for. They are my partners-in-crime, my go-tos, the ones with whom I share my hopes and dreams, and the ones who bring me back to reality. We have countless memories and great laughs together. Without my best friends I don't know if I'd be who I am today. They are always there for me. I know that whenever I'm in a tough spot or in need of help or guidance, I can look to them for advice, and they always know what to say. No matter what mistakes I make, they never judge me and always allow me to realize my wrongdoings graciously. They respect me and my choices and are always there for me to lean on. Not only do I thank God for giving me such gracious and amazing best friends, I also thank Him for blessing me with ones who help me grow spiritually as well. My best friends help me realize that we can't always understand why God does certain things. Whenever I'm worried or sulking, they remind me and assure me that God has a plan and a reason for everything. They tell me to look to God when I have questions or whenever I'm worried. I pray that God will help me be as good a friend to them as they are to me. I also pray that everyone is lucky enough to have best friends like mine. I don't know what I'd do without them, and I hope that we are able to maintain our friendship throughout upcoming challenges and life changes. My best friend is Jesus, but He blessed me with His best. Isn't that so like Him?

Makenzie Thomas: 16, Sevierville, TN
First Baptist Church and Gatlinburg-Pittman High School, Gatlinburg, TN

# Dating

"Commit your activities to the Lᴏʀᴅ, and your plans will be achieved."
—Proverbs 16:3

Teenage dating. Every teenager has either observed it or directly experienced it. Consequently, everyone has his or her own personal perspective on the subject, regardless of his or her relationship status. We have all seen the positive and negative effects of teen dating. Some of the positive effects can include actually receiving a valentine on Valentine's Day, being able to sit next to a special some-one in class, and getting a smooch of encouragement every once in a while. Teen dating can also produce a sincerely treasured companionship, improved maturity, and responsibility to each other. Some of the negative, more frequent effects of dating include extreme confusion, a consumption of time, and most commonly, intense awkwardness: "Do you want to go to the movies?" "My mom can pick us up at 6:00?" "Are we Facebook official?" "Should I hold his or her hand?" "Should we interlock fingers or clasp hands?" "What should I say?" "How should I act?" "Should I text first?" "Should I say 'I love you' yet?" These are all common ques-tions that come up in a teenage dating relationship. However, whether in a relation-ship or not, there is one particular key to success: complete commitment to the Lord. In Proverbs 16:3 it explains that whatever we do, our focus should be on the Lord for success. In whatever you do, whether you are an athlete, singer, dancer, instrumentalist, or artist, if you are wholly committed to the Lord, you will realize that complete joy is found in obedience to Him. So today, whether dating or single, be sure that the center of your attention is the Lord.

Danielle Quesinberry: 15, Knoxville, TN
Valley Grove Baptist Church Youth Group, Knoxville, TN; The Kings Academy, Seymour, TN

# Temptation

"Stay awake and pray, so that you won't enter into temptation. The spirit is willing, but the flesh is weak." —Matthew 26:41

It can be hard on teens to know how to deal with temptation. Even though you are a Christian, you are still tempted; it is part of being human. Whether you are tempted to lie or cheat, or even by sexual sin, the Bible tells you how to deal with it. It may not specifically name the sin you are struggling with, but it tells you how to get through hard things. You should remember that we were born sinful, and being tempted is normal. Our response to temptation is what matters. Prayer is a great way to help fight temptation. As Matthew 26:41 says, "Stay awake and pray, so that you won't enter into temptation. The spirit is willing, but the flesh is weak." We are weak but God will always be with us and will not give us more than He knows we can handle. First Corinthians 10:13 says, "No temptation has overtaken you except what is common to humanity. God is faithful, and He will not allow you to be tempted beyond what you are able, but with the temptation He will also provide a way of escape so that you are able to bear it." God knows what you can handle and He knows how you work. In this verse He promises to help you and to provide a way out of your temptation. God will be with you through everything. I can't stress that enough. It is also good to have friends and family to help you. God is enough, but most people like being able to talk to a friend and get advice. Having good Christian people surrounding you and building you up makes everyone feel better. It also gives you more confidence to stand up to whatever is tempting you. God knows what you are going through, and He will be there for you.

*Allison Fisher:* 14, Raleigh, NC
Providence Baptist Church and Leesville Road High School, Raleigh, NC

# Worship Is More Than Singing!

"Therefore, brothers, by the mercies of God, I urge you to present your bodies as a living sacrifice, holy and pleasing to God; this is your spiritual worship." —Romans 12:1

Worship is a beautiful thing. I love worshipping with my youth group every Wednesday night. Singing songs of praise to God with a body of believers is really an amazing experience. For a while I thought that was all worshipping meant—singing! But I have found out differently. This verse tells us differently. Our spiritual act of worship, according to Romans 12, is to offer our bodies as a living sacrifice. So worship is a living experience. It is 24/7. Our worship should never end, because we should always be offering ourselves up to Christ, trying our best to be holy and pleasing in His sight. With this in mind, our worship in church, our singing, should just be an overflow of what is already taking place in our hearts and lives. To show up at church and lift our hands, close our eyes, sing and sway to the music is hypocritical if we are not living lives of worship. How do we live this life of sacrifice? By the mercies of God. It is only by His grace that we can live for Him. We aren't going to be perfect, holy, and pleasing to God all the time, but there is grace for each moment. He only wants for us to try our best and to strive to live for Him in every moment. I once heard it said, "Christ died for me, the least I can do is live for Him." This is our worship, to live for Him all the time. Let your life be a worship song sung unto the Lord.

McKenzie Sutton: 17, Waverly Hall, GA
Cornerstone Baptist Church, Ellerslie, GA; Homeschooled

# Purity

**"Take delight in the LORD, and He will give you your heart's desires."**
—Psalm 37:4

Purity is something often taken for granted. Teens today underestimate its value and therefore ruin it before they enter adulthood. Many give it away to the ones they date, either physically or emotionally. This, unfortunately, has become so expected of our generation that adults and teens are caught off guard when they meet someone who is saving their heart and body for his or her future spouse. Purity holds great value. Remaining physically pure has many benefits. Not only does doing so honor your future spouse, but it also prevents insecurities. The easiest way to maintain physical purity is to establish boundaries before entering into dating relationships. Setting these safeguards can save you from compromising yourself and your standards. Not only is physical purity necessary, but so is emotional purity. Giving away emotional purity is easy because it often happens without you realizing it. This process takes place very slowly as you begin to share your heart and dreams with the people you date. This is dangerous because a crush isn't meant to meet emotional needs. This is a huge mistake that many teens make when they first start to date. Once you start down this slippery slope, it's hard to regain your footing. If you haven't given away your purity, cling to it tightly. Never compromise, even when it's appealing. You are not alone. Maintaining purity is hard and tiring, but with God you can win! And if you have given it away, God can restore it, making you new again. Through the love of Christ we all have been redeemed and our sins have been forgotten. Only He can erase the shame. Christ came to set the captives free and heal the brokenhearted. Finally, be aware that no one is perfect; we all make mistakes.

*Carson Gregors*: 17, Albany, GA
Sherwood Baptist Church and Sherwood Christian Academy, Albany, GA

# Your Heart

**"Guard your heart above all else, for it is the source of life."**

—Proverbs 4:23

We are to be careful with what we allow to enter our hearts and minds. We must also be careful about giving our hearts away. If we give our hearts to someone too early, we risk losing pieces of our hearts. Every time you hold hands or kiss, you give away a little of your heart that you can never get back. Slowly, little by little, you can give away your heart. If you give little bits of your heart to several people before you are ready for a serious, committed relationship, what will be left for your future spouse? Broken fragments of a heart? While it is important to love people and care for them as Jesus did, we shouldn't be giving our hearts away to guys (or girls) frequently. As we guard our hearts, we are also to guard our minds and what we allow our thoughts to dwell on. You may not give your heart to someone, but you can constantly think on things that aren't pure, lovely, and commendable, and in so doing, give your heart away. "Finally brothers, whatever is true, whatever is honorable, whatever is just, whatever is pure, whatever is lovely, whatever is commendable—if there is any moral excellence and if there is any praise—dwell on these things" (Philippians 4:8). This verse shows us what we should be allowing in our thoughts. Guarding our hearts doesn't mean being cold and uncaring toward people. Jesus loves and cares for people. We should follow His example. We should love and care for people as Christians and friends. We can do this while still guarding our hearts.

*Tyra Ruisinger:* 17, Raymore, MO
Summit Woods Baptist Church, Lee's Summit, MO; Homeschooled

# Love that Is Evident

"By this all people will know that you are My disciples, if you have love for one another." —John 13:35

There are people in my life whom I would rather not love. People who have hurt me in the past; people who, in my eyes, don't deserve my love. But Christ's command is to love no matter what. Love for others is what we are called to do. The Bible tells us that love is what defines us as Christians and sets us apart from the rest of the world. Sometimes loving others can be easy. To love your best friend is easy. Maybe you like the same things and never argue about anything. She's always been there for you. So you love her—after all, she's your best friend. But what about those people who are hard to love? The grandma with Alzheimer's who lives with you, that family member who has turned away from everything your family cherishes and values, or the annoying neighbor across the street. Sure, you can say you love them, but do you live love toward them? Living love is what being a Christian is all about. God is love. To live love is to live Christ. When we love others who don't deserve it we are following the example of Christ. He loved us when we didn't deserve it. He loved us in the ugly mess of our sin. So "we love because He first loved us" (1 John 4:19). Love is a choice and an action. We can go to church, sing in the choir, or lead a Bible study, but if it is not done in love it is useless. Loving others is how people see Jesus in us. Let love be the very definition of your life. Live love today and every day.

McKenzie Sutton: 17, Waverly Hall, GA
Cornerstone Baptist Church, Ellerslie, GA; Homeschooled

# Social Media

"Do not love the world or the things that belong to the world.
If anyone loves the world, love for the Father is not in him."

—1 John 2:15

The world has a very big influence on the lives of teenagers, especially girls, and especially when it comes to social media and other outlets. We need to be careful about the music we listen to, the movies we watch, the celebrities we look up to, and how we use social media. They all influence our thoughts and our actions. The world tells us that things like money, vanity, sex, and self-interest are all fine. God can bring you out of your comfort zone and use you for His will. Are you willing to be used by God in any way possible? Do not let what the world says dictate your future. Vanity affects most teenagers. The Internet, television shows, and commercials, and every other form of advertisement tell us how to look and how to behave in a worldly, sinful way. God is not in them and they are often promoting a sinful agenda. Stay yourself, be who God made you to be. Glorify God in everything you do. Stay in His Word and let Him be your guide. The Bible tells us how to live godly lives. God loves you for you, not you trying to be someone else. We can't be so sheltered as to not notice what pops up on our computer screens, or what is thrown at us during television commercials, but we can be so aware of what God's Word says that He will guard our hearts and minds. The devil wants us to see and to listen to the world and accept what the world has for us. He wants to bring us down in any way he can. Keep your guard up, and ask God to help you make the right choices about what the world puts in your path.

Dianah Edwards: 16, West Monroe, LA
First West Monroe Baptist Church and Northeast Baptist School, West Monroe, LA

# The Stress of It All!

"Casting all your care on Him, because He cares about you."
—1 Peter 5:7

"What do you want to do in life?" "Have you decided where you want to go to college yet?" "Are you going to play soccer?" "Do you want to go to school out-of-state?" Now that I'm a junior, these questions seem to pop up everywhere I go. I really haven't put much thought into any of these questions. I'm not sure where I want to go, what I want to do when I get there, or even exactly what I want to be. I always knew these choices were coming up, and I knew how important they were, but I never realized that everything would happen so quickly. Knowing that I have to make these decisions, and make them soon, has really stressed me out. My future depends on these decisions. What I choose could really make or break me. How am I supposed to know what the best choice is? I have realized that I can't simply rely on my thoughts and opinions. "Now if any of you lacks wisdom, he should ask God, who gives to all generously and without criticizing, and it will be given to him" (James 1:5). God knows what's best for me even better than I do. If I seek His guidance to make my decisions, I know that I will be able to make the best choices for myself. Everyone has been stressed about something at one time, whether it is school, parents, friends, or sports, and God knows this. The important thing to remember is that God wouldn't put you through something if He knew you couldn't do it. Are you willing to cast your worries on God?

Makenzie Thomas: 16, Sevierville, TN
First Baptist Church and Gatlinburg-Pittman High School, Gatlinburg, TN

# Dear God . . .

"Now this is the confidence we have before Him: Whenever we ask anything according to His will, He hears us. And if we know that He hears whatever we ask, we know that we have what we have asked Him for."

—1 John 5:14–15

How often do you pray? Is it something you do every day? Do you pray every other day? Or do you only pray at church? Or, perhaps, you find that you forget to pray except when you're about to take a test or a family member is ill? Maybe you don't make time to pray because you don't think that it does any good. I've thought like that before. A few years ago, I stopped praying every day because I never got what I asked for. I started to wonder if God heard me or even cared about what I was going through. While looking for verses about prayer, I found 1 John 5:14–15, which says this: "Now this is the confidence we have before Him: Whenever we ask anything according to His will, He hears us. And if we know that He hears whatever we ask, we know that we have what we have asked Him for." It encouraged me to know that God not only hears me, but that He will answer me. I realized that I had made a mistake in praying only to ask for things for myself. God isn't a genie that gives us whatever we ask for. There is no magic in heaven! He wants us to pray for others and ask for His will to be done in our lives. Sometimes, even when we pray unselfishly, the answer is no. We have to learn to accept that and trust that if God says no, it's because He has something even better planned for us. Keep in mind next time you pray that God really does hear you, and be confident that He will answer.

*Kaylin Calvert:* 18, Medical Lake, WA
Airway Heights Baptist Church, Airway Heights, WA; Homeschooled

# Trust Issues

"Trust in the LORD with all your heart and do not rely on your own understanding." —Proverbs 3:5

Over the past couple of years I have developed trust issues. For me, trusting someone else is very difficult. Being the independent person I am, trusting another person makes me feel vulnerable. Perhaps you can relate to my situation. The moment I stopped trusting people was when I gave my heart to someone and that person trampled all over it. In that rough patch of my life, not only did I stop trusting people, I stopped trusting God as well. That year was one of the worst of my life. I built walls around my heart and didn't let anyone in. In my mind, I was far too weak to spend time in prayer talking to God, let alone spend time walking to Him to give Him my pain. The funny thing was that God didn't ask me to walk to Him, He came and picked me up and carried me. To this day, God still carries me from time to time, but I have also learned to walk beside Him. I still have trouble trusting people, but God is teaching me how. Now that I have begun to trust again, He has blessed me with the two best friends anyone could ever have. I always thought that asking for help was showing how weak you are, but that's not true. It's not showing how weak you are, but how strong God is.

Taylor Dillon: 17, Stafford, VA
Grace Life Community Church, Bristow, VA; Emmanuel Christian High School, Manassas, VA

# When We Ask "Why?"

"The Lord is near the brokenhearted;
He saves those crushed in spirit." —Psalm 34:18

When I was younger, I had a best friend who was like a sister to me. In the fall of 2007, my friend's father was diagnosed with lung cancer. The cancer was in its final phases. While her dad was in the hospital, I was often in her house. Eventually, my friend's father died. I remember it being so painful. We were all left in a state of grief. I wondered how God could allow such a godly man, a man so important to so many, to die and leave us. With the death of my friend's father, we were each placed in a situation where we had to learn to put our trust in God and to look to Him for comfort. Psalm 34:18 states, "The Lord is near the brokenhearted; He saves those crushed in spirit."

*Mallory McClearn:* 16, Leesburg, GA
Sherwood Baptist Church and Sherwood Christian Academy, Albany, GA

# Trust God

## "I am able to do all things through Him who strengthens me."
### —Philippians 4:13

There are a lot of things teens can worry about in high school, which can make trusting God difficult. For me, I worry about my grades, getting sick, disappointing my family, and whether people like me or not. When I worry, I like to pray. Every time I have to take a test, I sit at my desk and pray before I start. Some people look at me funny, but it is just something I do. It always helps me feel better. When I am nervous about a big test or going through something difficult, one of my favorite verses to think of is Philippians 4:13, which says, "I am able to do all things through Him who strengthens me." Listening to Christian music will lift your spirits. Two verses that encourage me are Psalm 27:1, "The Lord is my light and my salvation—whom should I fear? The Lord is the stronghold of my life—of whom should I be afraid?" and Deuteronomy 31:6 "Be strong and courageous; don't be terrified or afraid of them. For it is the Lord your God who goes with you; He will not leave you or forsake you." Christian music and Bible verses help me get through different situations and remind me to trust in God. I am an anxious person, so having these verses and songs to think of helps me feel God's peace. I hope that you will put your trust in God and remember He is always with you, even if you don't feel that He is. God has saved us from death, so we can trust Him with all things. Put all your faith in God and surrender to Him. Remember God cares about what you are going through and will help you through everything.

*Allison Fisher*: 14, Raleigh, NC
Providence Baptist Church and Leesville Road High School, Raleigh, NC

# Friends Do Care and Help to Carry the Load

## "Carry one another's burdens; in this way you will fulfill the law of Christ." —Galatians 6:2

Ever had a really bad day or had something bad happen to you? You go to unload on your friend about it. The whole time she looks annoyed and the look on her face is saying, "Hurry up already." As soon as you are finished, she goes on to tell you about how she was walking today and one of the heels on her favorite pair of shoes fell off. Uncaring, selfish, not a really great friend—these are some words that might describe that person. If you are a Christian and these types of words or situations describe you, then you are not fulfilling the law of Christ. His law is to love our neighbors as ourselves. We fulfill that law when we carry one another's burdens. I looked up the word *carry* in *Webster's* dictionary, and it has over twenty-five definitions, the very first being "to hold or support while moving." As Christ followers, lovers of Jesus, whatever you want to call us, we are commanded to hold or support each other. When one of our brothers or sisters in Christ is going through a difficult time, it is our job to be the hands and feet of Jesus to them, to love them and to walk (move) with them through it. By living for Jesus we express love for others, and what better way to love them than to be there for them. All throughout Scripture the church is called to love, be there, support, and encourage one another in the faith. We need one another. Be a caring friend who is always ready to carry someone else's burdens. Be the friend who always listens to the other person before going on about what's happening in your life. By doing this you will be imitating Christ, Who put us first and carried our burdens all the way to the cross!

McKenzie Sutton: 17, Waverly Hall, GA
Cornerstone Baptist Church, Ellerslie, GA; Homeschooled

# Being Tempted

"No temptation has overtaken you except what is common to humanity."

—1 Corinthians 10:13

Being tempted is part of being human. Everyone is subject to temptations, and there are no exceptions. Temptation is everywhere you look, in every situation you may find yourself in. It's on the computer, on the television, and sometimes even through your friends. Being the somewhat normal teenager that I am, I have been tempted more times than I can count. Christian teens, in my opinion, have more responsibility to refuse temptation than non-Christian teens. Not only do we represent God, but we need to be examples to the rest of the world. Sometimes, for me at least, the fact that I am not supposed to do worldly things is very annoying, but most of the time it keeps me out of a lot of trouble. Temptation is not a punishment; it is a test. The Bible says to pick up your cross daily. Being a Christian does not mean that you will not fall victim to the things of this world, because you will. To just say "no" is much easier said than done. Saying "no" to things you want to say "yes" to will not go unnoticed. God rewards those who serve Him. Resisting temptation will be difficult, but in the end it's so worth it.

Taylor Dillon: 17, Stafford, VA
Grace Life Community Church, Bristow, VA; Emmanuel Christian High School, Manassas, VA

# Rebel

"Flee from youthful passions, and pursue righteousness, faith, love, and peace, along with those who call on the Lord from a pure heart. But reject foolish and ignorant disputes, knowing that they breed quarrels."

—2 Timothy 2:22–23

Today, teenagers are mostly known for the rebelling stage of their lives. Everyone expects it. What if we stopped? What if all of us decided that enough is enough? Adults have such low expectations of us during our high school and college years, but do we really want that? What if we were the generation who stopped this? The thing is, though, we need to be unified. Unity is something the devil hates! If we are unified, we are constantly encouraging one another and reaching out to others as a group! The verse above clearly says that if we flee from youthful desires and chase after what God wants together, we won't face quarrels with each other. We would be unified and could accomplish so much. This week, I challenge you to rebel against rebellion and encourage your fellow believers to do the same! Start planning how to get more teens to join you! Have high expectations of yourself; go out and prove others wrong.

Hannah Thompson: 15, Leesburg, GA
Sherwood Baptist Church and Sherwood Christian Academy, Albany, GA

# 123

## Using Your Talents

"Based on the gift they have received, everyone should use it to serve others, as good managers of the varied grace of God." —1 Peter 4:10

God has blessed me with the talent of playing volleyball. When I first started playing I was awful, but with much practice I became very good. At the end of every game I would always get compliments on my serves and sets. At the time I was on junior varsity, and my coach always bragged on me and said that I needed to be on varsity. It didn't take long for those praises to go to my head. I stopped playing the sport because I loved it and started playing because people bragged on how good I was at it! I would walk the halls at school and know that I was the best at what I did. It was the best feeling in the world. When I went to practice that day, I had no idea how drastically my world of volleyball would change. About an hour into practice, my coach told us to begin our serving drills. About my third or fourth serve in, I could tell something was wrong. By the end of practice, I couldn't even get the ball to half court. I didn't know it at the time, but I had permanently inflamed my shoulder. The rest of the season my serves were useless. For quite a while after the season was over, I thought that God was punishing me. Now that I look back, I see it wasn't punishment—it was a lesson. He wanted me to remember that He gave me that talent and that He could take it away. I had forgotten that I wasn't always good at volleyball. And, I didn't get good on my own either. I went through about a year of being completely humbled. Now I will never forget Who the glory goes to.

Taylor Dillon: 17, Stafford, VA
Grace Life Community Church, Bristow, VA; Emmanuel Christian High School, Manassas, VA

# Sickness

"Even when I go through the darkest valley, I fear no danger, for You are with me; Your rod and Your staff—they comfort me." —Psalm 23:4

When I was nine years old, my mom had surgery to remove her gall bladder. Because the hospital where the surgery would take place was a few hours away, my parents decided to stay in a hotel near the hospital while my two older brothers and I stayed with our big sister for a few days. When Mom and Dad came back, they brought some surprising news. The doctors had gone in with a camera probe to see if there were any blockages anywhere. While the probe was in there, the doctors found a precancerous growth in my mom's small intestine that was about to become malignant. After cutting it several times, the doctors were able to remove the growth. But because there is still a possibility that the growth can come back, she has to go have it checked out every few years. The first feeling I had was relief. The next feeling was fear. I didn't know much about cancer back then. But I had seen people with cancer on television, and I knew that cancer kills a large number of people. And the ones who didn't die suffered through so much pain to live. I was worried that the growth would come back without us knowing and that it would turn malignant before we could get rid of it. And I still worry about it. But God keeps reminding me that I don't have to worry because her life and health are in His hands. Even if she does get cancer, I know that in the end she will be safe with God. It's hard when a person that you love and are close to is seriously ill. It's hard to watch and accept. Just remember that God loves them even more than you do and will be with them every step of the way.

*Sarah King*: 18, Gainesville, VA
Emmanuel Baptist Church and Emmanuel Christian School, Manassas, VA

# Your Example

"Let no one despise your youth; instead, you should be an example to the believers in speech, in conduct, in love, in faith, in purity."

—1 Timothy 4:12

I'm the youngest in my family, so I never thought of myself as a role model. But two years ago I noticed my now three-year-old niece copying me. I realized that whether we think so or not, people, especially younger kids, look up to us. Because of that, we have to carefully portray what being a godly Christian teenager looks like. That is our responsibility. We can't just go around disobeying and being disrespectful to people in authority over us or have our lives revolve around popularity and the latest celebrity gossip. The way they will act in the future as teenagers is partially determined by our influence in their lives and the way we conduct ourselves. There are two easy steps to being a good role model. The first is to behave in a godly manner. We are supposed to help show them how to live according to God's will. That does not mean that we have to be perfect angels. That's obviously not going to happen, since we're human. But we want to be like Christ as much as we possibly can so that we can tell those who look up to us what Paul said: "Imitate me, as I also imitate Christ" (1 Corinthians 11:1). The second step is to be involved in their lives. This doesn't mean that you have to be best friends and spend every second together. All you have to do is talk with them occasionally. A simple "Hi" or compliment can brighten their day. At first, I was nervous about being a role model. But God showed me that I would be good at it as long as I was following Him. And you will be too. We're already making a difference in their lives. Let's make it a positive one.

Sarah King: 18, Gainesville, VA
Emmanuel Baptist Church and Emmanuel Christian School, Manassas, VA

# Suffering

"We know that all things work together for the good of those who love God: those who are called according to His purpose."

—Romans 8:28

Suffering is not a popular topic, but it is an inevitable one. We live in a wicked world because of sin, and suffering is one of the consequences we have to face. But what you and I have to understand is that even in our suffering God can do great things in us and through us. One of the best stories I can think of that involves some major suffering is the story of Joseph. Joseph's story has a crazy amount of ups and downs. Joseph started out as his father's favorite and was sold into slavery by his jealous brothers. He then became Potiphar's go-to guy but ended up in prison because of Potiphar's wife, where he was promptly forgotten, abandoned, and left to rot for crimes he didn't commit. Years later, he was let out of prison to interpret Pharaoh's dreams. After interpreting the dreams, Joseph became second in charge and helped keep Egypt from suffering during a famine. During the famine, Joseph's brothers came to Egypt searching for food, and Joseph was able to supply them with all they needed. He says in Genesis 45:5–7, "And now don't be worried or angry with yourselves for selling me here, because God sent me ahead of you to preserve life. . . . God sent me ahead of you to establish you as a remnant within the land and to keep you alive by a great deliverance." Joseph went through much pain and suffering in his life. He was hated by his brothers, sold into slavery, and put in prison unfairly. In all of this, he remained faithful to God. And because of this, God used him to provide for his family and ultimately the Hebrews as a nation. So next time you suffer through something, remember that God hasn't abandoned you. He may just be preparing you for something great.

Gabrielle LaCognata: 19, Belleview, FL
Church @ The Springs and College of Central Florida, Ocala, FL

# The Shy Ones

"For it was You who created my inward parts; You knit me together in my mother's womb. I will praise You because I have been remarkably and wonderfully made. Your works are wonderful, and I know this very well."

—Psalm 139:13–14

Being shy is an issue that many teenagers struggle with. Believe me, I have had personal experience with being shy. Ever since I was little I was extremely shy. I was afraid that the other kids would think I had a weird personality or that I would do something to embarrass myself. Because of that, I barely talked to anyone and rarely got involved in group activities. I had one best friend who I was completely myself with, but I always got quiet whenever we were around other kids. As you can imagine, I tended to fade into the background and was easily forgotten by people. It hurt, but I would have rather had them forget me than dislike me. This went on for years, until something changed around four years ago. One day, I was thinking about the verse above, and I realized that there was no reason for me to be shy. There was no reason for me to fear rejection because God made me who I am for a reason. Ever since that day, I decided that with God's help my shyness would no longer stop me from enjoying who God made me to be. Now I have so many friends that I can talk with for hours, and I'm not embarrassed about all my little quirks. I'm just me. Don't let being shy or the fear of embarrassment get in the way. God made everybody different. It's a good thing.

Sarah King: 18, Gainesville, VA
Emmanuel Baptist Church and Emmanuel Christian School, Manassas, VA

# Lies Can Not Justify Anything!

**"As a dog returns to its vomit, so a fool repeats his foolishness."**

—Proverbs 26:11

The verse for today deals with repeating the same sins in life. As teenagers, we are constantly bombarded by the temptations of this world. After getting caught or getting into trouble, it is easy to say that we have changed our ways and ask for forgiveness. But as time goes on and the guilt fades, it is very easy to revert back to our old ways, just as a dog returns to its vomit. I have found it easier to lie in certain situations if it means avoiding confrontation or protecting someone's feelings. But the more I justified lying, the more I found myself taking the easy way out. For example, one time my friend asked me to spend the night at her house and I left my answer open-ended, but later another friend asked me to do something. I chose to go with the second friend because I knew we would have more fun, but I lied to the first friend and told her I had family in town. Eventually the truth came out. When she found out that I had blown her off, her feelings were deeply hurt. Different lessons like this have taught me that honesty is always the best policy. Even if the truth hurts, it is a lot easier to justify truth than to justify a lie. Proverbs 26:11 opened my eyes and showed me that the lying had to stop and that God didn't want that sin in my life. Once I started telling the truth, things became a lot easier, and I was happier because I didn't have the stress of trying to keep straight the truth from a lie. God will help you, too, if you are using lies to justify your actions.

Micki Werner: 16, Gatlinburg, TN
First Baptist Church and Gatlinburg-Pittman High School, Gatlinburg, TN

# Never Judge by First Impression

"Stop judging according to outward appearances; rather judge according to righteous judgment." —John 7:24

Mark 7:2–8 says, "They observed that some of His disciples were eating their bread with unclean—that is, unwashed—hands. (For the Pharisees, in fact all the Jews, will not eat unless they wash their hands ritually, keeping the tradition of the elders. When they come from the marketplace, they do not eat unless they have washed. And there are many other customs they have received and keep, like the washing of cups, jugs, copper utensils, and dining couches.) Then the Pharisees and the scribes asked Him, 'Why don't Your disciples live according to the tradition of the elders, instead of eating bread with ritually unclean hands?' He answered them, 'Isaiah prophesied correctly about you hypocrites, as it is written: These people honor Me with their lips, but their heart is far from Me. They worship Me in vain, teaching as doctrines the commands of men. Disregarding the command of God, you keep the tradition of men.'" We should never judge someone's personality by a first impression. When we do judge, we should use the Bible as a measuring stick, not society or our own whims. People are often very different from how they seem. For example, I was very shy when I was younger, and my shyness was mistaken for being antisocial. I actually loved being around people. Because I wore a lot of black people thought I was a very serious person, when in reality humor was and is one of my favorite things. Since I preferred metal music to pop or country, people expected me to be irritable or angry, etc. I was actually very cheerful. I have learned from personal experience that you should always get to know someone before making any assumptions about them. God looks on the heart, and we need to as well.

Faith Kurtz: 13, Holden, MA
Bethlehem Bible Church and Bethlehem Bible Church Homeschooled Co-op, West Boyton, MA

# Putting God First

*"No one can be a slave of two masters, since either he will hate one or love the other, or be devoted to one and despise the other. You cannot be slaves of God and of money."* —Matthew 6:24

We live in a world with amazing technology that helps us connect with friends and family and sometimes even strangers; but many of the things that connect us as humans disconnect us from God. Many people don't have time for God. There are too many sports, extracurricular activities, social activities, or technological activities going on for us to have the time to build up that heavenly relationship God wants us to have with Him. While many of us are connected to the Internet, we become disconnected from God, and we all know that a weak connection can become frustrating especially when nothing can be done to fix it. I'm sure God is disappointed when we refuse to pursue a relationship with Him because He left it up to us to choose which path we take. From the beginning of time, God gave us a choice of good and evil. Adam and Eve chose the wrong thing to do, and they lived with regret for the rest of their lives. Now we have to make the right decisions ourselves, turn off the Internet and television, open a Bible, and spend time connecting with God. Proverbs 3:6 says, "Think about Him in all your ways, and He will guide you on the right paths." In other words, "In everything you do, put God first."

*Abby Fortner*: 15, Gatlinburg, TN
First Baptist Church and Gatlinburg-Pittman High School, Gatlinburg, TN

# When Suffering Is a Good Thing

"Seeing that we suffer with Him so that we may also be glorified with Him." —Romans 8:17

Many times when we think of suffering, we view it as a bad thing. We pray desperately for God to deliver us from our trials. We want to live quiet and comfortable lives. Each trial we endure is different, and I don't pretend to know where you're coming from or what you may be going through now. However, Philippians 1:29 tells us that "It has been given to you on Christ's behalf not only to believe in Him, but also to suffer for Him." As a Christian, we are called not only to believe, but also to suffer for the sake of Christ. But why? Romans 8:17 tells us that "we suffer with [Christ] so that we may also be glorified with Him." God tells us that He allows our suffering in this world as a sign of our "deliverance" (Philippians 1:28) and eternal salvation. Christians should expect to face trials in this world—in fact we should rejoice in them! Again, we ask, why? The suffering and trials we endure reveal our faith in God. Romans 5:3–4 says, "We also rejoice in our afflictions, because we know that affliction produces endurance, endurance produces proven character, and proven character produces hope." Trials allow us to grow and mature as Christians. Very often they remind us of what is truly important in life—not the distractions put in front of us by the world, but the Lord and our relationship with Him. Jesus says these words to His disciples: "I have told you these things so that in Me you may have peace. You will have suffering in this world. Be courageous! I have conquered the world" (John 16:33). We can have confidence that Christ will always remain with us and give us the strength to get through our trials, helping us to grow in faith and devotion to Him.

Kristin Goehl: 18, Princeton, MA
Bethlehem Bible Church, West Boylston, MA; Princeton University, Princeton, MA

# Don't Discount Your Youth

"Let no one despise your youth; instead, you should be an example to the believers in speech, in conduct, in love, in faith, in purity."

—1 Timothy 4:12

Josiah became king when he was only eight. Daniel and his buddies Shadrach, Meshach, and Abednego were only youth when the Babylonian king summoned them to serve him. They took a stand for God and for righteousness in front of all the older people who served the king. David killed Goliath when he was, as the Bible describes it, "just a youth." Scholars believe that Mary, the mother of Jesus was between the ages of twelve and fourteen when she gave birth to our Savior. I think God loves to use teenagers. He wants to be involved in every part of your life right now, as a thirteen-, sixteen-, or seventeen-year-old. So often teens think they will serve God when they're older. I know I am guilty of this, guilty of thinking that God can't really use me until I am older and stronger in Him. In this passage of Scripture Paul is encouraging Timothy, a young pastor, to not let anyone despise his youth. He is saying to Timothy, and essentially to us, that we are to not let people look down on us because we are young. We are not to think that just because we are teenagers, and we don't have everything quite figured out, that God cannot use us. He loves to use small people in big ways. He wants to shine brightly in our lives now. Jesus does not want us to wait to serve Him. He tells us that now, while we are young, we can be examples to all believers. We can be an example in the way we speak, act, love, trust, and walk out purity. Don't hold back because you think you're too young. Don't wait to serve the Lord. He wants to use you—right now in your youth!

McKenzie Sutton: 17, Waverly Hall, GA
Cornerstone Baptist Church, Ellerslie, GA; Homeschooled

# Now and Later

"Don't worry about anything, but in everything, through prayer and petition with thanksgiving, let your requests be made known to God. And the peace of God, which surpasses every thought, will guard your hearts and minds in Christ Jesus." —Philippians 4:6–7

I am the queen of stressing out. On my sixteenth birthday, I began having awful stomach pain and I could hardly walk. I had to leave school, miss volleyball, and go to the doctor. Like so many times in my life, I was a medical mystery. My doctor could not figure out what was wrong with me. After drinking two disgusting barium smoothies, we discovered that my only problem was stress. I had been stressing out so much over school and volleyball, my whole system was messed up. I spent my sixteenth birthday in the hospital! After that lovely experience, I decided I needed to stop stressing out. Then I thought, *Me? Stop stressing out? Like that's ever going to happen!* But I knew I had to. I read Philippians 4:6 quite often. It says not to worry about anything! I can't grasp that concept. I love to think about college, getting married, and how I will spend my time as an old lady. Even though I think those are harmless little thoughts, those are the ones I stress about the most. I've learned I must focus on the now, not the later. I still don't have the concept mastered, but I am working on it every day. I give it to God so that verse 7 above can come true. Jeremiah 29:11 says, "'For I know the plans I have for you'—this is the Lord's declaration—'plans for your welfare, not for disaster, to give you a future and a hope.'" God has each of our lives planned to the tee. It's our job to know the plan and to sit back, relax, and enjoy all that He has in store for us.

Hannah Savage: 16, Tarpon Springs, FL
Calvary Baptist Church and Calvary Christian High School, Tarpon Springs, FL

# Losing Friends

"A man with many friends may be harmed, but there is a friend who stays closer than a brother." —Proverbs 18:24

Eventually, we will let people down. The question is, who's going to stick around even through the hard times? Who's going to love you and forgive you no matter what? When you go through difficult times in your friendships, those are the kinds of questions you need to ask yourself. I've lost so many people in the past two years. Each person I lost I was close with at one point in my life. They truly meant a lot to me. After a time, all of them just threw me away. The worst part was that each of them did it to me at one time. It was one of the hardest things I've been through. When you lose friends, that's when you need God the most. God is always there, and He will easily reveal that to you if you simply let Him. If you're going through something like this right now, it will get better. Although it took me so long to get over all of those people, I finally did. This experience helped me realize how to be a good friend. Proverbs 17:17 says, "A friend loves at all times, and a brother is born for a difficult time." When everyone leaves, who is left? Those who are worth keeping. If you are currently trying to cope with losing a friend, I know how it feels—empty. This is when you really need Christ to help. Voice your thoughts to God and begin relying on Him. While going through this, look to the people who are staying with you and keep them. They're there for a reason. If you're currently not going through this, all friendships still need prayer. Continuously pray to God that all of your relationships will remain strong. Most of all, pray that you will remain a good friend to your friends.

Angela Stanley: 17, Woodbridge, VA
Dale City Baptist Church, Woodbridge, VA; Emmanuel Christian School, Manassas, VA

# Confronting Others

"If I say to the wicked person, 'You will surely die,'
but you do not warn him—you don't speak out to warn him about
his wicked way in order to save his life—that wicked person will die
for his iniquity. Yet I will hold you responsible for his blood."

—Ezekiel 3:18

The thought of confronting your friends about sin in their lives can be scary. I've been there. You're afraid of how they might respond, what it'll do to your friendship. The weight of Ezekiel 3:18 is incredible! God is pretty much saying that we will be held accountable for the times when we let fear win and don't confront our friends. Now I don't know about you, but I'd much rather be uncomfortable for a few minutes with a friend than have the Creator of the universe upset with me. There are some things to remember when confronting someone. Be loving (1 Corinthians 13:1–7), be humble (1 Peter 5:5), and offer to pray with them and for them. No one wants to be told that they're wrong, but looking back, that person will remember you as a true friend if you go about it in a Christ-like way. You need people in your life who will walk alongside you with Christ and who aren't afraid to confront you either. The first time someone confronts you, it's going to sting a little. That's just the prideful nature we've been given. But take it to heart, and let them help you grow in your walk. You will be so much closer to that person afterward than you would be with someone who is afraid to tell you the truth because they don't want to hurt your feelings.

Christa Morgan: 17, Alabaster, AL
Westwood Baptist Church and Thompson High School, Alabaster, AL

# Forgiveness

"Then Peter came to Him and said, 'Lord, how many times could my brother sin against me and I forgive him? As many as seven times?' 'I tell you, not as many as seven,' Jesus said to him, 'but 70 times seven.'"

—Matthew 18:21–22

Sometimes the problems we face are caused by other people and not just our circumstances. There are people I could not get along with throughout my school life. I always found it hard to get along with a couple of people in my school, even though we are together a lot. Even when there are good reasons for us to be friends, getting close to some people just seems impossible, no matter how hard we try. Sometimes people just annoy one another. Some of my peers have been difficult to be friends with, and they have left school. So now that I'm older I would love to make amends, but I can't. I really wish I had the opportunity to tell them that I am sorry for not being a kind person. Matthew 18:21–22 are some of my favorite verses. God is telling us that we should forgive people every time they don't treat us right. I have forgiven these two in my heart, but I would love the opportunity to ask them to forgive me. Forgiving people can be a very difficult thing to do. It can even be hard to forgive people you love, such as your brother, your sister, or your parents. However, we must always remember to forgive others because that's what God wants us to do. We must not hold grudges, and we must forgive the bad things others do to us, no matter who they are. Forgive!

Michaela Reed: 15, Albany, GA
Institutional First Baptist Church and Sherwood Christian Academy, Albany, GA

# What's the Point?

"Don't be deceived: God is not mocked. For whatever a man sows he will also reap, because the one who sows to his flesh will reap corruption from the flesh, but the one who sows to the Spirit will reap eternal life from the Spirit. So we must not get tired of doing good, for we will reap at the proper time if we don't give up."

—Galatians 6:7–9

There have been times in my life when I've looked at my peers and asked myself, "What's the point of living the way God wants me to?" God has high standards, and there have been times that I was tempted to just give up because I could never live up to them all. Besides, I can't lose my salvation, so why bother doing good works? Many people who aren't Christians seem to have more fun than I do because they don't have to follow Christian standards. Whenever I start to think like this, I remember Galatians 6:7–9. So yes, sometimes it may seem that living the way God wants you to is no fun, but remember that it's also for your good. Living for yourself might feel good at first, but when harvest time comes, you won't have anything good from it. Instead, let's live for the Spirit and reap eternal life.

*Kaylin Calvert:* 18, Medical Lake, WA
Airway Heights Baptist Church, Airway Heights, WA; Homeschooled

# All Sin

## "For all have sinned and fall short of the glory of God."

—Romans 3:23

As Christians, whether we recognize it or not, someone is always looking up to us. It might be our younger siblings, or maybe friends who aren't Christians, or people we come in contact with at the mall and other places we go. I've had many weird looks given to me by clerks at a store simply because I've said thank you to my mom for buying me an outfit. It has become a habit for me, but not so common anymore for many teens. Sometimes with my Christian label it can be hard to minister because people think, *Oh well, she is a Christian. She thinks she's perfect, and I don't want to be friends with her.* They don't understand that just because I'm a Christian doesn't mean I don't sin or that I'm very different from them. Everyone sins, which is a proven fact! We are all at fault, and we all need God. There is no such thing as a perfect Christian. Even your pastors and youth pastors sin, and they are not perfect either. Because we all sin and we all need a Savior, God sent His Son to take our place on the cross. He is available to do the same for everyone if you will just call on Him and repent and ask Him to save you. He's ready, are you?

Megan Medford: 14, Bryant, AR
The Church at Rock Creek and Bryant High School, Little Rock, AR

# The Proverbs 31 Woman

"Charm is deceptive and beauty is fleeting, but a woman who fears the LORD will be praised." —Proverbs 31:30

Most of us have heard of the Proverbs 31 woman. The phrase describes a woman who meets the standards described in Proverbs 31 and is a shining example of what it looks like to live out her faith. I know a woman like this. Katie was a senior at my school when I was in seventh grade. At the time, my best friend and I ran cross-country, as did Katie. My friend and I used to talk about how we wanted to be just like her. I didn't know much about Katie, but there was one thing that everyone could see from the way she lived. She loved Jesus with everything. She was involved in many ministries and leadership organizations. There was just something different about her countenance and the way she treated people. My friend and I met her because she sought us out and asked if she could be our mentor. I had heard about other girls my age that had someone older than them give them advice and encouragement, but I never imagined that someone would intentionally seek me out for this purpose. Katie poured into our lives and helped me in more ways than I could write about. I hope everyone knows someone like Katie. She helped me see the value in being a godly woman. Society constantly tells me that I'm too tall, too quiet, too smart, should have blonde hair, and wear a size 00. I'm told that I should focus on pleasing others and meeting their expectations. I know now that all of those things, like charm and beauty, are fleeting, but what will last is my relationship with God. Living a truly godly life impacts people's lives forever, and that is far more valuable than pleasing this world.

Alaina Clem: 14, Albany, GA
Sherwood Baptist Church and Sherwood Christian Academy, Albany, GA

# Parents and Pressure

## "Honor your father and mother so that you may have a long life in the land the LORD your God is giving you." —Exodus 20:12

Parents are the second best thing God gave us. Too bad most teens would disagree. I've concluded that parents and pressure go hand-in-hand! I know they always say they want what's best for us. It's not like I don't believe them, I just think they try and pressure us into doing the things they think are best for us. When asked to write for this book, I didn't think twice about it. But when I actually started writing it, I realized I really didn't want to do it. My mom told me to pray about it. I did and God gave me ideas. I still wasn't sure. My mom and dad prayed with me. Instead of lifting the choice to God, as I hoped she would, Mom prayed that God would give me words to write. To me that meant my mom hadn't listened at all to what I was trying to tell her. I wanted her to lift it to God and not make the decision herself. I didn't want to feel like she was pressuring me into it. I obeyed my mom and, thereby, obeyed God. Exodus 20:12 says, "Honor your father and mother so that you may have a long life in the land the LORD your God is giving you." I spent a lot of time praying over the next few days, and finally I was at peace of heart and mind. God told me my mom just wanted what was best for me and what would bring glory to Him. If you're going through something similar with a parent, I ask you to go to prayer as well. Just remember your parents love you. Love looks different to teens than it does to adults, but we can trust God in our Christian parents.

Deanna JL. Davis: 13, Fairchild Air Force Base, WA
Airway Heights Baptist Church, Airway Heights, WA; Medical Lake Middle School, Medical Lake, WA

# Sold Out

**"Love the Lord your God with all your heart, with all your soul, and with all your mind."** —Matthew 22:37

Many teens say they want to be sold out to Christ, but they often don't grasp the true meaning of this phrase. Being sold out to Christ equals surrendering your all to Him. *All* means everything, which means no partiality. If you want to give Christ your all, there can be no room in your heart for worldly things. This may filter which books you read and movies you watch. The latest movie and book fads won't satisfy the hunger inside you. They always leave you wanting more. Maybe this means changing the way you treat others around you, including your parents, siblings, and people you typically don't get along with.

Another scenario involves investing your time and energy into something that brings honor to God. Although this process is incredibly hard, the result (growing in your relationship with God) makes it worth the effort. After disposing of the junk in your life, you may find extra time in your day. This is good because taking the next step involves filling your life with godly things. Reading your Bible daily and praying to God consistently strengthens your relationship with Him. Understand your friends might not feel the same way about growing in their walk with the Lord. At first, they may try to persuade you to compromise, but stand firm. As one draws close to God, He reveals things that need to be cut out of that person's life, such as an activity, a personality trait, or even another person. When He does show these things to you, don't hesitate to obey. He is not trying to make you miserable but more like Him. Ask God to help you despise all the world has to offer. Then ask Him to draw you closer to Him. Be certain this is something you really desire because this is a prayer He loves to answer.

*Carson Gregors*: 17, Albany, GA
Sherwood Baptist Church and Sherwood Christian Academy, Albany, GA

# Not Strong Enough

"We are pressured in every way but not crushed; we are perplexed but not in despair; we are persecuted but not abandoned; we are struck down but not destroyed." —2 Corinthians 4:8–9

Freshman year was not good, but I've overcome a lot since then. I was the new kid, and they say it's supposed to be OK if you're new and a freshman. It was not! I was overwhelmed with a sense of loneliness. I had difficulty making friends and, even though I've never considered myself weird or abnormal, I had a very difficult time fitting in. For some reason I wasn't accepted, and for a time I felt completely alone and as if everyone was against me. So I retreated from the world into a little cave of self-pity and emotional turmoil. I tried to not think about my predicament by writing it off as something normal. After leaving public school I began to come out a bit more, but even then it sometimes felt like I was carrying a big burden. Now, I realize it was my own sin and shame, my pride that wouldn't let me let God carry the burden. He had already carried the world on His back and paid the price for sin. Jesus did that at Calvary, and it's a good thing because none of us can carry such heavy burdens. Our strength is not our own. Whatever burden you think you are supposed to carry, you can make the choice to accept Christ and let Him carry you through life. In the midst of my darkness, when I felt the world was closing in around me, I was forced to turn to God. But you shouldn't allow yourself to fall into the dark place, making God your last hope. Turn to Him now, and through His power there will be no obstacle that cannot be overcome. Pray and ask God to carry your burden, guilt, shame, and pain. In the end, none of us are strong enough without Him.

Hannah Arrington: 15, Borger, TX
First Baptist Church and Texas Virtual Academy, Borger, TX

# Give Thanks

**"Give thanks in everything, for this is God's will for you in Christ Jesus."**
—1 Thessalonians 5:18

Lilian is an exchange student from Africa that goes to my school. My family and I were involved in the process of bringing her to America. It was a long process, but she was finally able to come a few months into this school year. Lilian and I became fast friends. She told me about her life in Kenya, her family and her friends, and I shared with her as well. Lilian, now my best friend, is a shining example of God's faithfulness and provision. One night, Lilian and I were texting about the upcoming holidays. I asked her about how they celebrate Christmas in Kenya, and she told me this would be the first time she remembered receiving Christmas presents. I thought about all the Christmas presents I have ever received. I don't even remember what half of them were, yet at the time they were of utmost importance to me. I thought about all of things teens place so much value in—clothes, iPhones, the newest Nike product, or this and that. All of these things that are so dear to us hold no eternal value, and often we offer no thanks for them. Imagine all the things that others around the world, like Lilian, are denied the privilege of having—things like a nice, comfortable house, running water, a bed, and so much more. The amazing thing about Lilian, though, is she is so thankful for everything. Her story challenges me to stop and be thankful for all that I have. Whenever we are consumed with worldly desires to have the newest whatever, we should stop and think about all the Lilians. We need to thank Jesus Christ for all that He has blessed us with because we have been blessed with much!

*Alaina Clem*: 14, Albany, GA
Sherwood Baptist Church and Sherwood Christian Academy, Albany, GA

# God-Given Talents

**"The word of the LORD came to me: I chose you."** —Jeremiah 1:4–5

Many parents start their little kids in activities that they want them to be good in: sports, music, martial arts, dance, or crafting. The goal is to help them tap into their God-given talents, so that one day they can excel in it and be the best they can be. When they start junior and senior high school, there are more choices for activities than they can count! You can join any team or club you want: basketball, cheerleading, band, robotics club, and the list goes on. But if that child has already figured out their God-given talent, they will be motivated to go beyond average.

The same thing happens as we grow in our faith as teenagers. God has given each of us certain gifts that He knows we will excel in. Some of you might be thinking, *How did God know what I would be good at before I was even born?* In the first chapter of the book, when Jeremiah was only thirteen, God told Jeremiah that He chose him in the womb and set him apart from everyone else before he was even born. God appointed Jeremiah as a prophet to the nations while he was still a young boy. God has so many great plans for our young lives, and He wants us to live our best lives for Him using the gifts that He has given us. As teenagers, we are in the best position to let God work through us to minister to others. He has blessed us with the tenacity and energy we need to work for Him. All we have to do is open our hearts and minds to His call, and let Him use us to bring glory to His name.

*J'Yanna Janai Jackson:* 15, Slidell, LA
Franklin Avenue Baptist Church and Salmen High School, New Orleans, LA

# Chosen

**"But you are a chosen race, a royal priesthood, a holy nation, a people for His possession, so that you may proclaim the praises of the One who called you out of darkness into His marvelous light."** —1 Peter 2:9

God has specifically chosen Christians to have relationship with Him. Life is full of choices, and we aren't the only ones making them. God chose us, but we still have to make the decision to choose Him. Once we choose to live for Jesus, our choices should reflect Him. Choices are a very important part of our lives, but sometimes we don't notice them because they are so common. As Christians who have made the choice to accept God, we should look to Him in making all our decisions. We should be making decisions that bring glory to God. Pray about the choices you have to make. Ask for wisdom and guidance for the right decision. If you are not sure about a choice you have to make, ask a parent or pastor to help point you in the right direction. If you are making the right choice, God will let you know. God knows if we will make the decision to obey Him or not, but He still gives us free will. *Free will* means that we have the freedom to make whatever choice we want. God does not force us to do anything; however, He will point us in the right direction. We can still ignore Him and choose to go against Him, but we should remember that He has a plan for us, even if we can't see it. God's plan includes us being His chosen. If you look at the last part of 1 Peter 2:9, God also called us to praise Him for saving us. He made the choice to save us, and we should make the choice to glorify Him for it.

*Brenna R. Strain*: 15, Spokane, WA
Airway Heights Baptist Church, Airway Heights, WA; Medical Lake High School, Medical Lake, WA

# Made in God's Image

"So God created man in His own image; He created him in the image of God; He created them male and female." —Genesis 1:27

We are made perfectly in God's image. But teenagers struggle to come to this realization. Knowing that you were made perfect can feel like a tough standard to live up to. I struggle with that almost daily. I will wake up in the morning and look in the mirror and say to myself, "Why is this wrong with me?" or "Why did God have to make me like this?" I feel like I need to cover up with makeup or put on flashy clothes to make myself look better. I look to the girls around me at church or in class for acceptance, which only makes me paranoid about what I'm wearing or what I'm doing. But I feel this way because I have forgotten who I am in Christ and that God has made me so incredibly special and unique. He made me in His image! He made me to be me and He loves me for it. He looks down on His children and says, "Wow, do you see that fifteen-year-old, brown-haired, green-eyed girl? I made her, and she is beautiful. She has so many great gifts and talents that she will be able to use for My glory." Our God is not someone who casts people aside because they are different or there is something wrong with them. He created every human being from the Creation and until Resurrection. Tomorrow morning when you wake up, look in the mirror and tell yourself, "I am special. I am beautiful. I am made in God's image." During the day when people treat you badly and don't accept you, remember that it does not matter what they think, because God is the one who made you. He sees you as perfect and He does not make any mistakes. You are beautiful in His eyes.

Hailey Culberson: 17, Tulsa, OK
Evergreen Baptist Church, Bixby, OK; Homeschooled

# Worrying

**"Don't worry about anything, but in everything, through prayer and petition with thanksgiving, let your requests be made known to God."**

—Philippians 4:6

Worrying is the easiest thing to run to when there is a problem or when you do not know what's going to happen in a certain situation. We can worry about the smallest things or the biggest things. Worrying about things means we are taking them into our own hands. If we are worrying, we have not given the situation or problem to God. The wonderful promise we all need to remember is that nothing takes God by surprise. Paul says in Philippians to not worry, but to pray about each request we have. God will listen and He knows the exact way to take care of everything. God sees the bigger picture and is far better equipped than we could ever be to handle it, so it makes sense for us to trust Him with all our cares, problems, and worries. Don't you agree that if He is able to take care of things that we need to live on this earth that we can trust Him with our problems as well? Instead of us moaning all day about how bad things are, we can give them to God and watch Him work things out, and we don't have to worry at all. We all need to learn how to trust and rest by giving God everything. It is not easy, but it is a much better way to spend our time. Trusting God will never go wrong.

*Taylor Glow*: 17, Albany, GA
Sherwood Baptist Church and Sherwood Christian Academy, Albany, GA

# Love Thy Neighbor

"I give you a new command: Love one another.
Just as I have loved you, you must also love one another."

—John 13:34

People often say that *hate* is a strong word. What exactly makes one word stronger than another? Can a word be considered too strong? I know that everyone is guilty of getting angry and doing things out of anger. Everyone gets angry at someone or something almost daily. For me, there's this one person. My day could be going perfectly, and this person would do something. There will always be a person who, at some time in our lives, does something to make us think our lives are ruined. When this happened to me, it caused me to react in a hateful manner. I was ready to attack. I was allowing one person to control my mood and, basically, my life. The Bible says that we should love our neighbors, but how am I supposed to love someone when I truly don't even like them? I'd never thought that I hated anyone, but I was actually using the word *hate*. Matthew 5:44 reminded me, "But I tell you, love your enemies and pray for those who persecute you." To truly become a woman of Christ, I needed to learn to love my enemies and I needed to pray for them. I not only asked God to help me love my enemies, but also to help them. I asked Him to guide them like He guides me. When Jesus was being crucified He said, "Father, forgive them, because they do not know what they are doing" (Luke 23:34). Jesus asked God to forgive His murderers. If He could do this, surely I could forgive someone who simply angered me. Are you willing to forgive your enemies? Ask God to help you forgive those who do you wrong. With God's help anything is possible.

Makenzie Thomas: 16, Sevierville, TN
First Baptist Church and Gatlinburg-Pittman High School, Gatlinburg, TN

# Healing

"But those who trust in the LORD will renew their strength; they will soar on wings like eagles; they will run and not grow weary; they will walk and not faint." —Isaiah 40:31

Recently, a little boy I know was diagnosed with brain cancer. He is eleven, soon to be twelve. He was the top scorer for his and my brother's basketball team last year. He is now immobile. The only thing he can do is smile. He, in a sense, is trapped and wants to get out. His sickness has brought together a community and led many people to rethink their lives. The healing hasn't come yet, and we don't know if it ever will, but we must keep our faith and not give up hope. Whatever comes of this, God will bring good. This terrible situation has taught us to appreciate life and not to take a single day for granted, because we don't know when something like that could happen to us. Many people go through struggles that may be too big for them to handle, and that is where God takes control. We may not know what God has in store, and we may not know why He puts us through difficult times. We simply have to trust Him. It can be frustrating at times, but He is in control. Proverbs 3:5 says, "Trust in the LORD with all your heart, do not rely on your own understanding." Relying on your own understanding can lead to even more problems and struggles.

*Abby Fortner*: 15, Gatlinburg, TN
First Baptist Church and Gatlinburg-Pittman High School, Gatlinburg, TN

# Family

**"Tell the whole community of Israel that on the tenth day of this month they must each select an animal of the flock according to their fathers' households, one animal per household."** —Exodus 12:3

When I think of a perfect family, I see a nice couple, both who have great jobs, two or three well-behaved children, living in a pretty suburban home, with a pet dog and maybe some goldfish. But that's just me, just the way I think. Everyone has their own vision of the perfect family, but it's usually not the family they have. Maybe you only have one parent, or live with another family member. Maybe your siblings are horrible toward you. Or maybe you don't have any at all. We teenagers feel like we don't belong at our own house sometimes, but God put you exactly where you are for a reason. He knows what He wants you to do and when. Maybe you should share the gospel with your family or tell them how you feel. Being open and transparent is often the best way to share your faith, especially with family. Family is very important, and you only have one. Love them while they are around, because as you get older things change. Family is always family, but oftentimes they become separated by miles keeping them from being as close. Treasure the time with them now, and God will help you to share with them.

**Clara Davis:** 14, Little Rock, AR
The Church at Rock Creek and LISA Academy, Little Rock, AR

# Trusting God in Every Situation

"I will bless those who bless you, I will curse those who treat you with contempt, and all the peoples on earth will be blessed through you."

—Genesis 12:3

We all have something special that we love to do. For me it's dance. When I jump, I'm flying; when I do a hard piece of choreography, I'm ecstatic; and when I'm staring the judges in the face, I feel power coursing through my veins. We all have something that gives us this joy, but it only can last so long. I can face the judges, but later I may have trouble facing my classmates. God can give us this joy at a much greater level. The joy and love that God provides stick with us in every situation. God will be there to pull you through. We know that God is there, but it's sometimes hard to put your faith in a God we can't see. When I'm struggling with putting my faith in God, I usually try looking for Him in the little things. Like when someone does something out of character for you or something good you weren't expecting comes your way. If you do see Him, you will get this feeling in your gut and all you will be able to think is, "That was God." In eighth grade, I had a really hard English teacher. I'm talking about a grammar nazi. His idea of a good essay was written in your own blood and sweat. A year later, out of the blue, I really wanted to thank him for working me so hard. So I sent him an e-mail and his reply was: "THANK YOU!!!!! I just had a rough day of students not wanting to do their work. This e-mail was exactly what I needed." I had previously said that I would never send him a thank-you e-mail. But I did. I immediately got that gut feeling and knew that God had just comforted one of His children through me. Wow!

*Erin France:* 14, Anchorage, AK
First Baptist Church and Eagle River High School, Anchorage, AK

# Loving One Another

"Dear friends, let us love one another, because love is from God, and everyone who loves has been born of God and knows God. The one who does not love does not know God, because God is love." —1 John 4:7–8

You know that one kid who always gets on your nerves, the one who constantly makes fun of you for what you believe? I have one of those, and sometimes that one person can really get under my skin. It's hard for me to be kind when all she does is make me feel really bad about myself. I know, though, that God is there for me, and He's on my side because I'm a believer in Him. It is a constant battle for me to show some people God's love through my own love. I feel like they may never come to know Christ, so why bother? God tells us to love everyone. And when He says "everyone," He means *everyone*! It reminds me of the time when Jesus was hated by His people for no reason. They talked about Him behind His back and said cruel things to Him, but Jesus loved them! We are commanded to love those who do wrong to us, just as Christ loves us in spite of our wrongs. We need to model our lives after 1 John 4:7–8. We have to remember to love everyone with unconditional love, because God loves everyone more than we can even begin to comprehend. So why can't we at least try to love others as much as God loves us? We just need to remember that, as believers, we have a love that others don't have because we are set apart from them and have Jesus Christ in our hearts.

Nellie Otoupalik: 17, Spokane, WA
Airway Heights Baptist Church, Airway Heights, WA; Homeschooled/Co-op and Spokane Virtual Learning, Spokane, WA

# Self-Esteem

**"I will praise You because I have been remarkably and wonderfully made. Your works are wonderful, and I know this very well."**

—Psalm 139:14

Self-esteem! Oh, boy, there's that word again. *Self-esteem* is how a person thinks of or sees him- or herself. What do you think of yourself; how do you see yourself? Like many teens, I struggle with self-esteem. I don't think I'm good enough or pretty enough. Recently, I realized that God made me to be me, and nobody can change that. But I'm still not always happy with my looks. I decided to change my attitude about my looks by embracing who God made me to be. Psalm 139:14 has some key phrases: "I will praise You" and "I have been remarkably and wonderfully made." "You" is God. He made us exactly how He wants us. He made us remarkable, and He made us wonderful. No matter what others think of you and how you look, no matter what you think of you and how you look, you are perfect to God, and that's all that matters. Look at the second part of the verse: "Your works are wonderful, and I know this very well." God's work is wonderful. This means that we are wonderful, so why is it hard for us to see ourselves this way? I challenge you to change the way you think about yourself. Don't think about it in terms of self-esteem, but in terms of praising God. When we treat ourselves well we bring glory to God, and that gives us the opportunity to share Him with others. That's what the Christian life is about. So, again, here's my challenge: Change how you think of and see yourself, praise God for the remarkable and wonderful person He made you to be, then use that person to share Him with others. Try it and see how it feels. I can guarantee it's worth it.

*Brenna R. Strain*: 15, Spokane, WA
Airway Heights Baptist Church, Airway Heights, WA; Medical Lake High School, Medical Lake, WA

# The Truth

**"Your works are wonderful, and I know this very well."**

—Psalm 139:14

When I was about twelve, I started to think I wasn't skinny enough. I never thought I was really overweight, but I always felt that if I could just lose a few pounds I would look like a model. The world has an impossible standard set for young women. Every single day we're bombarded with photo-shopped pictures of women who have perfect yet unnatural bodies. The truth is that Satan has twisted and contorted God's idea of beauty into something unobtainable. We're never going to be content with our bodies or feel beautiful if we're trying to reach the world's standard of beauty, because it isn't how God created our bodies to look. In Psalm 139:13–16 it says, "For it was You who created my inward parts; You knit me together in my mother's womb. I will praise You because I have been remarkably and wonderfully made. Your works are wonderful, and I know this very well. My bones were not hidden from You when I was made in secret, when I was formed in the depths of the earth. Your eyes saw me when I was formless; all my days were written in Your book and planned before a single one of them began." This psalm reminds me of God's perfect design and plan for us. If you look up "Dove Evolution" on YouTube (if your parents are OK with it), you can see what a model goes through to look like she does on a billboard. The video is eye-opening. First Peter 3:4 says our beauty, "should consist of what is inside the heart with the imperishable quality of a gentle and quiet spirit, which is very valuable in God's eyes." I challenge other girls to ignore the lies of the world and live confident, pure lives, and for guys to encourage us in this effort.

*Tara Greene*: 16, Fort Belvoir, VA
Guilford Baptist Church, Sterling, VA; Homeschooled

# Trust

> "Trust in the LORD with all your heart, and do not rely on your own understanding." —Proverbs 3:5

A lot of teenagers struggle with trust problems. They've been hurt by their parents, felt that they were betrayed by a friend, or even had promises broken by one they trusted their most personal thoughts with. I began to have problems with trust because my family had to move a lot. From one town to another, over and over again I had to begin building new relationships and get adjusted to everything. Moving from school to school six times left me angry with God at times. I wondered why He would do this to me. What was the purpose of this? The truth is, we can't and won't know all the answers all the time. We have to trust Him, and I needed to trust Him in my parents. We have to let go and let God take over. Trusting can be hard to do and it takes time to earn trust, but God earned our trust before we were even born. His plans for us are so magnificent, though we don't see it yet. God has everything in the palm of His hand, so why not trust Him? Throughout my moves I made lots of friends and have been able to impact many lives. I can now count it all joy because of all that I have learned about people and places—all because I trusted God.

Megan Medford: 14, Bryant, AR
The Church at Rock Creek and Bryant High School, Little Rock, AR

# Court Case of Life

"Do not show partiality when deciding a case; listen to small and great alike. Do not be intimidated by anyone, for judgment belongs to God. Bring me any case too difficult for you, and I will hear it."

—Deuteronomy 1:17

When at school, I feel a little like I'm in court. The teacher is judge. Your teacher, no doubt, has more respect for a person who dresses nicely than a person who wears sweats and a T-shirt every day. But this is the image a lot of people go for. Then there is the jury. The jury may include people that you see every day that have an impact on how the law is enforced and who your classmates are. They are judging you too. We are constantly being judged at school. Their opinions vary, so we can only please a few people at a time. We cannot please everyone, as you have probably figured out already. When I find myself dressing a certain way in order to please someone, I go with what I like best. Chances are, if they don't like what I like, we will not become great friends anyway.

We should try to remember not to judge others. Sometimes when I get all dressed up for school and someone else wears sweats and a messy bun in their hair, I have the tendency to feel like I am better than they are. I need to remember that God is the only Judge that really matters, so why should I worry? Back to the court analogy: we forgot the defense lawyer: God! Some choose family or their best friends. However, God knows what you want and, more important, He knows what's best for you. His judgment is the important opinion, so having Him as a defense in any of the court cases of life is really awesome.

Erin France: 14, Anchorage, AK
First Baptist Church and Eagle River High School, Anchorage, AK

# Doubting My Savior (Part 1)

"The Lord is my rock, my fortress, and my deliverer, my God, my mountain where I seek refuge, my shield and the horn of my salvation, my stronghold." —Psalm 18:2

As a young Christian, I used to have doubts about God. Everyone goes through a phase of doubting Him and His works at certain times in their lives. My doubts came when I became more active in church and I felt that I was being torn down. I began wondering how I could believe in something I cannot see or if there really is a God. If He is real, then why does He let me go through all of this hurt and pain? The doubts I had were actually affecting my walk of faith and every part of who I am. If you or anyone you know is having trouble doubting our Savior, it will never get better unless you seek help! I thought that not sharing my concerns about Jesus and just going to church more would answer all my questions, but it didn't. After a while, my doubts turned into serious frustration, and at that point I realized that I needed help. I talked to a Christian adult about my concerns and she helped me understand that God does everything for a reason. When you hear that statement you automatically think, *Well, what is the reason?* I could not see it then, but later I realized that what she said is true. Sometimes God's reason is for you to help those who are going through what you have already been through. God wants us to be an example for those who do not know Him and He uses what we have learned to help others.

Reagan MiCole Brashears: 17, New Orleans, LA
Franklin Avenue Baptist Church and Eleanor McMain Secondary School, New Orleans, LA

# Doubting My Savior (Part 2)

"The LORD is my rock, my fortress, and my deliverer, my God, my mountain where I seek refuge, my shield and the horn of my salvation, my stronghold." —Psalm 18:2

I understand that it's hard to believe and have faith in something you cannot see, but you just have to pray and trust in God and His Word. God loves us and He will always be there for His children. Doubts are not wrong. They are a part of every Christian's life. Asking questions and really thinking about your faith can actually make you a stronger Christian. We must trust the Lord to be our rock, our fortress, and our deliverer; and then take refuge in God who is our rock. He is our shield and the horn of our salvation, and He is our stronghold. No matter what we are going through, God will be there for us to lean on. He is our motivation and He will protect us from all harm as long as we follow, obey, and trust Him. If you struggle with doubting God, read Psalm 19:1–4. Do not push away your thoughts about God; think them through with another Christian to deepen both of your faith. Having a partner to learn with and to help hold you accountable in this Christian journey will make things much easier! Doubts will still come, they always do. But they will be easier to deal with because you will know the truth, and that will help you make the best decisions.

Reagan Mi'Cole Brashears: 17, New Orleans, LA
Franklin Avenue Baptist Church and Eleanor McMain Secondary School, New Orleans, LA

# The Problem!

**"I will not set anything worthless before my eyes."** —Psalms 101:3

Outbursts of violence have taken place throughout America over the past decade, the most recent in Newtown, Connecticut, at Sandy Hooks Elementary. Attacks like these are becoming more violent and frequently cause chaos and confusion. After the initial shock sets in, victims and spectators begin to question how these disturbing events can happen. The shootings at Sandy Hook made me wonder what pushed the shooter over the edge. I will never understand why this man thought he had the right to take the lives of those people, but I think a factor that could have impacted his mind-set, as well as that of many other murderers, is that today kids are given video games jam-packed with gore and intense violence. The highest-rated box office movies are often filled with fight scenes, and the TV series with the highest ratings tend to be ones based on criminal activity. Our culture craves violent entertainment because Hollywood has made it look glamorous. It's ironic that our culture approves violent entertainment but is shocked when individuals live it out. Consumption of violence has reaped negative consequences in our country, devaluing life and portraying the idea that killing is OK. Watching movies and playing games filled with violence engrains rage into our brains, increasing the likelihood that we might respond similarly. Wouldn't it be amazing if Christian teens across America honored the lives of those lost to violent crimes by taking a stand against violent forms of entertainment? If a generation would refuse to spend money on entertainment that belittles life and dishonors God, then violent entertainment would create no profit. Maybe if we choose to help in bringing it to an end, then it wouldn't have as great an effect on future generations.

Carson Gregors: 17, Albany, GA
Sherwood Baptist Church and Sherwood Christian Academy, Albany, GA

# Relationships

"For this is God's will, your sanctification: that you abstain from sexual immorality, so that each of you knows how to control his own body in sanctification and honor." —1 Thessalonians 4:3–4

A relationship can be a great thing, but it can also hurt you. So many times someone will tell you that they love you and that you are the best thing that has ever happened to them. They will tell you anything just so that they can have you. I have been told by many boys that they loved me and cared about me. When people say stuff like that, be careful. Ask God to help you make a decision about whether a relationship with that person is a good idea. You may also be that person who people refer to as "forever alone." That is the biggest lie I have ever heard. You are never alone; God will always be with you. He cares about you and He loves you. If you are in a relationship, be sure that God is the center of your relationship. If He is not the center, He gets jealous. You are His wonderful creation that He wants to spend time with. When God is not the center of your relationship, it will bring you down. You are vulnerable to temptation, which the devil will throw at you. The devil wants you to fall and get hurt, and you will get hurt if God is not at the center of your relationship. Your body is a wonderful piece of art, with God's signature on it. He wants you to cherish it and take care of it. When you are not in the right relationship, it is easy to give up your body for another person. God's wish is that you give your body to your spouse. When you save yourself for your spouse, you are obeying God.

Dianah Edwards: 16, West Monroe, LA
First West Monroe Baptist Church and Northeast Baptist School, West Monroe, LA

# Failure

"For I am persuaded that not even death or life, angels or rulers, things present or things to come, hostile powers, height or depth, or any other created thing will have power to separate us from the love of God that is in Christ Jesus our Lord!" —Romans 8:38–39

If you were to ask me what I think about when you say "fears," failure would be one of the first. In everything I do, I strive for perfection. That may not sound like a bad thing, but it can be. I actually fear failing at anything. The thought of not meeting other people's expectations of me or not meeting my expectations for myself is very scary to me. This fear can cause me, especially in athletics, to not push myself to reach my full capability. I'm afraid that if I push as hard as I can, I might still fall short of my own or my coaches' expectations of me, thus failing. Recently though, God has been teaching me something that completely eradicates this fear. I think that one of the main reasons I struggle with this is that it feels like other people's (such as coaches, parents, or friends) love for me is determined by whether or not I meet their expectations. I know this is not always true, especially with parents, but this is often how it feels. For example, I have to make perfect grades and keep my room immaculately clean for my parents to be pleased with me, or I have to play a perfect soccer game and not miss any serves in the volleyball game for my coaches to be pleased with me. But through these verses in Romans, God showed me His love for me is unconditional. His love for me is not determined by whether or not I meet anyone's expectations of me. What I believe to be my failures can never change the love that God has for me! That is the most liberating thing I have ever learned.

Alaina Clem: 14, Albany, GA
Sherwood Baptist Church and Sherwood Christian Academy, Albany, GA

# Taking a Stand for God

## "Who stands up for me against the wicked?
## Who takes a stand for me against evildoers?" —Psalm 94:16

The psalmist asked two questions that we need to ask ourselves: "Who stands up for me against the wicked?" and "Who takes a stand for me against evildoers?" I believe God places us in situations to test us and to make us realize how strong our faith is. The first day of my new semester of school, I walked into a class unprepared for what was about to take place. I am not an argumentative person, I do not like confrontation. My teacher informed me that it was a discussion class, and everyone had to participate. Our first discussion was on gay marriage, and people who didn't agree were to raise their hands. I raised my hand, so she called on me to explain why I disagreed. I gave my reasons from a biblical standpoint, and there were people who backed me up. There were also people who disagreed with me. People should have the right to choose, but it felt like I was being backed into a corner. Even though people disagreed, it was my job, as a Christian, to share the Word of God with them and to not back down. I knew God had my back, and when I opened my mouth it was like God was speaking through me. Don't be afraid or back away when someone disagrees with you on an issue, when you know it's wrong in God's eyes. That is when you need to take a stand for God.

Brianna Carter: 19, Sharon, SC
Hillcrest Baptist Church and York Technical, York, SC

# Hypocrites

## "I do not sit with the worthless or associate with hypocrites."

—Psalm 26:4

Ever been called a Bible thumper? At my school, that's what people call the openly religious kids. I really don't like it when people say stuff like, "I am most definitely a Christian!" but then go on to skip class and use swear words when they talk to others. A lot of the time, you just want to tell those people off, but then you realize that would make you just as bad as they are. Psalm 26:4 says, "I do not sit with the worthless or associate with hypocrites." Don't let yourself get involved with those people. If you are like that, take a step back and think about how you can improve as a Christian. When you say you are a Christian, watch how you act, because you are setting a reputation for Christians. If nonbelievers see that all the Christians at school are mean to others and are just bad students, then why would they ever want to be one? You should stay away from hypocrites, but if you are already involved with them, invite them to church, and pray for them and for how God wants you to share the gospel with them. God will help you handle it. If people at school make fun of you for being religious, don't worry about it. The Lord knows your heart, and He also knows theirs.

Clara Davis: 14, Little Rock, AR
The Church at Rock Creek and LISA Academy, Little Rock, AR

# Outward Beauty

"Charm is deceptive and beauty is fleeting, but a woman who fears the Lᴏʀᴅ will be praised." —Proverbs 31:30

During my time in middle school and high school I have noticed that girls in almost every grade wear makeup. Some girls have stopped wearing glasses and now wear contacts. Some of them tend to get upset when they haven't straightened their hair. Makeup is not my thing. I wear glasses and have no plans for contacts. However, I have never considered myself to be very pretty. Acne is a problem for me, my eyes are very big, and I used to be overweight. I have been tempted to wear eye shadow or eyeliner many times, because it makes my eyes look pretty. I also don't wear clothes the way most girls do. My clothes are modest and not what the fashion designers dictate, and I rarely wear jewelry. You may be thinking that it is strange that I don't really care for makeup or beauty, but I have been tempted to make myself pretty several times. You may feel this way too, and have sudden urges to beautify yourself. There is nothing wrong with that, provided we remember that God is interested in inner beauty. I have to remind myself that God loves me just the way I am, and He created me like this for a reason. It is only natural for humans to want to fit in, especially teenagers. This applies to both girls and boys, because we want people to like us. Everyone is beautiful in their own way, but if you believe in God and praise Him and trust Him in your heart, that is what is really important.

Michaela Reed: 15, Albany, GA
Institutional First Baptist Church and Sherwood Christian Academy, Albany, GA

# A Trustworthy Friend

"A man with many friends may be harmed, but there is a friend who stays closer than a brother." —Proverbs 18:24

Have you ever known someone you thought was your friend, but then they turned on you? If you have, you know the disappointment of that experience. You thought that person was on your side, only to find out they weren't. Don't get me wrong, we all can mess up relationships. Still, when people act this way toward us, it affects our trust in them. We are less likely to tell them things we are going through, less likely to want to be with them. Sometimes I wish I had a perfect friend—someone who would always listen to me, not talk about me behind my back, and not leave me to go be with the popular kids. I want to tell you that, as Christians, we have this friend! His name is Jesus. I know, you're probably thinking, *I can't see Jesus, and I can't hear Him, so what kind of a friend is that?* Remember when we were talking about a person who turned on you? Here's something to think about: You are like that person, and Jesus is the one you turned on. Hard to believe, right? But it's true. Everyone has sinned. And guess what? Even though you turned on Jesus, He left the glory of heaven and came to earth. I don't know about you, but if I was in heaven, I don't think I would want to leave. Not only did He come to earth, He also became human. Of course, Jesus was still God, but He was also human. Not only did He become human, He died for you. And not a peaceful death. He endured a horrible death, to save people who had essentially turned on Him. Jesus proved His love for us when He died for us. You can trust Jesus. He loves you, and He is the best friend you could ever have.

Isabella Bako: 14, Anchorage, AK
First Baptist Church, Anchorage, AK; Homeschooled

# Clean It Up!

**"For you were once darkness, but now you are light in the Lord. Walk as children of light."** —Ephesians 5:8

Imagine you and a friend are going to eat at a restaurant. As soon as you walk into the lobby, they ask for your name and how many is in your party. You tell them two. They hand you a beeper and say the wait is ten minutes. You walk over to the waiting area and notice that the room is full of trash. Chairs are scattered everywhere, some are broken and unsafe to sit in, others are turned upside down. You straighten the chairs and find a place for you and your friend to sit. As you wait, you look down and notice that there are cockroaches scurrying across the floor and crawling all over your shoes! Do you stay to eat? Why not? This is just the waiting area, does it really have anything to do with the kitchen or how the food is being prepared? Of course it does! If the waiting area already looks like a war zone, you can only assume that the food preparation area is in similar shape! If this would be true of restaurants, wouldn't it also be true for our lives? Why would we assume that we could live haphazardly and sin in whatever way pleases us, yet still have a well-ordered spiritual life? How could we believe that we can stack up trash of the world on one side of our brains, and store up heaven on the other? "What has light to do with darkness?" The world is supposed to see our "good works that glorify our Father in heaven!" But if we don't have any, or people can't see them because their view is blocked by the garbage we've piled up in our lives, then we're making the gospel a joke! We have to surrender completely to the will of God! That means everything about you! It's time for the children of God to be children of God!

**Hannah McGee:** 15, Springdale, AR
Cross Church Springdale Campus, Northwest, AR; Shiloh Christian School, Springdale, AR

# Vices vs. Verses

"And whatever you do, in word or in deed, do everything in the name of the Lord Jesus, giving thanks to God the Father through Him."

—Colossians 3:17

Do you like having fun? Cool, me too. I like playing video games, reading, baking, watching movies, shopping, and hanging out with my friends. Maybe you like to play basketball or ride your dirt bike or swim. Whatever you like to do, you like having fun, right? Spending your time doing something you enjoy isn't usually a bad thing, but if it makes you forget who you are in Christ, it can be. First Timothy 4:12 says, "You should be an example to the believers in speech, in conduct, in love, in faith, in purity." This means that we have a responsibility to act in a way that honors God, even when we're having fun. We also need to pick our forms of entertainment carefully and make sure we're not filling our heads with things that are destructive to our spiritual health. This can be hard to do sometimes. It might mean not watching certain movies or listening to certain bands, which can be especially tough when all your friends are talking about them. We also need to make sure that we make some time for God in our schedules, which might mean choosing to read your Bible over playing that next mission or reading that next chapter. I know that choosing to spend time with God over a hobby can be difficult, but how will we know how God wants us to live if we don't listen to Him? And how will we ever grow in our faith if we don't live it out? Let's have fun, but above all, let's remember what's really important.

Kaylin Calvert: 18, Medical Lake, WA
Airway Heights Baptist Church, Airway Heights, WA; Homeschooled

# The Vinedresser

"I am the true vine, and My Father is the vineyard keeper. Every branch in Me that does not produce fruit He removes, and He prunes every branch that produces fruit so that it will produce more fruit." —John 15:1–2

Going through hardships and struggles is never fun or enjoyable. You never hear people say that they want those things to happen in their lives. Yet, as Christians, God puts us through hardships and struggles so that we can become even closer to Him. Jesus said in John 15 that God will prune those who bear fruit so that they can bear even more fruit. The pruning process involves branches that are dead and withered to be cut from the vine. Sometimes in the pruning process the vinedresser would even have to cut off the branches that were bearing fruit, so that when the new branch grew back it would bear even more fruit. Back in Jesus' time, the vinedresser was the equivalent of a shepherd. He knew each of his vines and their branches and what they were capable of. He knew that some branches would be more prosperous and fruitful than other branches. He knew just how much he should prune each one to get the best results. The point of the vinedresser was to protect the vines and each year to make them stronger. God is our vinedresser. He knows how many hardships and struggles to put us through in order to get the best results. God knows what we are capable of and, in the end, He just wants us to come out as a better person than before. The vinedresser always had a purpose for what he did to his branches, and God is the exact same way.

Taylor Glow: 17, Albany, GA
Sherwood Baptist Church and Sherwood Christian Academy, Albany, GA

# Vanity

"Your beauty should not consist of outward things like elaborate hairstyles and the wearing of fine clothes; instead it should consist of the hidden person of the heart with the imperishable quality of a gentle spirit, which is very valuable in God's eyes." —1 Peter 3:3–4

Fashion and style are everywhere you look: television, ads, websites, magazines, and more. Pop culture tries to tell you that you need a ton of clothes, seven pounds of makeup, the perfect weight, the latest bag, the coolest hat, the shiniest jewelry, and the latest kicks. And if you don't have those things you won't be the best or the most popular, so too bad for you. So many kids are obsessed with looks. The boys and girls who have those things commonly make fun of the boys and girls that don't, making them feel terrible about things that don't matter even a little bit. Don't get me wrong, the shoes and clothes are exciting. But the Bible states that we should not worship any idols before God. Not exactly little, golden chubby statues, but also things we would never notice. With clothes, maybe you're taking money you should be giving to God and spending it on yourself instead. In this world today with the "YOLO" (You Only Live Once) attitude, it is easy to get caught up in the false idols of this world. The challenge is to recognize them, face them, and overcome them. Honestly, it might not make you the most popular kid on the block, but you would be a very smart one. Embracing the Savior before anything else is a noble and rare thing to do. Be proud of who you are and proud of Who gives you life with or without the thirty pairs of jeans and twenty pairs of shoes.

Leah Harris: 16, Kodiak, AK
Frontier Southern Baptist Church, Kodiak, AK; Homeschooled

# Identity

"LORD, You have searched me and known me. You know when I sit down and when I stand up; You understand my thoughts from far away."

—Psalm 139:1–2

As teenagers, most of us at some point struggle with identity. I spent many nights the first semester of my junior year wondering who I was. I felt as though I had become someone I really wasn't as a way to avoid pain and to try to fit in. I recently went to a conference where the speaker made a statement that I agree with. He said that we cannot know ourselves until we know who Jesus is. I feel like in order to know who God is, we must live our lives constantly seeking Him. The better we know our God—the God who knows us—the better we know ourselves. I was praying semi-desperately one night when God showed me that I had to trust Him with all of me before I could be who He made me to be. He showed me that I needed to give Him the fears that I had hidden and struggled with all of my life. I decided to trust Him. Since then, I have seen such joy in my life. I have begun to see opportunities to become more like who God made me to be. In order to know yourself in Christ, you must come to a place where, from the depths of your being, you want to become who God wants you to be more than anything else. Be honest and ask God to show you what is holding you back from following Christ completely. What keeps you from God is often what keeps you from knowing who you are. If you give whatever it is to God, you are freer to be yourself. Do you struggle with knowing who you are or feeling like you are faking life? Are you willing to let God show you who He wants you to be for Him and to fulfill the plan He has for your life? He can.

Rebekah Byrd: 16, Tulsa, OK
Evergreen Baptist Church, Bixby, OK; Homeschooled

# Your Life

"You don't even know what tomorrow will bring—what your life will be! For you are like smoke that appears for a little while, then vanishes. Instead, you should say, 'If the Lord wills, we will live and do this or that.'" —James 4:14–15

Sometimes we need a reality check in our lives, because we all tend to live for what we want and can be terribly self-absorbed! It's a fact that we will all die someday. It could be soon—in the next twenty minutes—or it could be later. But we honestly don't know when it will be or how it will happen. The Bible says that we do not know the time we will be called from this life to the next. So, don't assume anything regarding things that might shorten your life here on earth, because it happens in the blink of an eye and then what are we? Instead of worrying about that day, we are called to live each day to the fullest of what God has for us, not to the fullest of our own sinful desires, like the world would have you do. Therefore, "You are to act justly, to love faithfulness, and to walk humbly with your God" (Micah 6:8), so that when the day does come and you are standing in front of the throne of the Lord Almighty, He will know you, welcome you into heaven, and congratulate you by saying, "Well done, My good and faithful servant!"

Emily Pitts: 16, Palm Harbor, FL
Calvary Baptist Church and Calvary Christian High School, Clearwater, FL

# Easy For You to Say

"I give you a new command: Love one another. Just as I have loved you, you must also love one another. By this all people will know that you are My disciples, if you have love for one another." —John 13:34–35

It seems we talk a lot about loving family more than friends and peers. Some must have perfect families and boring adult friends, which makes it easy for them. It seems like my family members are selfish, and my friends are nice to me. Is it wrong if I want to be with my friends instead? In reality, though, each of us is imperfect. That is why we need Jesus. It hurts that we are sinners, just like our siblings and parents. (And by the way, if we had to live with our friends, we would not think they were so wonderful, either). We fail our families daily, and if we don't it's because we aren't with them enough. We have all heard John 13:34 countless times: "Love one another." It sounds simple, right? Even when we mistreat our families, we still love them deep down. But often we forget what Jesus said in John 13:34, "Just as I have loved you, you must also love one another." Christ loved us by giving up His rights to live in heaven, and by sacrificing His life for ours. He treats us like friends, even though we are undeserving of His friendship. "By this all people will know that you are My disciples, if you have love for one another" (v. 35). If a nonbeliever witnessed your interaction with your family, would they be impressed? We are to love as Jesus loves, which means not expecting kindness in return. Our behavior, good or bad, toward others is a witness to nonbelievers. We must fulfill our responsibility in Christ.

Hannah Cooksey: 16, McMinnville, OR
Valley Baptist Church, McMinnville, OR; Homeschooled

# The "P" Word

"For this is God's will, your sanctification: that you abstain from sexual immorality, so that each of you knows how to control his own body in sanctification and honor, not with lustful desires, like the Gentiles who don't know God." —1 Thessalonians 4:3–5

One problem facing a majority of the teens in this present age would have to be purity—or lack thereof. Songs, movies, and even books try to brush off sex as something that happens naturally as a result of true love. This is both true and false. God designed sex as a way for a man and woman to express their love for one another and to "be fruitful [and] multiply" (Genesis 1:28). The only condition is that this be done within the bonds of marriage. In 1 Corinthians 7:2 Paul says, "But because sexual immorality is so common, each man should have his own wife, and each woman should have her own husband." Marriage is a moral way to fulfill sexual desires, but that does not give allowance for teens or anyone else to rush into it or take it lightly. I know this sounds a little unorthodox, but marriage is meant to be a lifelong commitment! As teenagers, society tells us that it's our job to live and be a little careless because we're only young once, but God calls us to be leaders even now! "Let no one despise your youth; instead, you should be an example to the believers in speech, in conduct, in love, in faith, in purity" (1 Timothy 4:12). Being a virgin until marriage should be something to strive for! Although you walk with Christ, temptations will still arise, but according to 1 Corinthians 10:13, all temptations can be triumphed. Purpose in your heart today to abstain from sexual relations until marriage. When temptation tries to draw you in, you can rely on God and His promises to rescue you!

Kelsey Roberts: 18, Albany, GA
Sherwood Baptist Church and Sherwood Christian Academy, Albany, GA

# Looking for Love

"Young women of Jerusalem, I charge you by the gazelles
and the wild does of the field: do not stir up or awaken love
until the appropriate time." —Song of Songs 2:7

Love's complicated! Social media tells us one thing, but as Christians, love takes on an entirely new depth of meaning. God gave the ultimate demonstration of love when He sent His Son as a sacrifice for us. How does this relate to romance? It is an example of the ultimate loving relationship. The Bible may not discuss dating specifically, but it gives guidelines for relationships, stressing the importance of friendship. Proverbs 17:17 says, "A friend loves at all times." Love is the basis for any strong friendship, and vice versa. As close friends, you can easily see each other's strengths and flaws, demonstrating love through encouragement and accountability. Christian girls should treat young men as brothers in Christ and as another's potential husband. Both should work to honor God first through actions (Hebrews 10:24). Keep in mind the end goal—not only the possibility of marriage but also the eternal glorification of God. There's a saying: "A woman's heart should be so lost in God that a man must seek Him in order to find her." Put God first and He will be faithful to bring the right man to you. "Flee from youthful passions, and pursue righteousness, faith, love, and peace, along with those who call on the Lord from a pure heart" (2 Timothy 2:22). As we wait for God's choice for a husband we can show love to our future husband by our conduct toward other young men and our attitude toward God. Psalm 119:9 says, "How can a young man keep his way pure? By keeping Your word." By abstaining from premarital sex, dressing modestly, and following God's commandments, you honor God and love the man with whom you'll spend the rest of your life!

Kristin Goehl: 18, Princeton, MA
Bethlehem Bible Church, West Boylston, MA; Princeton University, Princeton, MA

# Vast, Unmeasured, Boundless, Free

## "But God proves His own love for us in that while we were still sinners, Christ died for us!" —Romans 5:8

I think we've all been subject to that one chemistry or calculus problem. You've been working hard for over an hour, but somehow the concept doesn't sink in. *I can't understand this,* you may be telling yourself. Regarding spiritual things, there are some topics that we simply do not have the ability to understand (Psalm 145:3). One of these topics is the love of God. R. C. Sproul notes, "However accurately we may speak about the love of God our speech is limited by our human perspective. Whatever God's love is, it is not exhausted by our concept of it" (R. C. Sproul, *Loved by God* [Nashville: Thomas Nelson, 2001], 5). It is impossible for us to comprehend the love shown to us when Christ died to redeem His people. Surely it was this love on the mind of S. Trevor Francis when he penned the words of one of my favorite hymns:

*O the deep, deep love of Jesus, vast, unmeasured, boundless, free!*
*Rolling as a mighty ocean in its fullness over me!*
*Underneath me, all around me, is the current of Thy love*
*Leading onward, leading homeward to Thy glorious rest above!*

I want to remind you today that, as a believer, you are loved with a love so deep that you cannot understand it! Romans 5:8 says that while we were in sinful rebellion and ignorance of our great need of a Savior, Christ poured out His life for us. In spite of our sin, Christ sacrificed Himself in order to reconcile us with God, that we might be adopted and live for eternity with Him. Pray that the Holy Spirit will increase your understanding of Christ's love until the day we meet our Savior face-to-face.

Emily Sherrod: 17, Mobile, AL
Christ Fellowship Baptist Church and Stanford University Online High School, Mobile, AL

# Make Up

"For it was you who created my inward parts; you knit me together in my mother's womb. I will praise You because I have been remarkably and wonderfully made. Your works are wonderful, and I know this very well."

—Psalm 139:13–14

Look at yourself. You are such a wonderful masterpiece, beautiful inside and out. You should favor your body with everything you have, and do not let people tell you otherwise. Do not listen to the people who bring you down. You are such a beauty. You do not need makeup to make a new you. Be who you are, which is what is important. Do not try to act like someone you are not. Show the people around you the real you and be proud that God made you so wonderfully. Many girls bring themselves down because they listen to what people say to them. Clothe yourself in God's Word, shine out His glory and power. Show love and kindness to others around you, for that is the great beauty people want to see. God is so proud you are His child, He shows you off to the world. Do all that you can to please your Father in heaven, for you are the example of His greatness. When people look at you, they will see God in you and in your actions. You do not need to wear the latest fashions or newest trends. You do not need to be like the world. In fact, be different from the world, not like everyone else. Just look at the world right now. We are kind of like robots walking around wearing the same things, talking the same way, even doing the same things. It kind of gets annoying, doesn't it? Everyone being alike? Why don't we just be who God wants us to be? Ask God what He wants you to do every day; ask Him how to handle a situation, to work through you in everything you do. You have a mighty purpose; do your best to fulfill it.

Dianah Edwards: 16, West Monroe, LA
First West Monroe Baptist Church and Northeast Baptist School, West Monroe, LA

# Life Through the Spirit

"But the fruit of the Spirit is love, joy, peace, patience, kindness, goodness, faith, gentleness, self-control. Against such things there is no law."

—Galatians 5:22–23

So as Christians were called to live fruitful lives, right? Yes! So why is it that our lives often look absolutely nothing like the lives of Christians in the Bible? We have the same power living inside us as they did. For the longest time I struggled with this question. I would sit in a sermon about having more patience, feel convicted because I really struggle with this, and the next day nothing would change. I would get so irritated with myself because no matter how hard I tried, I could never be patient. I would read this passage in Galatians, and even ask God to help me be more patient. This summer, I finally heard God laugh and say, "Daughter, I already have!" You see the fruit of the Spirit is just that—the fruit of the Spirit. Paul didn't write it was the fruit of Paul or the fruit of Annalise. When Jesus ascended into heaven. He left us with a helper, the Holy Spirit. It is only through the power of the Holy Spirit we can live this Christian life. Yes, I need be a leader. Yes, I need to love greater. Yes, I need to more patience. But, if I ever try to accomplish all these things by myself, I will always come short. I can never posses the fruit of the Spirit without the help of the Spirit! Instead, the fruit comes when I walk in intimacy with Jesus Christ. The overflow of an intimate relationship with Christ is a fruitful life.

*Annalise Clem*: 17, Albany, GA
Sherwood Baptist Church and Sherwood Christian Academy, Albany, GA

# A Time for Everything

"There is an occasion for everything, and a time for every activity under heaven." —Ecclesiastes 3:1

Have you ever had a time in your life when you just felt like nothing is going right? Or a time when you just felt happy and content, and you just didn't know why? Well, Solomon tells us that there is a time for everything, a season for every activity under heaven. This means that there will be times in your life when you will want to cry, to dance, to laugh, to be silent, and to love or hate. Have you ever heard the phrase "everything happens for a reason"? Well, it's true. Everything does happen for a reason, in the exact time God means it to. He uses each of these feelings as a season in your life that will help you in the future. So when you cry out to God, wondering if all this grief you are feeling will ever end, know that it will. When Solomon says "a season for every activity under heaven," he doesn't mean seasons like the weather. With the weather, you always know that it will be hot in the summer and cold in the winter. But the seasons of our lives that Solomon is referring to are completely unpredictable. You could be laughing and happy one day, but crying out for God to save you the next. It's all part of His perfect plan for your life. He uses each of these seasons to help you grow. In the midst of grief, you may wonder how in the world God will use this for good, but He will. We may not know His plans, but we have to remember that they are perfect and everything He does is for our good. So, the next time you can't figure out why God is letting something happen to you, remember that whatever it is you're going through is God's perfect plan to help you grow. Everything that happens is for a reason, even if you don't see it right away.

Hannah Abernathie: 15, Tulsa, OK
Evergreen Baptist Church, Bixby, OK; Homeschooled and Cornerstone Tutorial Center, Tulsa, OK

# A Lukewarm Christian

"So, because you are lukewarm, and neither hot nor cold,
I am going to vomit you out of My mouth." —Revelation 3:16

I have been attending church since I was born. My membership has changed a few times, but I've always gone to church. I thought that just attending church and making sure you were a Christian was all that it took. Being raised in church, I felt obligated to say the sinner's prayer and get baptized, so I did. When the older people in church would stand up and shout or raise their hands, I honestly thought it looked kind of crazy. *Do they not realize they're drawing attention to themselves?* I thought this until I was fifteen years old. My friend took me to a Christian concert called Hearts on Fire. I changed at that concert. I had never raised my hands and praised or cried tears of joy for God. That night, when they had the altar call in that huge room, I went down. I made an adult decision and gave my life to Christ for real that night. I felt like a new person, because I was a new person. When I went back to my church, I told the congregation what had happened and, as soon as possible, I was baptized. God says in Revelation 3:16 to not be a lukewarm Christian or He will "vomit you out." By this, He means that He wants you to not only know that you *know* you're a Christian, but to do things to show that you're for real about Him. Don't be afraid to express your love for Jesus. People may look at you funny, but God loves it, and they're going to want what you have. They'll get curious. Since the concert and my baptism, I have struggled to not go back to being a lukewarm Christian. I am proud to say that now I am on fire for God.

Breanna Smith: 17, Sharon, SC
Hillcrest Baptist Church and York Comprehensive High School, York, SC

# Let God Know What Your Requests Are

"Don't worry about anything, but in everything, through prayer and petition with thanksgiving, let your requests be made known to God."

—Philippians 4:6

As teenagers, we are faced with so many decisions every day. Some of the choices we make can be as simple as what to wear to school on any given day, but others, such as where to go to college and what to major in, can be life-changing. But what I think God is saying in the verse above is to trust Him and look to Him for guidance in every area of our lives. We cannot expect good things to happen without doing the work that is required. In school, we cannot expect to score a 100 percent on a test just by praying and not doing anything to prepare for it. We need to do what is required of us. As a junior in high school, I have a lot of anxiety about what the future will bring. I am trying to be prepared by volunteering, organizing my résumé, and practicing for my ACT and SAT. I will work hard to do my very best in these things, but I will ultimately trust that God will guide my way and help me make the best decisions for my life. This gives me great comfort and takes away the stress I have in my life. Knowing and trusting God in your life is the most important thing that you can ever do. He's ready, are you?

Michi Werner: 16, Gatlinburg, TN
First Baptist Church and Gatlinburg-Pittman High School, Gatlinburg, TN

# Come Out, Come Out Wherever You Are

## "Get up! Go to the great city of Nineveh." —Jonah 1:2

Have you ever tried to avoid something you know is right? Have you ever been called to leave your comfort zone, but just couldn't force your way out? Many people spend their lives running from God and what He is telling them to do. Are you hiding from God? In Jonah 1, God told Jonah to go to Nineveh and call on the Ninevites to repent, but Jonah ignored Him and, instead, hopped on a boat going the other way. Why would Jonah hide from God? He hid for the same reason most do—going to Nineveh would not be easy. The Ninevites were a people full of sin. They were evil, and preaching to them meant that Jonah would have to leave his security and comfort. Jonah was not able to flee God's presence, however. God caused a great storm to come upon the sea, and Jonah was thrown overboard. Running from God will not put you in a good place. You must stop running from God and trust that He knows what is best for your life. Are you running right now? Are you on the path toward ending up in the belly of a fish? It is never too late to turn around and start listening to God. It literally took Jonah hitting the bottom of the sea before he realized he couldn't flee from God. Stop running and trust God. Do what you have been told to do. He is calling you to come out of your comfort zone and live boldly for Him.

*Laura Roggenbaum:* 17, Palm Harbor, FL
Calvary Baptist Church and Calvary Christian High School, Clearwater, FL

# Sticks and Stones May Break My Bones, but Words Will Never Hurt Me

"... to reward with rest you who are afflicted, along with us. This will take place at the revelation of the Lord Jesus from heaven with His powerful angels." —2 Thessalonians 1:7

We all have experienced a moment when we find out that words do hurt. In fact, they hurt us more than sticks and stones. How do words hurt more than sticks and stones, you say? Glad you asked. It is because words stick with us forever. All of us can remember a time when someone spoke cruel words to us, even if it was just a joke. We remember the feeling that came attached to those words more than the feeling that came from a little stick or stone. Therefore, unlike wounds from sticks and stones that heal, wounds that are made from cruel and harsh comments seem unlikely to ever heal. The attacks keep coming and the words keep playing over and over in our heads until we finally believe those words. Is there a cure? Yes. And there is hope as well. God tells us that if we hold tight to Him and stand up against those comments, then great will our reward be in heaven. In 2 Thessalonians, the disciples give encouragement by telling us that although a relief or a reward may seem unlikely to ever come, God is just and loving. He sees us where we are and is there for us when we call. He will give us the relief we need from our troubled hearts and the hope and endurance to continue on. Therefore, we are not alone in our trouble; God is right by our side. So, yes, words do hurt, but God will rescue us from the pain we experience and will heal our wounds. Hold on to His promises, trust in His timing, and stay strong in the faith.

Haley Smith: 16, Tarpon Springs, FL
Calvary Baptist Church and Calvary Christian High School, Tarpon Springs, FL

# What's Your Passion?

"We know that all things work together for the good of those who love God: those who are called according to His purpose."

—Romans 8:28

Everyone has a passion for something: that one thing that they are good at and they love doing. Mine is cooking. My best friend's passion is to be a singer. Another friend doesn't know what she wants to do with her life. It's hard for her to see that when I have mine practically planned out. One thing that I have to remember is that what I do with my life isn't my plan, it's God's. So, if you haven't found that one thing, just wait. God will show you His perfect plan for you eventually. He can be trusted. If you wonder if you will find your passion, it is easy to think that maybe you have no purpose, that God made a mistake with you. But that isn't the case! God loves you and put you here for a purpose. Another thing to remember is that our purpose in life is to point to God. That's the most important thing you will ever do: live your life for God. When you find your passion, whatever it may be, you can use it to live for God—whether it's cooking, singing, the medical field, or even acting. God can use you in any way to live for Him. So, find that one thing that you absolutely love doing. No goal is too big or too small, especially if you really want it. And, of course, nothing is too big for God to handle.

Hannah Abernathie: 15, Tulsa, OK
Evergreen Baptist Church, Bixby, OK; Homeschooled and Cornerstone Tutorial Center, Tulsa, OK

# Gratefulness

"Shout triumphantly to the Lord, all the earth. Serve the Lord with gladness; come before Him with joyful songs. Acknowledge that Yahweh is God. He made us and we are His—His people, the sheep of His pasture. Enter His gates with thanksgiving and His courts with praise. Give thanks to Him and praise His name. For Yahweh is good, and His love is eternal;, His faithfulness endures through all generations." —Psalm 100:1–5

We wake up to beautiful things every day. A lot of the things we take for granted, like sunrises, rain, fog, safety, warmth, and food. Americans are known to be the people with more than enough. Even with that, oftentimes we are still unappreciative. Until recently I was blinded to all the great gifts I have. I live on a very small island in Alaska called Kodiak. I was used to sun and heat and lots of places to go, but Kodiak is so much different. It's rainy and small. It's an "everyone knows everyone" kind of island, with only a few restaurants and one small Walmart. When we moved here, I thought I had just given everything up that was fun: my gymnastics, my mall, my warm summer days, and my tan. But what I didn't realize is that I had gained a different set of good things. I gained mountains and oceans, great Alaskan people, and record beautiful sunsets and sunrises. Sometimes it's hard, but no matter what place or situation you're in, there will always be a God-given blessing. That is what makes your day delightful. Don't treat the little things like nothing. Give thanks and praise.

*Leah Harris*: 16, Kodiak, AK
Frontier Southern Baptist Church, Kodiak, AK; Homeschooled

# Dealing with Hatred

"If the world hates you, understand that it hated Me before it hated you."

—John 15:18

We can only guess why some people dislike us. Society tells us that when people hate you that it means they desire what you have. The Bible tells us that we will not be liked and will be treated differently because we are Christians, but we can't let that bother us. It's more difficult for teens to deal with being an outcast because of our need to feel accepted. The truth is, you will never be accepted by this world! How can you fit in with something that you are not a part of? Being a Christian is supposed to make us stand out and be different, so don't stress about who likes us. My advice for anyone dealing with people that mistreat you is for you to pray for those individuals as well as yourself. Ask God to help you love them anyway, because this world teaches us to hate those who hate us. Those who mistreat us do not know any better, because of what they are taught by the world. The Bible says in Matthew 5:44, "But I tell you, love your enemies and pray for those who persecute you." In order for us to impact others in a godly way, we have to ignore what the world says. We want to honor God while on earth. Instead of being rude to those who treat us badly, let's be kind! It will puzzle them, and then it will really make them desire what you have! God knows we will not be liked by everyone, but we are to spread the gospel to everyone. Remember to act out of Christian love, whether people like you or not, because Christ showed unconditional love for us when we were sinners.

Reagan M'Cole Brashears: 17, New Orleans, LA
Franklin Avenue Baptist Church and Eleanor McMain Secondary School, New Orleans, LA

# Everything Has Changed

"Love is patient, love is kind. Love does not envy, is not boastful, is not conceited." —1 Corinthians 13:4

My friend and I both liked the same guy. It was a tricky situation to be in. We swore we'd never let a guy come between us. Problem was, this particular guy happened to be my ex-boyfriend. I still had feelings for him, but I wanted my friend to be happy. I talked to the guy and we decided that we weren't going to get back together. I didn't want to have an "if I can't have him then nobody can" attitude, so I didn't stop him when he asked her out right in front of me. This was toward the end of the school year, so I only suffered a month of seeing them together. I tried my best to remain friends with both of them, but jealousy took over. I thought I loved them, but love does not envy. So I kept my thoughts and feelings to myself, since the Bible says that love is patient and kind. They continued to date over the summer, but I didn't really keep in touch with either of them. All of it was too much to handle. Even though I lost two friends because of that, God taught me a valuable lesson: Jealousy tears people apart. Throughout the Bible, God states that envy is a sin. That situation seemed doomed to be bad but, looking back, I might still have their friendships if I hadn't had a jealous heart.

Callie Spencer: 14, Broken Arrow, OK
Evergreen Baptist Church, Bixby, OK; South Intermediate High School, Broken Arrow, OK

# Faith in the Midst of Doubt

"Now without faith it is impossible to please God, for the one who draws near to Him must believe that He exists and rewards those who seek Him." —Hebrews 11:6

On a windy evening, Jesus commanded Peter to walk on water—and Peter did. Later, Peter began to doubt the power of the Lord and immediately began to sink. Do you question your trust in Christ? Does your faith seem weak, causing you to doubt and leaving you with terrible feelings? You must stay strong in your faith, even when experiencing doubt. Everyone struggles with doubt. In fact, even Jesus' closest friends doubted at times. Peter doubted. Thomas doubted. In the Old Testament, Eve doubted. Gideon doubted. Abraham and Sarah doubted. I'm sure you can think of a time when you've felt alone in your doubt, like you're the only one questioning God. The devil wants us to doubt, which is one reason it is so difficult to overcome. Mercifully, God is greater than Satan and will help you conquer your doubts. The Bible tells us in Psalm 116:5 that "The Lord is gracious and righteous; our God is compassionate." He commands mercy on those who doubt in Jude 22. However, it is not OK to dwell in doubt. You must replace your doubt with faith because, as we learn in Hebrews 11:6–7, God will reward your faith with righteousness. When struggling with doubt, actively read the Word of God. The Gospels are the best help, because the words of Jesus while He was on earth penetrate the heart. It is helpful to have a wiser and more mature Christian as a confident you can go to. Most important, you must pray for God to strengthen your faith and gift you with perseverance. Who knows, someday you may develop faith which can move mountains.

Laura Roggenbaum: 17, Palm Harbor, FL
Calvary Baptist Church and Calvary Christian High School, Clearwater, FL

# You Are His

**"But you are a chosen race, a royal priesthood, a holy nation, a people for His possession, so that you may proclaim the praises of the One who called you out of darkness into His marvelous light."** —1 Peter 2:9

"You are not good enough." "You weigh too much." "You get on my nerves." "You have no talent." "You are ugly." Do any of these sound familiar? These bashes are among many that the world will throw at you to make you feel unwanted or unloved, and in high school we will pretty much do anything to fix ourselves. Have you ever skipped lunch, gotten a new haircut, or bought a whole new wardrobe in order to make yourself feel acceptable? Nothing will ever satisfy you, nothing will ever make those people see the real you, but I know Someone who will. His name is Jesus and, guess what—He is crazy about you! He says "You are beautiful." "You are worthy." "You are Mine." He chose you over life; He died for you. You can do nothing to merit His love, and He will never leave you. Rather than trying to fit in with the crowd, spend time getting to know and exalting the One who loves you, the One who made you. You no longer have to live in darkness or in pain. Pain will come your way, but you can rest in the Lord. Develop a relationship with and learn to love God. He will wipe your tears, laugh with you, teach you what is right, and be your best friend. The unsaved have nothing to compare to the Almighty Father. You belong to Him, so show the world the fearless, pure, and whole relationship you have with the Lord, and let His presence radiate through you.

*Reagan Bell:* 17, Tuscaloosa, AL
Valley View Baptist Church and Hillcrest High School, Tuscaloosa, AL

# An Honest Heart

"Guard your heart above all else, for it is the source of life. Don't let your mouth speak dishonestly and don't let your lips talk deviously. Let your eyes look forward; fix your gaze straight ahead."

—Proverbs 4:23–25

I recently asked a male friend of mine, "If you could give one piece of advice to Christian girls, what would you say?" His answer surprised me: "Be honest with yourself and others." Though unremarkable, his statement actually was quite deep. First: honesty with yourself. In these hectic years, it's important to recognize your motivations, faults, and strengths. It is especially important for Christians to be honest about troubles and sin in your life, and to be able to examine yourself (2 Corinthians 13:5). Once you recognize your needs and blessings, you can then communicate freely with God. Though God knows everything, relationship with Him matures through openness in prayer and by studying His Word. Second, be honest with others—primarily, your parents. Matthew 19:19 says, "Honor your father and your mother." Honor comes through obedience; be open with them and they will support and guide you. Honesty also builds friendships that can last for many years with people who help build you up spiritually. Finally, honesty with guys is very important. Young men are affected by the way young women interact with them. It is important for you to be honest with them about your feelings. Set emotional and physical boundaries and they will respect you and value your efforts. Honesty vanishes when sin enters. "Whatever is true . . . dwell on these things" (Philippians 4:8).

Kristin Goehl: 18, Princeton, MA
Bethlehem Bible Church, West Boylston, MA; Princeton University, Princeton, MA

# What's My Purpose?

"But get up and stand on your own feet. For I have appeared to you for this purpose, to appoint you as a servant and a witness of what you have seen and of what I will reveal to you." —Acts 26:16

One question I've heard some of my friends ask lately is, "What is God's purpose in their lives?" Not only my friends, but I've also had that question floating around in my brain. God doesn't really send us a nice little letter describing to each of us what He wants us to do. Although that would be incredible, that's just not how He operates. However, God does talk to us a lot through His Word, the Bible. You would probably be surprised at how many verses there actually are that describe our purpose. One well-known verse is Jeremiah 29:11. It is great and definitely worth checking out. Also I like this one above found in Acts. God doesn't tell us our exact career choice, but He does tell us what our purpose should be, before our careers. My youth pastor often says, "The point of your life is to point to God." That is incredibly true! We are called to be an example of Christ to others and share our faith with them. If our priority is being servants and witnesses for Christ, then God will direct the rest of our lives. We give our lives to Him, knowing that He will use us to do something great for the Kingdom. We may not know the next step in our journey, but we can be assured that He does. And because He does know, we can absolutely trust Him to steer us in the way we ought to go. So, always keep in mind your sole life purpose, and God will surely direct the rest of your life for His glory!

Amy Meeks: 16, Tulsa, OK
Evergreen Baptist Church, Bixby, OK; Mingo Valley Christian School, Tulsa, OK

# Time

"I gain understanding from Your precepts; therefore I hate every false way. Your word is a lamp for my feet and a light on my path."

—Psalm 119:104–105

I'm very busy taking piano lessons, teaching piano lessons, taking harp lessons, being at church every Sunday and Wednesday, doing my job, babysitting, being active in Bible quiz, doing school work, teaching three-year-olds in Sunday school, and I can never clean my bunny's cage too much! There is nothing wrong or sinful about these things, but I still need my quiet time with God. I have to manage my activities and make sure to make time for God above all the other things I do. I don't have it all figured out, and I don't always make time to read and study God's Word. It is important, and I need to make my personal time with God a priority. I can't just do everything else and then hope that there is time left in the end to spend with God, or just hope to squeeze it in sometime during the day. I must deliberately set aside the time I am going to spend with God. Then I must use that time that I have set aside wisely, focused on God, and without distraction. This is important because it will have eternal value. Not only will it bless you, now and in eternity, to spend time in God's Word, but it will also bless others. They will see the ways God is working in your life as you are being sanctified. They will see changes in the way you act and treat those around you. It will hopefully inspire them to spend time in God's Word too.

Tyra Ruisinger: 17, Raymore, MO
Summit Woods Baptist Church, Lees Summit, MO; Homeschooled

# The Gospel

**"He made the One who did not know sin to be sin for us, so that we might become the righteousness of God in Him."** —2 Corinthians 5:21

The world distorts who Christians are and what we believe. The apostle Paul summarizes the gospel in 1 Corinthians 15:3–4, saying: "For I passed on to you as most important what I also received: that Christ died for our sins according to the Scriptures, that He was buried, that He was raised on the third day." Our basic beliefs should be clear! In Isaiah 43:15, God says, "I am Yahweh, your Holy One, the Creator of Israel, your King." Not only is God perfectly holy and without sin, but He also rules over us. Since He is holy, nothing sinful can enter His presence. Romans 3:23 tells us that we are all sinners because of Adam and Eve's fall and are separated from God. God loves us because He created us, and He sent His Son, Jesus, to live a perfectly sinless life and then to die on the cross, taking the payment for our sins. In order to receive this gift, we must respond by recognizing the truth in the gospel: that we are sinners and must put our faith in Christ. Romans 8:1–2 says, "Therefore, no condemnation now exists for those in Christ Jesus, because the Spirit's law of life in Christ Jesus has set you free from the law of sin and of death." Once you understand the gospel of Christ, you are able to tell it to others. Though difficult, you don't want to break friendships or offend others. We are to teach God's message, even if others reject it. The gospel is how God saves sinners like us. Praise the Lord, without it we'd be lost!

*Kristin Goehl:* 18, Princeton, MA
Bethlehem Bible Church, West Boylston, MA; Princeton University, Princeton, MA

# Stressed Much?

### "Commit your way to the Lord; trust in Him, and He will act."
—Psalm 37:5

Do you regularly feel stressed? I know I do. I really try not to let it get to me, but sometimes I just can't help it! I'm a very organized person, so when things become too much for me to handle or don't work out according to my plans, I often end up feeling defeated and drained. And you know why that is? It's because I've been trying to do it all on my own! How silly it is of me when there is a loving Savior just waiting and, more important, wanting to take on all my cares and worries so that I don't have to lean on my own understanding! Teenagers often stress way out about worldly things, such as getting all our homework done in time to watch the latest show or achieving the highest grade on Tuesday's history test by staying up until 2:00 a.m. and skipping out on our quiet time with God. When we do these things, we are implying that we don't fully trust God's control over our lives and that the things on our to-do lists are more important than having a strong faith in Him. So, the next time you start feeling worried or anxious about something, stop and be still with God, surrendering your whole self to Him and trusting that He'll help you through it! When we commit all our ways to God, trusting in Him, He will act on our behalf. What a great promise that is for us to meditate on.

Emily Pitts: 16, Palm Harbor, FL
Calvary Baptist Church and Calvary Christian High School, Clearwater, FL

# God's Stock Market

> "Taste and see that the LORD is good.
> How happy is the man that takes refuge in Him!"
>
> —Psalm 34:8

Like most people, I go through dry spells in my walk with God, and I also have times when the Lord is teaching me and I feel spiritually full. One big key for me to grow in Him and experience those close times is for me to invest time in my relationship with Him. I think of it like God's stock market. If we invest a tiny bit of time, just enough to flip open the Bible and read a verse, we will reap a distant relationship with God. But He is waiting for us to talk to Him, and He is ready to spend time with us. Instead of spending time with Him, we think we have more important things to do, like school, time with friends, or checking Facebook. Social networking systems like Facebook and Twitter are created to meet our need for friend time. We need to let God be our best friend, because the return is better. Years from now, how many minutes we spent texting or playing around with friends will seem an utter waste compared to how many minutes we spent with God. If we would only invest more into God's stock market, we would profit from a much closer walk with Him, and our lives would be so much fuller. I like what Psalm 34:8 says: "Taste and see that the LORD is good. How happy is the man that takes refuge in Him!" Try it sometime; just "taste and see," and God will reward you. James 4:8 says, "Draw near to God, and He will draw near to you."

Hannah Cooksey: 16, McMinnville, OR
Valley Baptist Church, McMinnville, OR; Homeschooled

# Overcoming Giants

## "Don't let anyone be discouraged by him; your servant will go and fight this Philistine!" —1 Samuel 17:32

Whether fear, insecurity, jealousy, or bullies, everyone will face giants at some point. The question is how can these giants be overcome? First Samuel 17 tells the story of David and Goliath. When the Israelites saw Goliath, they all ran from him in fear. David had a different perspective on this giant, however. David looked at this man as someone who had defied the Lord. He looked at the giant and said, "You come against me with a dagger, spear, and sword, but I come against you in the name of Yahweh of Hosts, the God of Israel's armies—you have defied Him" (v. 45). He knew that God was on his side and had faith that God would help him to overcome Goliath in the name of the Lord Almighty. When facing giants in life, David's example is one that will help us. Don't fear these challenges as you take a stand against those things that hinder your relationship with God. Why would you not want to defeat something that is blocking the path between you and the Lord? God wants you to take a stand against your problems and He promises to be with you every step of the way. If God is for you, nothing can be against you. Just as Goliath began as a little baby, all giants begin small. It is best to face them right away, not to hide from them. So, when trying to overcome giants, trust in God. With Him, there is nothing we cannot overcome.

*Laura Roggenbaum*: 17, Palm Harbor, FL
Calvary Baptist Church and Calvary Christian High School, Clearwater, FL

# Holding on to the Eternal

**"I have fought the good fight, I have finished the race, I have kept the faith."** —2 Timothy 4:7

Esau was hungry. No, actually, he was famished. So hungry that he was going to die. He had been working all day and was exhausted. His brother Jacob had stayed home and was cooking when Esau got home. What could be better than coming home to a nice warm pot of stew? Esau asked Jacob for some stew, and Jacob agreed to give him a bowl in exchange for Esau's birthright. A birthright was a huge deal back then. It gave the firstborn son his father's rank in the family and property when he died. Esau agreed to sell. In that moment, he made a decision that would impact the rest of his life. He traded immediate happiness for what would matter in the long run. Don't let your fallen appetite get in the way of your eternal necessities. There have been so many people who have let the devil tempt them into following the world and their sinful desires, when they should be following Jesus. Do not be tricked into trading your faith and trust in God for the things the world throws at you, whether it be an offer for power, possessions, or pleasure. It is not worth losing eternity with your Savior. Be strong in the Lord so that in the end you can say like Paul in 2 Timothy 4:7, "I have fought the good fight, I have finished the race, I have kept the faith."

*Laura Roggenbaum*: 17, Palm Harbor, FL
Calvary Baptist Church and Calvary Christian High School, Clearwater, FL

# God's Plan (Part 1)

"For we are His creation, created in Christ Jesus for good works, which God prepared ahead of time so that we should walk in them."
—Ephesians 2:10

Although I'm only sixteen, my family has moved ten times because my dad is in the Air Force. The hardest part of moving, for me, is trusting God to provide a home, church, and friends. When I have no idea of what's going to happen to us in the upcoming months, it's hard to not grow anxious or fearful. Solid churches are difficult to find, and it takes about a year to really make good and close friends. We might move to a new home that's smaller than or not as nice as the one before, and sacrifices might have to be made to make it work. Saying good-bye to friends is one of the easiest parts of moving, because I'll not only see them again, but I now have precious friends all over the world. An invaluable lesson I've learned through moving is that my siblings and parents are my best friends, and they are always there. They are going through the same things and ready to support and encourage me. I've learned and seen something far more precious though, which is that God is sovereign and nothing is out of His hands.

Tara Greene: 16, Ft. Belvoir, VA
Gilford Baptist Church, Ft. Sterling, VA; Homeschooled

# God's Plan (Part 2)

"For we are His creation, created in Christ Jesus
for good works, which God prepared ahead of time so that
we should walk in them." —Ephesians 2:10

Moving brings with it the opportunity to learn about so many different places, which is helpful in certain classes, like history and geography. Isn't it wonderful that in God's creation He allowed for these valuable lessons? He provides for every single need, and we get to see our prayers answered in tangible ways. It's absolutely incredible to see the people that God has handpicked for us to meet in all the different places we have lived. He's not only chosen the people, but the church and ministry opportunities, and prepared them for us, as Ephesians 2:10 says, "ahead of time so that we should walk in them." Knowing that God has a perfect plan for our next move and every single person we encounter there makes moving exciting. Although moving brings with it some hardships, it's amazing to see the hand of God working through our lives and the lives of others in our many moves. If you're moving, or have moved, I would challenge you to start thinking of the good works that God has prepared for you, and get excited to see God's breathtaking work take place in every one of the new places He sends you to.

Tara Greene: 16, Ft. Belvoir, VA
Gilford Baptist Church, Sterling, VA; Homeschooled

# Priorities

"An unmarried woman . . . is concerned about the things of the Lord . . . but a married woman is concerned about the things of the world—how she may please her husband." —1 Corinthians 7:34

"I wonder if Chester would like this outfit." "Oh, Millard is looking at me!" "Maybe if I talk about Lamborghinis more, Fletcher would think I'm cool." I have realized lately how much of our time is wasted wondering what boys think of us. What is your first thought when you pick out an outfit or make a choice in life? Is it "What will Wendell think of this decision?" First Corinthians 7:34 is convicting because time is so precious, and we can never live our teen years again. Paul said he wrote that verse "so that you may be devoted to the Lord without distraction" (1 Corinthians 7:35), but are we? Instead of focusing on what boys think, we should focus on what God thinks. He cares what we say and how we act. "No foul language is to come from your mouths, but only what is good for building up someone in need, so that it gives grace to those who hear" (Ephesians 4:29). He cares about what we wear, too. First Timothy 2:9 says, "The women are to dress themselves in modest clothing, with decency and good sense." Notice that it doesn't say, "Wear whatever draws guys' attention." To replace our unnecessary thoughts, we can pray and meditate on Bible verses. I don't mean we should be meditating with our eyes closed while we are walking down the sidewalk, but in bed, in the shower, while driving, and other times like that are perfect for spending time with God. Think about how much time and energy we would have to spend on God and His Word if we didn't waste it!

Hannah Cooksey: 16, McMinnville, OR
Valley Baptist Church, McMinnville, OR; Homeschooled

# For All My Fellow PKs

## "Serve with a good attitude, as to the Lord and not to men."

—Ephesians 6:7

"First to arrive, last to leave." The life of a pastor's kid (PK), is something many don't understand. You aren't alone; I know what you're going through. It is tough living in the fishbowl we call life. Everyone is looking into our bowls, and tapping on the glass. Sometimes our lives remind me of *Finding Nemo.* When the dentist's niece, Darla, gets a new fish, she shakes the poor little fish to death. The church gets us, in our little fish bag, and shakes everything out of us. We have to attend every event, babysit every child, know the answer to every Bible question, and the name of every person that comes and gives you a hug. On top of that, as PKs we know all the drama going on in the church. We see the toll it takes on our fathers, and it makes us resent the people of the church. We tire of church, of people, and of being expected to do everything for everyone. We feel we need to be perfect because everyone sees every little thing about our life. We can't be normal teenagers, because everywhere we go a report somehow gets back to the people in our church, and they end up complaining to our dads. If you aren't going through this, show a little sympathy for those of us who are. Hard as it is, it is worth it! Take every annoying task as a task specifically ordained by God. I believe God chose us PKs because He knows we can do it. Many people believe we're super-crazy rebellious children. Let's prove them wrong and God right. Be ready to make war against all the stereotypes and judgmental people. Flaunt your fishbowl, shake it off if things don't go right, and remember to serve with a good attitude.

*Hannah Savage:* 16, Dodge City, KS
First Southern Baptist Church and Dodge City High School, Dodge City, KS

# Acceptance

"How happy is the man who does not follow the advice of the wicked, or take the path of sinners, or join a group of mockers! Instead his delight is in the Lord's instruction, and he meditates on it day and night."

—Psalm 1:1–2

We want to be accepted. We're human! We want to feel liked and we want to feel the approval of the people we care about. The problem is that a lot of the time we seek approval from the wrong people. I lost most of my friends after some terrible high school drama. I felt like such a loser because I didn't have my big group of friends anymore. So I became best friends with the first interesting person I found, but that friend was a terrible influence. She did drugs, drank, partied, and had sex with multiple guys. Eventually, I was doing not quite everything she did, but acting like I did. Then I could get in with her crowd and have that big group of friends. I was accepted, but for what gain? So I could walk down the school hallway with people instead of by myself? My reputation took the biggest hit. I was called so many names. People I didn't even know existed judged the most personal parts of my life. After a while I didn't care anymore. If people thought that of me, I might as well do it, right? I gave my heart to different guys that didn't even care to spend time with me. I didn't care about family, grades, my violin, or doing anything productive. The sad thing is that I didn't even notice how my life had gone downhill. But through teen pregnancy and the death of my daughter, God helped me turn my life around and get back on the track that will benefit me now and in the future. Once I turned to Him, I realized that God's acceptance was the only real acceptance I was actually searching for.

*Leah Harris:* 16, Kodiak, AK
Frontier Southern Baptist Church, Kodiak, AK; Homeschooled

# Stay Strong

"Therefore, as you received Christ Jesus the Lord, walk with Him, rooted and built up in Him and established in the faith, just as you were taught, overflowing with gratitude." —Colossians 2:6–7

The Christian life may seem glamorous, problem-free, laid-back, or easy. Well, I hate to tell you this, it is anything but. The devil seeks you every day, throwing temptation at you constantly. As a Christian, it seems a huge target is placed on you. The devil wants to hit your bull's-eye, to weaken you, or to make you second-guess your faith. Friends may call you snobby, tell you that you are trying to be better than you really are, or they may disown you or stop acting the same around you because you are "that Christian." Some family members don't understand, and may not like the choice you have made. But God is with you, walking with you when the going gets hard, lifting you up out of the pits, and providing what is needed to be strong. We need to consume the Word, pray without ceasing, and meet Christian friends. Jesus will change your whole perspective on life; things that seemed important won't any longer. You may find yourself staying at home to watch a movie instead of going out to a party, or helping a sibling instead of fighting with one. You may even find yourself going to church! Living for Christ will not be easy, but it will be awesome. You may not see it in high school; people may reject you until the moment you graduate. But trust me, one day you'll go from being "*that* Christian" to being "that Christian." So stay strong, never give up, and always remember God is right there with you.

Reagan Bell: 17, Tuscaloosa, AL
Valley View Baptist Church and Hillcrest High School, Tuscaloosa, AL

# God Is Love

## "The one who does not love does not know God, because God is love."

—1 John 4:8

Recently, I sat in the back row of a dark, crowded movie theater as I watched the film *Les Misérables*. I fought back tears as the characters sang of law, grace, redemption, and mercy. For me, the most moving moments of the film were when the characters displayed unremitting love and forgiveness toward one another. These actions symbolize the love God has for His chosen people. Scripture reveals certain aspects of this great love of God. First John 4:8 says that God Himself is love. God the Father manifested love to us when He sent His Son to this sinful earth. As Christ took the sin of His chosen people on Himself and bore the wrath of the Father, He poured out the greatest love the universe will ever see (John 15:13). So, God's plan of redemption manifests the love of God, but God is also the foundation for the love displayed by His creatures. According to R. C. Sproul, 1 John 4:8 refers to the fact that God is "the source, the ground, the norm, and the fountainhead of all love" (R. C. Sproul, *Loved by God* [Nashville: Thomas Nelson, 2001], 5). Movies like *Les Misérables* remind me not only of the great love of my Savior, but also of our responsibility to show this love to those around us. Jesus commands us to love one another (Matthew 22:39), but we can't do it on our own. Love is a fruit of the Spirit—something we can only display though the grace and work of the Holy Spirit. Ask the Holy Spirit to produce love in your heart. Then reflect the great love of Christ to those around you.

*Emily Sherrod*: 17, Mobile, AL
Christ Fellowship Baptist Church and Stanford University Online High School, Mobile, AL

# Rebellion

"... so that it may go well with you and that you may have a long life in the land." —Ephesians 6:3

Teens go through rebellion. Rebellion means going against the rules. Have you ever stayed up past your bedtime sneaking around behind your parents back? I have, even though I don't like to admit it. I think the verse above means that we are to do good things so that our foolishness will not keep us from having a long life in this world. The Ten Commandments tell us to honor our fathers and mothers. Teens tend to have trouble with rebellion, and it often starts by not honoring our parents. Some kids have a boyfriend or girlfriend even though their parents told them not to. Is that right? No it's not. You should always be able to tell your parents anything! You should look up to them. They should be your role models, representing Christ. C'mon, haven't you ever wanted to be like your mom or dad when you grow up? I do! I look up to my parents, and I can tell them anything. Some teens can't be open with their parents. Sometimes this is because their parents are not Christians, and they do things that are wrong. But God tells us to honor them—we don't get to make the decision to not honor them. You might pick someone else to be your role model, but you still have to honor your parents. Even though you disobey and suffer the consequences sometimes, they still love you! We teens need to stop rebelling and learn to trust and honor the parents God gave to us. It will be good for us in the long run.

Beraiah Benavides: 14, Sevierville, TN
Pathways Baptist Church, Sevierville, TN; The King's Academy, Seymour, TN

# Created for Love

**"God saw all that He had made, and it was very good."** —Genesis 1:31

Isn't God amazing? Look at creation, how everything works, and especially the beauty. Look at how God loves us and how creation shows this. God made everything to work perfectly, but He also made it enjoyable. Many religions believe differently about creation, but Christians know the truth. God's truth is the only explanation that makes sense. God spoke the world into existence. Can you even imagine that? "Then God said, 'Let there be light,' and there was light" (Genesis 1:3). Amazing! We need light; we can't function the way we do without it. God created light before He created humans. He took care of us before there was an "us." He loved us enough to think of us before He made us. God spoke all of creation into existence, except humans. Genesis 2:7 tells us, "Then the LORD God formed the man out of the dust from the ground and breathed the breath of life into his nostrils, and the man became a living being." Genesis 2:22 says, "Then the LORD God made the rib He had taken from the man into a woman and brought her to the man." He obviously loves us and cares enough about us to have a personal relationship with us. No other god in any other religion is like our God. Even though mankind has often turned their back on Him, God still loves and cares for us. God provides for His children and the world as a whole, including the many people who don't even know Him. Isn't it great to have a God who loves and cares for us? No one can ever take away the fact that our God is truly an awesome God.

*Brenna R. Strain:* 15, Spokane, WA
Airway Heights Baptist Church, Airway Heights, WA; Medical Lake High School, Medical Lake, WA

# Light of the World

"No one lights a lamp and puts it under a basket, but rather on a lampstand, and it gives light for all who are in the house."

—Matthew 5:15

We are the light of the world. As Christians, we must be a light in this dark place. Think of a dark cave, in the forest, in the middle of nowhere. You can't see a thing, not even your hand five inches in front of your face. You turn on your flashlight—light. The light defeated the darkness. How often does light defeat darkness? Ten times out of ten. So if the world is cold and dark and we are the light, what should we do? Shine! We all know the children's song "This Little Light of Mine." A verse in the song says, "Hide it under a bushel? No! I'm gonna let it shine!" Light is not meant to be hidden. Luke 11:33 states, "No one lights a lamp and puts it in a cellar . . . but on a lampstand, so that those who come in may see its light." We are to be the light to this world's darkness. What does it mean to be light? Do I have to carry a flashlight with me wherever I go? In Matthew 5 it says that our light should show others our good deeds so that they may praise God. Light defeats darkness as good deeds defeat bad works. This world will notice our light; they will notice the good deeds we do. Once they realize we are different, it is our job to point them to God and give Him the praise. Our goal as Christians is to bring God glory, to point others to Him. Figuratively speaking, we wave our light around until people notice it, then we point our flashlight up to heaven so that those watching can see God. "In the same way, let your light shine before men, so that they may see your good works and give glory to your Father in heaven" (Matthew 5:16).

Sarah LaCognata: 14, Belleview, FL
Church @ The Springs, Ocala, FL; Homeschooled

# Memory: God's Gift to You

### "I have treasured Your word in my heart so that I may not sin against You." —Psalm 119:11

We memorize every day without realizing it. Maybe it's a phone number, terms and definitions for a test at school, your best friend's birthday, or the lyrics to your favorite song. God has gifted each of us with a memory, where we can store whatever we wish. When God gave us that memory, His main purpose was for us to memorize His living and active Word, not the names of all the presidents or the formulas for algebra, although those are good things. Joshua 1:8 says, "This book of instruction must not depart from your mouth; you are to recite it day and night so that you may carefully observe everything written in it. For then you will prosper and succeed in whatever you do." God commands us to not let the Word depart from our mouths; what better way to fulfill this than to have it memorized! He says that if we recite it day and night then we will be able to carefully observe everything written in it. He promises success in whatever we do, which is pretty amazing. We all want success! Here are some simple steps to start immersing yourself in His Word: Set aside a little time each day to learn a new section of Scripture. It could be a verse, a part of a verse, or several verses. Review your verses while in the car, the shower, or during a boring lecture at school. (Just kidding about the last one.) Meditate on Scripture before you fall asleep, even if it is just for a short while. By meditating, I mean thinking deeply and slowly about the meaning of the verses. But above all, to really be in His Word, you must have devotions with Him every morning. To live a life devoted to Christ, we must give Him the first part of our days.

*Hannah Cooksey:* 16, McMinnville, OR
Valley Baptist Church, McMinnville, OR; Homeschooled

# Beauty in His Image

*"You are beautiful, my darling, with no imperfection in you."*

—Song of Songs 4:7

God loves you just the way you are. No matter how you look, He will love you. Don't listen to what other people say. You are beautiful in your own way. Don't let anybody put you down and say you're not pretty, and don't do that to yourself. I struggle thinking that I'm not pretty, but my friends say that I'm beautiful. Don't get upset over wearing glasses, and don't try to overdo trying to make yourself look a certain way to satisfy your peers. A little makeup might be good, but that doesn't mean you need to put makeup on to look pretty. The Lord created us in His image. Don't change yourself for a guy. You want him to love you for you and not some pretend person. You will know when the right guy comes along. He will love you with or without makeup, because the right guy will love your heart. We need to focus on our inner beauty that matters to God and to others. Remember, it's your opinion that matters and what's inside your heart. The Lord looks on the inside, not the outside. Have confidence in yourself. Believe. Pray to God and say, "Thank You, God, for making me in Your own image, and help me to focus on the person You are developing in me. Amen."

Beraiah Benavides: 14, Sevierville, TN
Pathways Baptist Church, Sevierville, TN; The King's Academy, Seymour, TN

# God Is Near

**"The LORD is near the brokenhearted, He saves those crushed in spirit."**
—Psalm 34:18

A morning not different from most: husbands and wives kissed each other good-bye, kids were dropped off at school, and some went to work while others boarded planes. They didn't imagine that would be their last day to do those things. Probably while their coffee from that morning was still hot, the planes those passengers boarded crashed into their office buildings. The horrible events of 9/11 changed so many lives. America was shaken to the core. Almost three thousand moms, dads, sisters, brothers, daughters, sons, aunts, and uncles died that September day. Many Americans turned to God for comfort, hope, and healing, and when they did, He was there. He is near to the brokenhearted. Didn't He promise in His Word that He would never leave nor forsake us? Perhaps He just seems more near when we are brokenhearted, because that is when we come to Him. I think it takes a tragedy to get us to come to God, to break us of our pride, and to show us our need for Him. That's what September 11, 2001 did. It broke us. It made us think twice about the next time we hugged someone good-bye, because we were horribly reminded that it could be the last time. It showed us that America is not invincible—that our motto "In God we trust" still needs to be our motto. We grieved together for the lives we had lost, for the first responders who gave their lives for victims. We grieved, and we learned, and we prayed. We thanked God for being near to us, and set our hope on the truth that despite all that happened to our country that day, He was and is on the throne!

*McKenzie Sutton*: 17, Waverly Hall, GA
Cornerstone Baptist Church, Ellerslie, GA; Homeschooled

# Finding Acceptance in Others

"All of you, take up My yoke and learn from Me, because I am gentle and humble in heart, and you will find rest for yourselves."

—Matthew 11:29

Teenagers look for acceptance from others. We are willing to do anything to be let into a group or invited to a party. We risk our entire futures on the idea that we need one more person to like or accept us. I began to talk to my parents about this issue. They told me that it does not get any easier, that I will struggle with trying to get people to accept me for the rest of my life. But there is a solution to this problem. It may sound like a typical church answer, but the honest answer is Jesus. We are to find our acceptance in Him. He is gentle and humble and willing to work with you along the way. He picks you up when you fall and helps you continue your journey. But it is incredibly hard to rest in the fact that God's is the only opinion that matters. Pray and ask God to show you how you can trust Him. Allow Him to work in your life. He wants you to trust Him. It does not matter if the most popular girl in school lets you join her group or if your cute neighbor decides he likes you. The only thing that matters is your spiritual life with God. After you die and go to heaven it will not matter that you had the most coveted boyfriend in school or were a part of the most popular group. The Bible says that those things will fade away. But we will always have Jesus. That is why it is so important to realize that you are accepted by God. He did create you, after all!

Hailey Culberson: 17, Tulsa, OK
Evergreen Baptist Church, Bixby, OK; Homeschooled

# Teen Responsibility

"When I was a child, I spoke like a child, I thought like a child,
I reasoned like a child. When I became a man, I put aside childish things."

—1 Corinthians 13:11

The variety of people groups in high school is interesting and overwhelming. There are honor students, I-don't-care-at-all students, in-between students, some socially awkward students, and just about any other kind of student. No matter what group, there are always at least a few kids from each group that have either tried, done, or are doing drugs and alcohol. A lot of parents don't even realize it. I know some nice, popular, Christian girls who are steady underage drinkers and do the occasional drug. Others of my friends are on the honor roll and have also gotten drunk quite often. The funny thing is, the parents of all these kids think that their children are perfect angels. Not that I blame them; honor roll doesn't scream drugs at all. And that's another thing that makes it so difficult to say no to drugs. With the added freedom of being in high school, you have a lower risk of getting caught doing things you know deep down you shouldn't be doing. I'm sure you all know the downside of drugs and drinking. Drugs are addicting, illegal, you get them from the not-too-great side of town, they consume your life, and so on. Drinking is also illegal underage, fairly dangerous, not good for your health, and it goes on. We've all heard the reasons not to do those things. It gets pretty tiring to hear them sometimes. But God gave us these authorities to protect us. Our teachers and parents aren't actually trying to make us miserable. Find out who you are and what you love in this world. With teenhood comes freedom, and with freedom comes responsibility.

Leah Harris: 16, Kodiak, AK
Frontier Southern Baptist Church, Kodiak, AK; Homeschooled

# Swing Set and Jesus

"Then Jesus said, 'Leave the children alone, and don't try to keep them from coming to Me, because the kingdom of heaven is made up of people like this.'" —Matthew 19:14

Recently I got on a swing set for the first time in years. Swinging was my favorite thing to do as a child. I would get on and go as high as my legs could get me. I felt like I was flying. Swinging made me remember how simple my life used to be. Even my faith was simple. God loved me. I loved Him. He gave His Son for me; I gave my life to Him. It was simple. But it seems like the older I get the more complicated life and faith become. There are questions that need answering, many things to know. If we aren't careful, we can get so bogged down with the questions and answers that we forget the simplicity of our faith. Paul writes this to the Ephesians in chapter 2:4–5: "But God, who is rich in mercy, because of His great love that He had for us, made us alive with the Messiah even though we were dead in trespasses. You are saved by grace!" We were dead in our sins and God, who is rich in mercy, made us alive in Christ. Our faith is simple. Is it easy to understand? No! Why would God send His only perfect Son to a world full of sinners? But that's what He did. That's how much God loves us. Our response doesn't have to be complicated. I believe that if we all had the faith of a child we would trust God much more than we do. Children almost always trust their parents. Why don't I completely trust God? So next time you are tempted to make your faith complicated, remember what Jesus said in Matthew. He wants us to have faith like children, completely surrendered and trusting Him with all we have.

Gabrielle LaCognata: 19, Belleview, FL
Church @ The Springs and College of Central Florida, Ocala, FL

# Perfectionism

"Then I heard a loud voice from the throne: Look! God's dwelling is with humanity, and He will live with them. They will be His people, and God Himself will be with them and be their God. He will wipe away every tear from their eyes. Death will no longer exist; grief, crying, and pain will exist no longer, because the previous things have passed away."

—Revelation 21:3–4

Good grades have come easy for me, and I have been labeled as a goody two-shoes. I don't mind studying; in fact, I actually love it. I love school and making good grades so I can prove my potential. Ever since I can remember, I've always felt pressure from my parents to do well in school and in my music. Given, my parents weren't really trying to exert pressure on me, and it's not that I didn't want to succeed, but sometimes I couldn't help worrying. I constantly feared that I wouldn't be acceptable and would lose my parents' respect for me as a "good child." If I could, I would spend my entire life simply making people laugh and smile. I never told anyone about my feelings, because I didn't want to burden anyone. Soon, my fears developed into paranoia and depression. I never felt that I was good enough; I could always be just a bit better. Don't get me wrong, all humans can improve. But when you focus solely on that, it begins to eat away at you. On the outside, it appeared as if nothing had ever fazed me; I behaved just as I always had. I often felt alone deep inside, but then I'd remember today's verses, which I ardently love. They give me hope and motivation to continue doing the best I can. We can't please everyone, but we can place our worries on the Lord, and He will reward us for our efforts.

Emily Matlock: 15, Springdale, AR
Cross Church Springdale Campus and Shiloh Christian School, Springdale, AR

# Being a Leader in Christ

"A man's heart plans his way, but the LORD determines his steps."
—Proverbs 16:9

The idea of speaking in front of people or even opening up to people scares me. I always let my fears get in my way. My church's youth group went on a winter beach retreat and it was a life-changing experience. I not only grew closer with the Lord, but I learned that He had blessed me with the talent of leadership. Every night, the youth in room 206 would sit in the floor and talk about that night's lesson. I could feel my fear taking over when the other girls were opening up and sharing their stories. Something inside of me knew I had the right words to help those girls. So before I knew it, I was talking and the girls were crying. I loved that the girls grew closer and opened up. Each night we discussed our problems, our joys, and even our mistakes in life. I knew this was God's way of making us grow closer. He also showed me that I helped those girls by showing them good leadership and being a good role model. I still get nervous at times, because I want to be the best leader to them. I know that God has great plans for me and the youth group. He has great plans for you too. It is important to find out what that plan is and to ask God to lead you toward a future that is pleasing to Him and a joy to you.

Brianna Carter: 19, Sharon, SC
Hillcrest Baptist Church and York Technical, York, SC

# Hatred

## "Love your neighbor as yourself. There is no other commandment greater than these." —Mark 12:31

"Love your neighbor as yourself." Love and treat others as you love and treat yourself. Teens struggle with this because we struggle with anger. Have you said things you wish you could take back? The problem is you can't! But we can trust God, through the Bible, to help us. Hebrew 4:12 says, "For the word of God is living and effective and sharper than any double-edged sword, penetrating as far as the separation of soul and spirit, joints and marrow. It is able to judge the ideas and thoughts of the heart." The bad part about not being able to take back hurtful things we say is that we have to deal with those words. My mom and many others have said, "If you don't have something nice to say, don't say it at all." Also think about what you're going to say before you say it. Sometimes it helps to say what you want to say to a friend in your mind, so when you do talk, you can speak without hurting them. God does not want us going around hurting people with our tongues. Please! Don't break your friend's heart because you didn't think about what you were going to say. Words can sound a lot like hate, so remember to be careful. Asking God to help you to control your tongue is the best way to not say things that will hurt. We don't want to push people away, so we need to be careful to choose our words carefully, before we speak. Think!

Beraiah Benavides: 14, Sevierville, TN
Pathways Baptist Church, Sevierville TN; The King's Academy, Seymour, TN

# Trust

"Our fathers trusted in You; They trusted, and You rescued them. They cried to You and were set free; They trusted in You and were not disgraced." —Psalm 22:4–5

It's difficult to trust God all the time, and it's an issue I've struggled with for years. I believed that God could provide and that He could do miracles; what I had trouble with was would He do it for me? How do we trust God? When people teach on trusting God they seem almost vague, telling you to trust God but never how. You're left feeling guilty and full of unanswered questions. Why is it so hard to trust God? Trusting is difficult because we fear what God will do with us if we trust Him with everything, so we tend to hold back. We make up clever excuses for why we do not submit. If you want what is best for your life, you must trust God's will, forgetting whatever it is that you fear to give to Him more than you want your way. There is no shortcut to trusting God. If you really trust Him, you will give Him every-thing. God isn't satisfied with even 99.9 percent of you. He wants all of you. He wants you to trust Him so that He can do wonderful things with your life. When you trust God, be specific as you pray. Tell Him in your own way, "God, I trust You with my fear of rejection. I give You this trip, it is Yours to fund or not fund as You will." When you honestly assess your life and entrust your entire life to His complete control, God gives peace, joy, and an attitude of praise. The more you trust God, the easier it gets to trust Him. God can be trusted with your life because He is good all the time. Are you willing to trust God with everything in a constant, even daily way?

Rebekah Byrd: 16, Tulsa, OK
Evergreen Baptist Church, Bixby, OK; Homeschooled

# God Is Your Nightlight

## "Your word is a lamp for my feet and a light on my path."
—Psalm 119:105

When going through rough times, you feel like you are in the dark, and the dark can be scary. It could be trouble with friends or family, a loved one passing away, or maybe even a reason you can't identify. If you go down a dark hallway, or dark street, your mind automatically starts thinking about all the things that could happen, or pop out and attack you. You know, the bogeyman jumps out and terrorizes you. Ghosts come out and spook you. Monsters of all shapes and sizes attack you. It's in those times that your mind starts to doubt what you know to be true. You start to wonder if the darkness is ever going to end. But it will end, because God is light. And where there is light, there can be no darkness. We should rejoice in these rough times, because in them we are weak; and when we are weak, we rely on God more. When you trust in God, He allows you to see the light at the end of the tunnel. Instead of giving up, continue to persevere and trust God that the dark will end. When it does, you will be stronger and closer to God than you were before. When you go down a dark road, physically or spiritually, remember that God is the light that allows you to see truth. He is the dawn that scares away the creatures of the night. He also knows exactly what you are going through and just when you need that burst of light that gives you hope. Pour out your heart to God and tell Him your feelings and anxieties, and He will fill you up with peace and hope. So let God be the nightlight that lights your path.

*Hannah Abernathie*: 15, Tulsa, OK
Evergreen Baptist Church, Bixby, OK; Homeschooled and Cornerstone Tutorial Center, Tulsa, OK

# Facing Hardships

"I have told you these things so that in Me you may have peace. You will have suffering in this world. Be courageous! I have conquered the world."

—John 16:33

We will run into hardships that we will have to overcome. That is a bleak-sounding future. If I just heard that line, I would probably think, *That is definitely not a religion that I would want to follow.* Who wants to jump into something that will lead them down a dark path, right? Wrong! Although the Bible tells us that we will face trials, we have nothing to fear. In fact, our fear of troubles is an awful excuse for not wanting to follow Christ. This sounds really dark, but there is light at the end of the tunnel, if you choose to respond in a godly manner. One awesome thing about our God is that He will never leave us nor forsake us. Wow, can anyone else make that kind of promise?! No. Although Jesus basically tells us that we will have to face some rough times, He doesn't tell us that we will be left alone. In fact, He tells us to be courageous because He has already conquered the world. That just totally blew me away. Jesus has already conquered our hardships for us, so all we have to do is just look to Him for directions. Instead of dwelling on your troubles, try bringing them to God. He is the best listener. God knows us better than anyone else, so we don't have to approach Him in fear. He already knows all. I'm glad that I serve that kind of God. To sum it all up, there is no need to be afraid when you face hardships. Rather, you should praise God for them and give them to Him, because He can take care of the situation better than anyone else. There are certainly brighter days ahead!

Amy Meeks: 16, Tulsa, OK
Evergreen Baptist Church, Bixby, OK; Mingo Valley Christian School, Tulsa, OK

# Christian Mode

"The LORD is a refuge for the oppressed, a refuge in times of trouble."
—Psalm 9:9

When you look in the mirror, do you see a giant halo over your head? Sometimes we, as Christians, tend to think of ourselves as perfect in the eyes of the Lord. Despite this, five minutes later, we look back at the exact same reflection and make six million adjustments so that our peers at school will like us. Why do we do this? I'm not saying looking good is bad, but this should not overpower our devotion to the Lord. In the same way that we look at our reflections differently, we act differently when we're in church mode than when we are in regular teenager mode. At school, we tend to act like church mode doesn't really exist. When asked, we'll probably say, "Yes, I go to church," but we may still be ignoring church mode, which is obvious to those around us. At church we act as though the last week of regular teenager mode never happened. We get into the habit of thinking that just by going to church on Sunday we're somehow different from the people we go to school with, but we are able to act in the same way they do. So I propose a solution: Christian mode. I'm not saying you should wear robes and carry a life-size model of the cross with you when you go to school, but let the cross be seen through you. By taking refuge in the Lord, we have nothing to fear! So when you are at school and debate doing the thing that will help you fit in or sticking to Christian mode, remember that with the first you are on your own. When you stick to the Word, God is on your side. That's the best backup you can ever have.

Erin France: 14, Anchorage, AK
First Baptist Church and Eagle River High School, Anchorage, AK

# Involved

"And let us be concerned about one another in order to promote love and good works, not staying away from our worship meetings, as some habitually do, but encouraging each other, and all the more as you see the day drawing near." —Hebrews 10:24–25

Many schools, both public and private, have various clubs and organizations that are offered for extracurricular activities. In my public school, I am in CSU, which stands for Christian Students Union. We meet once a week for about an hour. We sing, then do a Bible study and fellowship. It may seem insignificant, but we are supposed to be involved in assemblies of Christians, even away from church, in order to strengthen our faith. Another option at my school is prayer circle. Every day before lunch, a group of unashamed Christians comes together to pray. We exchange prayer requests and praises, then we join hands in prayer. Both of these are great ways to get involved in fellowship with other Christians. Hebrews 10:24–25 talks about how God wants us to gather with other Christians and encourage each other. So I encourage you to seek out clubs and activities in both your school and community. If you feel God tugging at your heart and pushing you to join in fellowship with other Christians, don't be afraid—get involved!

Callie Spencer: 14, Broken Arrow, OK
Evergreen Baptist Church, Bixby, OK; South Intermediate High School, Broken Arrow, OK

# Loving Mercy

## "The merciful are blessed, for they will be shown mercy."

—Matthew 5:7

Mercy is not getting what you deserve. It is showing compassion to others, even when they mess up. Mercy does not show judgment, but works to make things better and reserves punishment. How often do you show others mercy? Do you like to help others in their trials? Do you enjoy serving? Do people trust you when they need help? When someone wrongs you, are you quick to forgive, or is your motto "an eye for an eye, a tooth for a tooth"? It can be very difficult to show mercy. There is definitely no way to show mercy on your own strength. You must look to God who is "the Father of mercies" (2 Corinthians 1:3). Put on a spirit of thankfulness. If you are thankful for what Christ has done for you by sacrificing Himself on the cross, it will be easier to put into perspective the little situations that are tough to show mercy in throughout the day. Say to yourself, "Who am I not to forgive when Christ has already forgiven everything I have done?" Another way to be sure you are showing mercy is to make Micah 6:8 your daily prayer. It says, "Mankind, He has told you what is good and what it is the LORD requires of you: to act justly, to love faithfulness, and to walk humbly with your God." Some versions say to love mercy. Love mercy. Write this on a note card, stick it on your bathroom mirror, or bookmark it in your Bible. Who have you withheld mercy from? I challenge you to begin showing mercy every chance you get, just as Christ has shown you.

Laura Roggenbaum: 17, Palm Harbor, FL
Calvary Baptist Church and Calvary Christian High School, Clearwater, FL

# Love

*"No temptation has overtaken you except what is common to humanity. God is faithful and He will not allow you to be tempted beyond what you are able, but with the temptation He will also provide a way of escape so that you are able to bear it."* —1 Corinthians 10:13

Boys and girls are so different—equally amazing, but so different. As a hormonal girl, I went through the same problems that we all go through in our own ways. What was my biggest issue? Boys. I thought that I needed a boyfriend to gain respect from my peers. I thought it made me look cool. I thought it would show that I'm not weird and people actually want to be around me. But I gave my heart to the wrong boys. The first boy I liked professed to be a Christian. He was from a nice Christian family, and they went to church and youth group every week. So it was perfect, right? Not really. I assumed that I could trust him with my whole heart. But, just like me, that boy was giving in to teen issues too, and eventually he pressured me into things that I wasn't comfortable with. After that, my heart was damaged. The term *broken heart* seemed too real to me then. I was so confused. I believed that if I had another boyfriend it would be OK again. I kept giving my heart over and over, to the point where I had no heart left to give. Fortunately, I had a relationship with God, the only One who will never ever fail me. Not only did He not fail me, but He fixed me too. Guys and girls need to wait for love. Treat yourself like what you're worth. Wait for the partner that God will give you.

Leah Harris: 16, Kodiak, AK,
Frontier Southern Baptist Church, Kodiak, AK; Homeschooled

# Come Away

"He said to them, 'Come away by yourselves to a remote place and rest for a while.' For many people were coming and going, and they did not even have time to eat." —Mark 6:31

We are constantly on the go with school, chores, sports, music lessons, church. Then we have to spend time with our family and friends. As teenage girls in this fastpaced era, we are constantly running, trying to keep up, trying to balance everything on our plates, and then find time to sleep. Have you ever been so busy that you didn't even have time to eat? That's how Jesus' disciples were, busy doing good things. They were serving the Lord and ministering to people. But Jesus is like, "Hey, guys, I think it's time to come away and spend some time with Me." I think Jesus meant these words directly to the disciples, but I think He also means them for us. The disciples were physically with Jesus all the time. They served and loved right alongside Him. They needed to retreat, to be alone with Him, and to rest. How much more do we need to do so? It's important to come away from the world daily and spend time with Jesus. It's important to get into His Word, to pray, and to commune with Him. An excuse many of us use is that we don't have any time left for God. It's hard to come away by yourself to a remote place and spend time with Him. We need to purposefully come away and spend time with the Lord. We have to let His Spirit refresh ours. We need Him. This world keeps us running, and we get weary. But Jesus' call to us is always the same: "Come away."

McKenzie Sutton: 17, Waverly Hall, GA
Cornerstone Baptist Church, Ellerslie, GA; Homeschooled

# Help My Unbelief

**"Immediately the father of the boy cried out, 'I do believe!
Help my unbelief.'"** —Mark 9:24

Have you ever experienced a painful struggle with doubt? It happens. It's part of our sinful nature. I grew up hearing about Christ's love for me and the forgiveness that comes in Christ alone. Having been raised attending gospel-centered churches and knowing Christ as my Lord and Savior, I can honestly say I have difficulty remembering when I wasn't saved. But at times I still struggle with doubt and unbelief. I'm not alone. If you have similar doubts, you are not alone either. John the Baptist was chosen specifically by God to pave the way for the coming of Christ and proclaim Jesus as the awaited Savior. "Here is the Lamb of God, who takes away the sin of the world," John declared at the baptism of Christ (John 1:29). Jesus said of John the Baptist, "Among those born of women no one greater than John the Baptist has appeared" (Matthew 11:11). What a compliment from the Creator of the universe! Would you believe this great man, John the Baptist, had doubt? In Matthew 11:3, John sent word to Jesus asking, "Are You the One who is to come, or should we expect someone else?" Jesus responded mercifully, referring to Scripture and confirming His Messianic identity. Doubt is not something peculiar to you or me. Even John the Baptist—chosen by God to prepare for and exalt His Son, Jesus Christ, as Lord and Savior—struggled with doubt. It is important to remember that faith is not something that we can muster up on our own. Faith is a gift of God. As one man beseeched Jesus to cast out a demon from his son, he cried out, "I do believe! Help my unbelief" (Mark 9:24). Be assured when doubt comes, that as a believer, God is available to call on His name for greater faith.

*Emily Sherrod:* 17, Mobile, AL
Christ Fellowship Baptist Church and Stanford University Online High School, Mobile, AL

# Thank God for Your Family

**"Dear friends, if God loved us in this way we also must love one another."**
—1 John 4:11

Your family is a gift from God put in your life for a reason. Love them with all of your heart, spend time with them. Going out with just your family can be such a great experience. When I was four, I was adopted by a family very different from me, and I felt like I didn't belong. I spent a lot of my life not wanting to be a part of family reunions. I realized that I could not do that my whole life. So I actually got to know my family. I realized what great people God had put in my life. I could not have asked for a better family fit. It is important to know your family and, believe me, you will not regret it. Your family was put in your life to build you up. A family is a team that knows each other and will do anything good for the other members. Always pray for your family members. Ask your family members how their day was, encourage them. Always be honest with them. Protect them from evil coming their way. Stand up for them when they are in trouble. Never ignore them when they are down. Ask God to help you keep a strong relationship with your family. Ask God to be the center of your family. That is the greatest thing you could ask for. He will be with your family in the struggles and pain. God is a member of your family too. He is your heavenly Father. He is watching over you and other families around the world. He cares about each and every one of you. He wants what's best for your family, as a whole. So, again, please do not disregard your family. They are the best thing you could ask for.

Dianah Edwards: 16, West Monroe, LA
First West Monroe Baptist Church and Northeast Baptist School, West Monroe, LA

# Prayer

"Rejoice always! Pray constantly. Give thanks in everything, for this is God's will for you in Christ Jesus." —1 Thessalonians 5:16–18

One of the greatest struggles Christian teens face is in his or her prayer life. Entering my teen years, I was distracted by the troubles and successes of my busy life, and I spent less time with God. Prayer became a crutch to be used in extreme circumstances. I found myself talking to God only when I had great achievements or problems. Don't go there! Prayer builds our relationship with our heavenly Father. Philippians 4:6 says, "In everything, through prayer and petition with thanksgiving, let your requests be made known to God." Prayer is a comfort for Christians, where we can put all our concerns in God's all-powerful hands. When we face troubles, the psalmist reminds us that prayer is also for praise. "Let us enter His presence with thanksgiving; let us shout triumphantly to Him in song" (Psalm 95:2). God promises to answer our prayers, though not always as we may expect or particularly want (1 John 5:14–15). Prayer helps us to know and do God's will, because He knows what is best for us (Colossians 1:9–10). We are in a constantly growing relationship with God, and talking to Him is an important part of that relationship. Think about how much time you spend talking to one of your friends through texting or online; isn't your relationship with God so much more important? Then you should talk with Him all the time about your life. God wants to connect with you because He loves you!

*Kristin Goehl*: 18, Princeton, MA
Bethlehem Bible Church, West Boylston, MA; Princeton University, Princeton, MA

# Facing Judgment

"Do not judge, and you will not be judged. Do not condemn, and you will not be condemned. Forgiven, and you will be forgiven." —Luke 6:37

Ever had a friend whom you love but could wring their neck at the same time? You are not alone. My friend and I fight all the time over silly stuff. Naturally we have been taught differently, but we tend to judge each other. As I've prayed, it has gotten better over the course of the year, but it's still a work in progress. I remember the first time I wore my combat boots to school. That summer I had gone on a work project, so they were covered in paint. When I got to school and showed my friend, she completely freaked out. She told me I shouldn't have worn those to school. She wasn't the only one at fault, though. I freaked right back at her. I would let no one tell me what I could or could not wear, except for my parents and certain other adults in authority. I yelled at her for being a bad friend and told her that she had no right. I realized I was at fault, so I prayed for forgiveness for what I said and the tone I used. Proverbs 15:1 says, "A gentle answer turns away anger but a harsh word stirs up wrath." At lunch I was still mad, but thanks to God another friend helped settle the problem. God used her to bring the two of us back together. Luke 6:37 says, "Do not judge, and you will not be judged." I realized I was at fault. By the end of the day we were besties again. My friend had just been trying to protect me in her own way. We both need to grow more in our Christian life. Everything turned out all right.

Deanna N. Davis: 13, Fairchild Air Force Base, WA
Airway Heights Baptist Church, Airway Heights, WA; Medical Lake Middle School, Medical Lake, WA

# Seeking Confidence Through Christ

*"For God has not given us a spirit of fearfulness, but one of power, love, and sound judgment."* —2 Timothy 1:7

Throughout my younger years, I was more of a quiet and shy kid. I would politely talk to adults, but never try to approach them. They intimidated me. I was drawn to the other quiet kids, or I would just hang out with my familiar friends. It never really occurred to me that I should go and try to talk with other people in order to overcome my shyness. I was totally content with my friends. But as I grew older, I realized that I didn't have to be shy. I could talk to other people if I really wanted to. I was the one keeping me from breaking out of my shy, closed-off self. Then I got to thinking, *How can I ever share the gospel with other people if I can't even approach the people near me?* Honestly, God didn't create us to stay bottled up. He wants us to go out to everyone we know and tell them the good news of Jesus. It's truly selfish of us if we just keep this kind of awesome, impactful information to ourselves. Many Bible verses remind us that God did not create us to be afraid and close-minded. We were created to worship and bring glory to Him. If we are to fulfill His plans for us, we have to break out of our old selves for Him. He's way more than worth it! So, don't be afraid to approach those people you normally wouldn't. They need Jesus just as much as you do. Also, don't be fearful of what other people think of you; your real value is in Christ. Break free from the shyness that is holding you down! God has so much in store for you if you do.

Amy Meeks: 16, Tulsa, OK
Evergreen Baptist Church, Bixby, OK; Mingo Valley Christian School, Tulsa, OK

# Sunrise

"But you are a chosen race, a royal priesthood, a holy nation, a people for His possession, so that you may proclaim the praises of the One who called you out of darkness into His marvelous light." —1 Peter 2:9

Some friends and I went to the beach recently to see the sunrise, but it was still very dark and we couldn't see anything. Finally, it started getting a bit lighter. We couldn't actually see the sun yet, but we could see its effects. The water looked lighter and it really was getting brighter. And then, there it was, a big, beautiful, pink sun rising over the water; welcoming a new day. My friend mentioned how similar a sunrise is to the day when the Son rose. All was dark. The followers of Jesus were without hope, without their leader, and without the knowledge of what to do next. Then Jesus rose, bringing light to a dark world—hope, life, and vision. Jesus gave them the command to "Go and make disciples of all nations." Their job was to take the light of Jesus to those who were living in darkness. For Christians today the same command applies. We are to take the light to the dark parts of the world. We have all heard the song "This Little Light of Mine." Why would we hide something as incredible as eternity with God in heaven under a bushel? C. S. Lewis once said, "I believe in Christianity as I believe that the sun has risen: not only because I see it, but because by it I see everything else." The world needs the Son, His light, the One who fills our dark lives with light. Look for opportunities to shine God's light in this world. So as the song goes, "Shine your light and let the whole world see. We're singing, for the glory of the risen King. Jesus."

Gabrielle LaCognata: 19, Belleview, FL
Church @ The Springs and College of Central Florida, Ocala, FL

# Rising Above

"We are pressured in every way but not crushed; we are perplexed but not in despair; we are persecuted but not abandoned; we are struck down but not destroyed." —2 Corinthians 4:8–9

It all started in sixth grade and went through eighth. It was really hard in the beginning, because I didn't know most of the people at my new middle school. After I got more comfortable, I decided to open up a bit. He seemed harmless from a distance, so I took the risk of falling for him. Big mistake. Turned out that this boy had power; he was popular. Well, he found out I liked him and decided that he hated me. So he told all of his friends to hate me too. Overall, he was responsible for ruining my chances at making many friends in middle school. Every day I went to school and he teased me, ridiculed me, and got all his buddies to join in. I was shunned, ignored, avoided, gossiped about, hated. Through it all, I couldn't stop having a crush on him. So I didn't put much effort into defending myself. Eventually I went to the principal, who claimed she couldn't help me. I was on my own. So I started ignoring him. Even though the tormenting didn't stop until the end of eighth grade, I coped. God stayed with me the whole time and helped me in ways that I didn't even notice then. Second Corinthians 4:8–9 talks about how many bad things happen to us, but God keeps them from being as bad as they could be. I learned something from that experience that affects me still today. There are going to be people in life who don't like you, but the Bible says many times that we should love our enemies and treat them well. Do not become like them. Instead, be the better person.

Callie Spencer: 14, Broken Arrow, OK
Evergreen Baptist Church, Bixby, OK; South Intermediate High School, Broken Arrow, OK

# Be Still

**"I will meditate on Your precepts and think about Your ways.
I will delight in Your statutes; I will not forget Your word."**

—Psalm 119:15–16

Were you ever in a time-out as a little kid? I spent some time there when I was younger, and it was a terrible punishment. I hated listening to the sound of the timer as it ticked down the seconds. I wanted nothing more than to get out of the corner and go and play with my brothers again. As I grew older, I became so busy with chores, homework, and 4-H that all I wanted to do with my free time was read or sleep. Isn't it funny that sitting still for a few minutes is something that we hated as a little kid, and yet it can be really nice now? In fact, making quiet time to spend with God can be one of the best ways to grow spiritually. In Psalm 119:15–16 the psalmist is saying that he will take time to think about God's ways and commandments and study His Word. Do you take time to be still and think about God, whether it's reading your Bible and thinking or taking time to pray and listen for God to respond? Even if it is simply spending some time being thankful for what you have, strive to be still for a moment today. Think about the things you do throughout the day. You always have five minutes free at any one moment. God doesn't care if you give Him the five between sports practice and the bus ride home. He doesn't care if you do it at lunch time while you eat. The important thing is to take that time to quiet your mind, to be still, and to know that He is God.

*Kaylin Calvert*: 18, Medical Lake, WA
Airway Heights Baptist Church, Airway Heights, WA; Homeschooled

# Dealing With Grief (Part 1)

"My eyes have grown dim with grief, and my whole body has become but a shadow." —Job 17:7

I hate grief. My father was always sick, really. He had problems with his back, and he had diabetes. When he got sick one week near the end of the school year in 2012, I really didn't think much of it. He had been sick before and had always gotten over it. Always! One day he got so sick he had to go to the hospital. I thought he would just get some medicine and come home, but he didn't. I honestly don't really know what happened at the hospital, but when I got there, they told me he had lung cancer. I tried my best not to cry, but I was so upset. Why my dad, whom I loved so much? My big sister told me he would be OK, but my dad wasn't OK. The cancer spread like wildfire and made its way to his brain. The day before he died, I sat with him and my family, but he was not the man we had all known. He was an old, bald, sick, frail man who didn't even remember he had cancer. My father passed away in the summer of 2012. His cancer was in advanced stages when he learned that he had it. It's hard to watch someone you love die, and it can turn you against God. Trust me; I know it is hard—so hard. God will help you; He will change you, and make you a better person. He knows that grief hurts, but it's not going to forever. My faith has grown because of my father's death, because God is the only one who knows how I feel. I trust Him to take good care of me here on earth and my dad in heaven. Please know this: God is always there and He will always care.

Clara Davis: 14, Little Rock, AR
The Church at Rock Creek and LISA Academy, Little Rock, AR

# Dealing with Grief (Part 2)

"Be gracious to me, Lord, because I am in distress; my eyes are worn out from angry sorrow-my whole being as well." —Psalm 31:9

Grief is one of the hardest things I think a person can go through. When I lost my dad to cancer, I was mad, sad, and I didn't understand why something like that would happen to my family. I was so confused and hurt and, for a while, I was even mad at God for taking my father away from me. Job 1:7–9 explains what I was feeling when it says, "The Lord asked Satan, 'Where have you come from?' 'From roaming through the earth,' Satan answered Him, 'and walking around on it.' Then the Lord said to Satan, 'Have you considered My servant Job? No one else on earth is like him, a man of perfect integrity, who fears God and turns away from evil.' Satan answered the Lord, 'Does Job fear God for nothing?'" Soon after my father's death, I had to go back to school and see all the people who were happy. Grief can push you away from God, but God loves you for exactly who you are. Everyone goes through trials and hardships, but God Himself will pull you through. "If this is so, then the Lord knows how to rescue the godly from trials and to hold the unrighteous for punishment on the day of judgment" (2 Peter 2:9). Know that God is there for you, and He truly understands what you are going through. Grief can be felt for numerous reasons: loss of a loved one, a friend, having to move, having someone you like break up with you. But remember, God is always there! He will never fail in helping you. He will never stop loving you. He lets us grieve and He can handle it with us and for us. Call on Him in times of grief.

Clara Davis: 14, Little Rock, AR
The Church at Rock Creek and LISA Academy, Little Rock, AR

# O What Love Is This!

"For God loved the world in this way: He gave His One and Only Son, so that everyone who believes in Him will not perish but have eternal life."

—John 3:16

Imagine you are responsible for the care of a group of kids for the next three weeks. You have to make sure all their needs are met: physical, emotional, financial, and spiritual. Now imagine that your favorite kid becomes suddenly ill and you have a choice to save his/her life by giving them yours, or you can watch them die. What do you do? Most of us would choose to give our own lives. But would you really? I only know of one person who did that. Jesus, God's only Son! I'm sure you know the story. God sent His perfect Son to save us from our sin, so that we might live in heaven with Him for eternity. Have you ever thought that God knew He was going to have to send His Son to die for you? He knew before Jesus was even born. God knew that it was impossible for us to obey Him. That's why He sent Jesus. He sent Him so it would be easier for us to accept Him! What favor He bestowed on us. Now, I'm going to paraphrase here, and I want you to do the same thing. "For God so loved Nellie in this way: He gave His One and Only Son, so that if Nellie believes in Him, she will not perish, but have eternal life." Now doesn't that sound better? Where I said my name, I want you to put yours in. God wants us with Him. He wouldn't have sacrificed His Son if He didn't. Now it's up to us to make the final decision. The time is right!

Nellie Otoupalik: 17, Spokane, WA
Airway Heights Baptist Church, Airway Heights, WA; Homeschooled/Co-op and Spokane Virtual Learning, Spokane, WA

# Fallin' in Love

"Then He said to them all, "If anyone wants to come with Me, he must deny himself, take up his cross daily, and follow Me. For whoever wants to save his life will lose it, but whoever loses his life because of Me will save it." —Luke 9:23–24

Have you ever seen two people who you could tell were deeply in love with each other? Maybe it's your parents, older siblings, a friend, or maybe it's you and that special someone! You can tell that all they want to do is be with each other. What makes them happiest is to see their true love happy. Isn't that what it should be like when we give our heart to Jesus? It should be a little more like "fallin' in love" and a little less like "something to believe in." I'm not talking about just praying a prayer, what I'm asking is if you have ever really, completely and totally, with reckless abandon, surrendered your life to Christ. Have all your dreams, hopes, ambitions, desires, and plans for your life and future have been given over to Him? He offers us unconditional love, no matter what. He wants us to love Him with all our hearts, souls, and minds. He wants us to deny ourselves and follow Him, taking up His cross daily. Losing our lives in Christ means that we will live eternally with Him.

Hannah McGee: 15, Springdale, AR
Cross Church Springdale Campus, Northwest, AR; Shiloh Christian School, Springdale, AR

# Love Your Enemies

"But I say to you who listen: Love your enemies, do what is good to those who hate you, bless those who curse you, and pray for those who mistreat you." —Luke 6:27–28

Is there someone at school, or at your church, who you absolutely cannot stand? There are plenty of people whom I really would not want to be friends with. Everyone has a person that annoys them or is mean to them. It's human nature to not like certain people, but God's Word tells us to do just the opposite of what our flesh would want to do. A lot of times, we judge someone by a first impression. I'm guilty because I do this a lot. Next time you encounter someone that you don't like or someone that is mean to you, try to get to know them, and be nice to them. The Bible tells us to bless our enemies! It doesn't matter that you don't know what is going on in their home, how they are feeling, or how desperate they are to have a friend, you are told to bless your enemies. There is also a reason behind an action. Pray for these people, and try to be their friend. I challenge you to find one person and befriend them. God has called us to love everyone, no matter how hard it may be. The blessing will be theirs and yours, and you might make a friend for all eternity!

Layne Coleman: 14, Little Rock, AR
The Church at Rock Creek and Little Rock Christian Academy, Little Rock, AR

# Putting on a Humble Heart

## "God resists the proud, but gives grace to the humble." —James 4:6

The smartest person in the school knew it, and she made sure everyone else did too. When the teacher made the slightest mistake, the girl would quickly correct him with a snooty attitude. She was talented. She got lead parts in everything she went out for at school. She told everyone that if they were as talented and smart as she, maybe they could get the best parts and rank high in the class. The one thing the girl did not have—friends. Nobody wanted to be around her because she was always bragging. Would you be around someone that was always putting their achievements up and you down? Probably not! You must humble yourself before God and others. God does not like such behavior. We can become more humble by looking at people positively, instead of trying to find the worst in them. The Psalms say that God will mock those who mock but, once again, He will give grace to those who are humble. Another way to practice humbling yourself is to be quick to admit that you have messed up. Proverbs 28 says that we are not to hide our sins, but that we are to confess them and then we will find mercy. Kindness is important, but it needs to be sincere. Put on a servant's heart, going into your community to serve others, and you will be humbled. C. S. Lewis said, "True humility is not thinking less of yourself; it is thinking of yourself less." Most important, give God the glory for all your gifts and talents. You haven't accomplished anything in your own strength. So, instead of being proud, be thankful. Humble yourself before God has to do it for you!

Laura Roggenbaum: 17, Palm Harbor, FL
Calvary Baptist Church and Calvary Christian High School, Clearwater, FL

# The Power of Words

**"There is one who speaks rashly, like a piercing sword; but the tongue of the wise brings healing."** —Proverbs 12:18

"Sticks and stones can break my bones, but words can never hurt me." I don't know who came up with that saying, but I'm going to guess they had never had anything negative said to or about them. I don't know about you, but out of all the hurts that I've experienced in my life, the ones that hurt the most involve painful words. They could've been spoken to me, about me, or even words that I regretfully remember saying myself. Anything and everything you say can either build up or tear down. The only "Bible" that some people will ever read is going to be you and me. If our words are not reflecting Jesus, then they cannot possibly know the true love of Christ. Words are powerful and they have the ability to either lift up or destroy. We all know when we are not speaking truth, or speaking harshly to or about someone; stepping across the boundary from building up to tearing down. Hold your tongue and think before you speak. People are watching you, make everything you say count. Proverbs 21:22 says, "A wise person went up against a city of warriors and brought down its secure fortress." Maybe we should reword that childhood saying to, "Sticks and stones can break my bones, but words, they can destroy a life."

**Hannah McGee:** 15, Springdale, AR
Cross Church Springdale Campus, Northwest, AR; Shiloh Christian School, Springdale, AR

# What Is Faith?

### "Now faith is the reality of what is hoped for, the proof of what is not seen." —Hebrews 11:1

Faith has been a popular topic of scholars for centuries. It's one of those characteristics that everyone has to some degree but no one can quite describe. You have faith that your bedroom floor will be there in the morning, you have faith that there will be enough air so that you can take a breath. We have (or should have) faith in God, but what does that mean, exactly? Have you ever thought about what faith is to you? To me, faith is putting my trust in God. It's being confident that He's there, that He can provide for me, that He loves me and has a plan for my future. There have definitely been times in my life that my faith was tested, and I'm sure there will be many more. I've had doubts before about whether Christianity was really the only way to get to heaven. I wondered what made it any better than any other religion. I felt guilty for a while for having such doubts, but James 1:2–3 says, "Consider it a great joy, my brothers, whenever you experience various trials, knowing that the testing of your faith produces endurance." Trials aren't any fun to go through, but the testing of our faith is a good thing. It's OK to ask questions and be unsure. If you ever have doubts about your faith, don't ignore them and hope they'll go away. Ask your pastor or another spiritually mature person in your life to point you toward an answer. Like a runner preparing for a marathon, we have to train our hearts to make it through the race that is life. We all have to go through the struggles of this world until God comes to take us home, so wouldn't it be nice to have some more endurance?

Kaylin Calvert: 18, Medical Lake, WA
Airway Heights Baptist Church, Airway Heights, WA; Homeschooled

# Wickedness

**"For the Lᴏʀᴅ says to the house of Israel: Seek Me and live!"**

—Amos 5:4

Wickedness! It is all around us. We see wickedness even in the church, but the church is a place we should not see it. You can always count on the church to make your faith grow, so we must pray and trust God to remove the wicked hearts! Wickedness is all over television, in video games, and in powers that are demonic. What about movies? We can go on and on about examples of wickedness. Hatred is another factor that leads to wickedness. Hatred can be a strong killer that grows in your heart. When we hate in our hearts that hate comes out as wickedness and it hurts. Besides, the Ten Commandments tell us to not hate, but to love God and others. Wickedness comes in a lot of forms that get in the way of us loving God: witchcraft, using His name in vain, holding a grudge, and so on. How do you deal with the problem of wickedness? You deal with it by asking God to help you and by reading God's Word, and get to know the Ten Commandments. God gave us those commands, or rules, to follow because He loves us and He doesn't want us to get hurt. It will also help to learn the fruit of the Spirit! Come on, you know what I'm talking about. When you were little you had a little song or jingle to it. The fruit of the Spirit is: love, joy, peace, patience, kindness, goodness, faithfulness, and self-control. So, control your tongue, and know God and the Bible to be able to deal with wickedness.

Beraiah Benavides: 14, Sevierville, TN
Pathways Baptist Church, Sevierville, TN; The King's Academy, Seymour, TN

# Self Image vs. God's Image

> "I will praise you because I have been remarkably and wonderfully made. Your works are wonderful, and I know this very well."
>
> —Psalm 139:14

When I was about eleven or twelve years old, it seems like one day I just looked in the mirror and decided that I was ugly. Ever since then, I have struggled with self-image. Everyone wants to feel important, and when you don't like the way you look, it is easy to feel that you are worthless. But you aren't! It took me a long time to realize that God made us exactly the way He meant to and, because of that, I am beautiful. I still struggle with it every once in a while, wondering if any guy will ever like me or ask me to prom. When you have thoughts like this, you start to feel alone and wonder if you have any friends. Believe me, you do have friends, even if it doesn't seem like it. Plus, you always have God by your side, and He's the best friend you'll ever have. If you've invited Christ to be your Savior, when God looks at you He only sees Jesus. God knows that we are beautiful. We are made in His image, after all. And He is perfect, glorious, and beautiful beyond our comprehension. So what does that make us? Precisely. Because we are made in His image, we are beautiful. Did God make animals in His image? No, He made humans in His image. So, don't worry about how you look. If you trust in God, He gives you confidence, so that you don't exactly care how your outside appearance looks. What really matters is what is on the inside, and that's the only place God looks. So go out into the world. Be confident. When you are confident, you can do anything with God's help.

Hannah Abernathie: 15, Tulsa, OK
Evergreen Baptist Church, Bixby, OK; Homeschooled and Cornerstone Tutorial Center, Tulsa, OK

# Strength

## "I am able to do all things through Him who strengthens me."

—Philippians 4:13

High school band is very stressful because it requires a lot of hard work. When I first started in ninth-grade band, I was overwhelmed by the new environment. All the new people—double the size of my middle school band. I admit that I didn't try as hard as I could have. I was scared that I wasn't good enough. So I hid in the background. Just like in life, you have to give your all in band. You either care or you don't. I struggled trying to figure out if I still wanted to be in band. It seemed like too much of a commitment for me, like just another thing to worry about. Philippians 4:13 says that we can do all things through God who gives us strength. Even though band is difficult, especially in high school, God can help me through it. If I trust Him and believe in His power, then He can give me strength. Strength is an essential thing to have in band. I figured that out pretty fast. Like all things in life, there are lessons to be learned. You should not just give up when things get hard. There are opportunities in life that shouldn't be passed up. Band is just one example of an opportunity that depends on how strong you are. Ask God to help you make hard decisions, to give you strength to persevere through difficult commitments. Don't let stress force you to give up on something you undoubtedly worked hard to achieve.

Callie Spencer: 14, Broken Arrow, OK
Evergreen Baptist Church, Bixby, OK; South Intermediate High School, Broken Arrow, OK

# Growth

**"Like newborn infants, desire the pure spiritual milk, so that you may grow by it for your salvation, since you have tasted that the Lord is good."** —1 Peter 2:2–3

On our kitchen wall, you can see a line of small pencil marks. This is not an unusual sight in homes. Many parents keep track of their child's height as he/she grows. We're expected to get taller as we spend more years in this world. Our Christian lives are very similar. We begin as children: "I assure you . . . unless you are converted and become like children, you will never enter the kingdom of heaven" (Matthew 18:3). New Christians, while often very excited for their faith, lack spiritual understanding in many areas. If you are young spiritually, listen to and learn from the more mature Christians. What you learn as a new Christian should also be different from what more mature Christians are learning (Hebrews 5:13–14). New Christians need to understand the basic principles of the faith, while experienced Christians should be studying the harder parts of God's Word so that they may continue to grow. All Christians should be growing and maturing daily. Someday you will be mature in your faith, and it will be your job to mentor and aid younger Christians. However, we are always learning; we are always growing in some way. Philippians 1:6 says, "I am sure of this, that He who started a good work in you will carry it on to completion until the day of Christ Jesus." Spend time in God's Word, speak to Him in prayer, and build your faith and relationship with Christ each day of your life, until the day you stand before Him and He says, "Well done."

*Kristin Goehl*: 18, Princeton, MA
Bethlehem Bible Church, West Boylston, MA; Princeton University, Princeton, MA

# Victory

"I have told you these things so that in Me you may have peace. You will have suffering in this world. Be courageous! I have conquered the world."
—John 16:33

I've played basketball since I was old enough to play junior pro. Right now, I am on the varsity team at my high school. The past seven years of my life have been full of blood, sweat, and tears in the gym. Countless hours have been spent working on my shot and, because of that, my role on the team is "the shooter." One season, I remember having two bad games in a row. I was really down on myself about it. Then my dad reminded me to keep my head up. He said, "You have worked long and hard to become what you are. Don't let two games define the rest of your basketball career. Keep shooting. Walk in the victory!" Being a shooter on a basketball team is just like being a Christian in this world. As Christians, we are called to be the light, but sometimes we are going to mess up along the way. We can't let the mistakes we make define the rest of our lives. Walking around with guilt is the last thing Jesus wants us to do. He has overcome the world. In Him, we already have the victory. Now we must walk in it.

*Victoria Davidson*: 17, Newton, GA
Sherwood Baptist Church and Sherwood Christian Academy, Albany, GA

# Do Not Worry

"Don't worry about your life, what you will eat or what you will drink; or about your body, what you will wear. . . . Look at the birds of the sky: They don't sow or reap or gather into barns, yet your heavenly Father feeds them. Aren't you worth more than they?" —Matthew 6:25–26

I struggle with worry, and I think everyone does. We worry about friends, college, money, getting cars, and so much more. Recently my dad lost his job, and I struggled with fear. My mom told me how God would use this time for us to trust Him. She said that God will provide what we need. On top of that, I was having trouble getting the money I needed for a mission trip I am taking this summer. A payment of $1,000 was due and I didn't have it. I couldn't understand why God didn't give me the money I needed. I knew He wanted me to go. A few days later I gave my trip to Him to provide or not provide for it as He saw fit. Just a few days later, someone put $116 in my Bible; more money followed until I had enough to make the payment. My dad still has no job and I don't have all my money for my trip, but I know God can be trusted because He has always proven faithful. If you're worried about a friend, pray for them; love them but trust God. Worry doesn't produce anything good; instead, it renders us useless. Give your worries to God and live continually "casting all your cares on Him, because He cares about you" (1 Peter 5:7). When you let Him take care of your hopes, fears, and even worries, you will find His peace.

Rebekah Byrd: 16, Tulsa, OK
Evergreen Baptist Church, Bixby, OK; Homeschooled

# Beauty and Looks

"But the Lᴏʀᴅ said to Samuel, 'Do not look at his appearance or his stature, because I have rejected him. Man does not see what the Lᴏʀᴅ sees, for man sees what is visible, but the Lord sees the heart."

—1 Samuel 16:7

I'll be the first to admit, it's not fun being a teenage girl. There are many things in the lives of teenagers that are stressful, but one of the worst parts for me is my looks. (Even some teen boys go through this!) I am very insecure. There are many days that I look in the mirror in disgust. I don't like a lot of things about my appearance, and what makes it worse is that I always end up comparing myself to every other girl around me. What does the Lord have to say about this? First Peter 3:3–4 states, "Your beauty should not consist of outward things like elaborate hairstyles and the wearing of gold ornaments or fine clothes. Instead, it should consist of what is inside the heart with the imperishable quality of a gentle and quiet spirit, which is valuable in God's eyes." God created us. He thinks we're a wonderful creation, so why would He care about how we look when He made us? Of course, it's not a bad thing to want to look good. Where you need to draw the line is how much you care about your looks and how it affects you. If you're not struggling with your looks, that's great. Keep on that positive track. If you are, however, here's my challenge: you need to begin by taking that up with God. Pray that you won't let your outward beauty take over your life, and ask Him to help you care more about what's inside of you—the things that truly matter.

Angela Stanley: 17, Woodbridge, VA
Dale City Baptist Church, Woodbridge, VA; Emmanuel Christian School, Manassas, VA

# Flee!

### "Flee also youthful passions, and pursue righteousness, faith, love, and peace along with those who call on the Lord with a pure heart."

—2 Timothy 2:22

I've never been the popular girl. I've never been the first girl that guys want to date. I used to be picked on for silly little things like my height, because I'm not exactly what you'd call tall. However, I know God knew what He was doing when He made me. Purity is a big thing and something my family is prayerful about. I'm held to very high expectations. Thankfully, I don't have to go around with the baggage of past boyfriend(s) who tried to tempt me. I don't have a gorgeous little baby on my hip. God says to run from lust. If you feel tempted, hightail it out of there! I get to actually say that I'm waiting until marriage. I get to proudly wear the purity ring that I got for Christmas from my boyfriend, whom I am grateful to be blessed with. If you are a girl who isn't as lucky as I, perhaps God wants to do something very special in your life as well. Your body may not be pure, but your heart is. God says we are His diamond in the rough. He loves you no matter what you've done. But, you do need to ask for forgiveness. And if you are blessed like me, congratulations! Girls, don't let a guy take advantage of you. Whether he says he loves you or whatever, God loves you more. Flee from the enemy and stay pure!

*Breanna Smith*: 17, Sharon, SC
Hillcrest Baptist Church and York Comprehensive High School, York, SC

# Outrageous Outbursts

**"My dearly loved brothers, understand this: Everyone must be quick to hear, slow to speak, and slow to anger."** —James 1:19

Did you ever think that the reason God gave us one mouth and two ears is because He wants us to listen twice as much as we speak? Take heed to the words spoken to you before you respond. We all have those moments in our lives when we let that one person or circumstance annoy or hurt us so badly that we just want to scream. Then, we allow ourselves to lose control of our tongues and tempers. The words that follow typically do not honor God. When we go off on people like that, our words can leave scars, they are like daggers to the soul. I'm sure we've all been both victim and perpetrator in this kind of circumstance. If you struggle with controlling your temper, remember, you can't do this on your own. Ask God to give you patience and a gentle tongue. Next time you face a situation where you just want to explode on someone, think about how God would want you to respond and how you could honor Him through it. When you respond in love to your enemies, they will see Christ in and through you and may even decide to accept Him as their Lord and Savior.

*Imani McBean*: 14, Leesburg, GA
Mt. Zion Baptist Church and Sherwood Christian Academy, Albany, GA

# Names of Jesus

"For a child will be born to us, a son will be given to us, and the government will be on His shoulders. He will be named Wonderful Counselor, Mighty God, Eternal Father, Prince of Peace." —Isaiah 9:6

Jesus has many names scattered throughout the Bible, in worship songs, on bookmarks, wall art, and numerous other places. But have you ever stopped and actually studied the meaning of several of His names? I did, and it was an eye-opener. You could literally go on and on forever about what each one means to us, but let's look at few. *Wonderful Counselor* literally means extraordinary advisor. We make mistakes, and a lot of them. But God can be our advisor. He can help us go out in the world and live for Him and make the right decisions. *Mighty* is defined on Dictionary.com as "having, characterized by, or showing superior strength or power; of great size; of great amount." That is how big and strong our God is. He is mighty and has superior strength like none other. God is bigger than all of your problems, worries, and enemies. God is our Eternal Father. *Eternal* means having no beginning and no end, like a circle. You already have an earthly father, but he's just that—earthly, human, just like you and me. God, our heavenly Father, is like no other. God is a Father that will never leave you and He will always be there to guide and protect you. *Prince of Peace* means someone who has supreme power but uses it free of conflict. You know Jesus is good when He has all this power, power beyond our comprehension, but is a peaceful King. Look up more of Jesus' names and research what they mean. You might learn something about God that you didn't know before, something that will bless you in your Christian life.

*Hannah Abernathie*: 15, Tulsa, OK
Evergreen Baptist Church, Bixby, OK; Homeschooled and Cornerstone Tutorial Center, Tulsa, OK

# The Hummingbird

"He will wipe away every tear from their eyes. Death will no longer exist; grief, crying, and pain will exist no longer, because the previous things have passed away." —Revelation 21:4

Have you ever felt helpless? It's a terrible feeling. A few months ago, my grandma's cancer had spread from her liver to her brain, leaving her very weak and in a lot of pain. For two weeks, my mom and I spent the days with her in her apartment in an assisted living complex, just so that she would have someone who was family there with her all the time. Though we had to help her do a lot of things, I still felt pretty helpless. There was nothing I could do to make her better, and we all knew that she probably wouldn't live much longer. I still spent day after day in that room, though. I was close to her and knew that I couldn't stand it if I knew that I hadn't been there for her if she needed me. The days passed by really slowly. Grandma mostly slept, Mom and I tried to distract ourselves with books and home improvement shows. On the day she passed away, my family and I were just starting to wipe the tears from our eyes when we saw something move outside the window. There, hovering around where my uncle had just taken the feeder down the day before was a little hummingbird. It was like God was reassuring us that my grandma was OK now. She wasn't in pain anymore, and God had wiped the tears away from her eyes. It hurts when someone that we love passes away, but if they're Christians, we can be certain that they're in a better place and feeling better than they ever felt on earth. If we're Christians, we can be confident that we'll see them again. And heaven is going to be awesome.

Kaylin Calvert: 18, Medical Lake, WA
Airway Heights Baptist Church, Airway Heights, WA; Homeschooled

# When Texting Becomes Talking

"Let your eyes look forward; fix your gaze straight ahead."

—Proverbs 4:25

With technological advances, it's nearly impossible to find someone without a cell phone. Maybe you have the newest iPhone, or the Samsung Galaxy, or maybe you're lucky enough to have just a prepaid. But no matter the phone, most all of them have texting capabilities. Texting has become an ideal form of communication because it allows for multitasking. It's quick, fast, and there are no long conversations on the phone. It's the instant messenger without the Internet. The average teen sends about sixty texts a day. When you're texting, it doesn't seem like all that much, but texting can become a distraction. We've all been warned about texting and driving, about how many teenagers have died in crashes while they were texting. Thirty-nine states have laws prohibiting texting while driving, and it's illegal to drive and use a phone in ten states. But more than 50 percent of teenagers have admitted to texting and driving, even with these laws in place. What harm could sending a text cause? There's nothing wrong with preferring texting to talking on the phone, but when it becomes a distraction it can hurt us. The Bible talks about distractions, how they can separate us from God. Face it, we humans have pretty short attention spans, so it's difficult for us to remain completely focused on God. Distractions become our undoing. I'm guilty of texting during prayer time in youth group. Fact is, you can't possibly expect to be completely focused and in tune with God when you let things like texting, talking, etc., drive you away from Him. So the next time you pick up your phone to text a friend, make sure that doing so doesn't distract you or them from something important, like spending time with God!

*Hannah Arrington:* 15, Borger, TX
First Baptist Church and Texas Virtual Academy, Borger, TX

# My Role Model

**"Make yourself an example of good works."** —Titus 2:7

At ten, my family moved to a new state. When we first visited our new church, I was surprised that even the girls who were eighteen would talk and listen to me. I had never experienced that before. Most teenagers don't want to be seen talking to anyone younger than they are. It helped me to be with people who were more mature than I, and they encouraged me to grow closer to God. I still spent time with the girls who were closer to my age, but any interaction that I had with older girls was beneficial. Recently the Lord has been showing me that now that I am an older teen, I have the same opportunity! I need to be like those older girls, listening to kids who need encouragement. I have been learning that a smile, a hug, or a word of praise can lift a younger girls' heart and encourage her. God commands us in Titus 2 to exhort those younger than we are and train them to live a Christlike lifestyle. We have the opportunity to impact the next generation by investing time in younger kids. In the same way that we should be exhorting younger girls, we should be exhorted and learn from those older. As teens, we can be way more impatient than older adults, but I encourage you to listen to older women sometimes. It is so worth it! Think about how many more years of life they have experienced than you. Even though they lived in different times, Solomon said, "What has been is what will be, and what has been done is what will be done; there is nothing new under the sun" (Ecclesiastes 1:9). You would be surprised what great wisdom older women have.

*Hannah Cooksey*: 16, McMinnville, OR
Valley Baptist Church, McMinnville, OR; Homeschooled

# Grace in Practice between Two Best Friends and God

"God, who is rich in mercy, because of His great love that He had for us, made us alive with the Messiah even though we were dead in trespasses. You are saved by grace!"

—Ephesians 2:4–5

Giving grace to those who don't deserve it is hard, but there is one person I know that has shown grace to me more than any other, my friend Rebekah. We have been best friends since sixth grade. But I haven't always been the best friend to her. I've cut her down and pushed her away over and over again. But she has always been there for me; praying, forgiving, and just being there even when I didn't want her to be. She has shown me the kind of grace that God gives. I don't deserve any of what she or God has done for me. But God has used her in so many ways to show me how sufficient His grace is for me through her.

Like Hailey said, we have been friends a long time. God's grace has taught me through our friendship. I'm not some amazing person with a never-ending supply of forgiveness. Learning to extend grace and to forgive is difficult. When I've been upset beyond words and frustrated to the extent that I didn't think I could make it, God has always been there. Hailey talked about the bad parts of our relationship and the difficulties that we have been through, but our relationship would never be as strong and as trusting if not for those struggles. Hailey is a godly, wonderful friend. The grace of God that has kept us together as friends is something that we hope you will experience too.

Hailey Culberson: 17, and Rebekah Byrd: 16, Tulsa, OK
Evergreen Baptist Church, Bixby, OK; Homeschooled

# Being the New Kid

"So they went out and traveled from village to village, proclaiming the good news and healing everywhere." —Luke 9:6

Being the new kid in school is not easy. You have to make new friends, your first impression effects the way people will think of you for a while, and you miss your old life and friends like crazy. When I move, I feel like screaming at God, "Why?!" God moved me both for personal reasons and to fulfill His will. In fifth and sixth grade I had an awesome friend, whom I still love today. But when I moved away from Florida to Washington, DC, I was devastated to leave her. The next place I lived, I had friends, but none as close. Then there was another move from Washington, DC, to Alaska, of all places. I was wary of the idea of living in a place known for igloos and darkness! God made sure I had nothing to worry about, and I fell in love with Alaska. Plus, I found another friend that I could practically call my sister. As awesome as God was to give me all this in my new life, He also put me here to fulfill a spiritual responsibility. Moving gives us opportunities to touch twice as many lives. Our words and actions need to show Jesus. However, this goes both ways. If you are the person who never has to move, then you need to help the people who are probably hurting spiritually because of a move. If you are the mover, always remember that God is everywhere, no matter where you go. If you are the comforter, always be ready to be the mouthpiece of God. Both of these types of people have the opportunity to touch people's lives, and this opportunity should never be wasted.

Erin France: 14, Anchorage, AK
First Baptist Church and Eagle River High School, Anchorage, AK

# God Wants Us

"This is eternal life: that they may know You, the only true God, and the One You have sent–Jesus Christ." —John 17:3

God wants us to know Him through an intimate, one-on-one relationship. The Creator of the universe wants to know you better than your best friend knows you. And we should want to know Him too. God will never leave us, He will always be there for us to lean on, and He will never tire of watching over us. God is our Protector. When we merely go to Him when we need help or we're in trouble, we make Him a resource instead of a relationship. We are His children and He wants to know us. What if we used our parents as just a resource? What if we had absolutely no relationship with them? Wouldn't that be sad? But we do that often, don't we? We may only go to our parents when we need extra money, or an extended curfew, and not just to talk or to hang out with them. But then, when we move away from our parents and move on with our lives, we might not have a relationship to go back to. When you go to their house to visit over Christmas you won't have anything to talk about, because you no longer need them as a resource and you don't have a relationship. Let it not be that way with God. Let us look to Him as a Father and a friend, not simply a way out of trouble. Praise God in times of happiness. If we do this, even when it seems our earthly friends have left us, we will always have an ever-growing relationship with our King. "My goal is to know Him and the power of His resurrection and the fellowship of His sufferings, being conformed to His death" (Philippians 3:10).

Sarah LaCognata: 14, Belleview, FL
Church @ The Springs, Ocala, FL; Homeschooled

# Forgiveness

"'Lord, how many times could my brother sin against me and I forgive him? As many as seven times?' 'I tell you, not as many as seven,' Jesus said to him, 'but 70 times seven.'" —Matthew 18:21–22

The verses above are on a difficult principle: forgiveness. When you were younger, your parents probably encouraged you to say, "I'm sorry" or "I forgive you" after arguments with siblings or friends. As you got older, however, you began to see that forgiveness is more than saying, "I forgive you." Forgiveness is a matter of whether you forgive someone in your heart, not just with your mouth. In the verses above, Peter asks Jesus if He should forgive someone as many as seven times. Jesus tells him not seven, but seventy times seven. Do you know what seventy times seven is? Seventy times seven is 490. Even though it seems impossible to forgive someone 490 times, I think Jesus actually meant us to forgive them every time. Seems ridiculous, right? Why would we forgive someone every single time they sin against us? It is hard to forgive people because we feel like they don't deserve forgiveness. This leads to something interesting: they actually don't deserve forgiveness, which means that you don't deserve forgiveness either. We forgive not because someone deserves it, but because God forgave us (Ephesians 4:32). If people got what they deserved, we'd all be in hell. Think about it. Without Jesus dying on the cross, we are still stained with sin. The problem with that is that God and sin don't mix. We are either of God or of sin, not both. Only through Jesus are we saved, by His blood we are set free from our sin. Next time you're having a hard time forgiving someone, remember how much Jesus has forgiven you. It just might help.

Isabella Bako: 14, Anchorage, AK
First Baptist Church, Anchorage, AK; Homeschooled

# Temptations

"No temptation has overtaken you except what is common to humanity. God is faithful, and He will not allow you to be tempted beyond what you are able, but with the temptation He will also provide a way of escape so that you are able to bear it." —1 Corinthians 10:13

At a high school football game there are many temptations that can arise. Sometimes we put ourselves in difficult situations, and other times they will arise unexpectedly. My situation happened when talking to a guy with my best friend. My friend and I don't curse, but he does. When he cursed, he turned to me and apologized, but not to my friend. I guess when you are the youth minister's daughter people tend to view you like you're a nun. I told him that it was fine, but I really wanted to show him that I'm not different from anybody else. I was offended that he thought of me differently and that he should apologize because I'm so "holy." I honestly wanted to curse, just to show him that I am not different from any other girl. The point is, when temptations arise, whether unexpected or not, make sure that your relationship with God is strong enough to resist those temptations. I probably would not have been able to resist that without God's help. Matthew 26:41 says, "Stay awake and pray, so that you will not enter into temptation. The spirit is willing, but the flesh is weak." My flesh is weak, but the spirit is strong.

*Abby Fortner*: 15, Gatlinburg, TN
First Baptist Church and Gatlinburg-Pittman High School, Gatlinburg, TN

# World Changers

"But you will receive power when the Holy Spirit has come on you,
and you will be My witnesses in Jerusalem, in all Judea and Samaria,
and to the ends of the earth." —Acts 1:8

In the verse above, Jesus tells His disciples that they will receive power when the Holy Spirit comes to them and they will be His witnesses to the ends of the earth. Jesus told this to eleven ordinary dudes: fishermen, a tax collector, etc. Know what? They did that! The gospel basically exploded from Jerusalem—from their city, country, region, and to the ends of the world. Now, 2,000-plus years later, we know the gospel! These ordinary men changed the world! They left their mark on millions of lives over time. So why can't we do the same? What would you do if you couldn't fail and money didn't matter? That's your dream. God has given each of us our very own plan for our lives. He's given us a purpose. If He didn't want us to do something on earth, wouldn't He just take us up to heaven when we were saved? Instead, He left us here for His glory and to bring others to Him. A world changer sees needs, meets them, and lets the Holy Spirit give them power. God has called all believers to go out into their communities, states, country, and to the ends of the world. Acts 1:8 does not say "or to the ends of the earth." It's a demand to go all over, spreading the news of the gospel. Andy Stanley says, "Do for one what you wish you could do for everyone." Go out into the world this week and change it by changing one. Then watch, because God will do some crazy amazing things we had no idea were possible!

*Hannah Thompson:* 15, Leesburg, GA
Sherwood Baptist Church and Sherwood Christian Academy, Albany, GA

# Good-bye Gossip Girl

**"A gossip goes around revealing a secret, but a trustworthy person keeps a confidence."** —Proverbs 11:13

I used to be Miss Gossip Girl. By no means was I pop (a popular girl), but I did gossip with friends. I talked about how people messed up or got into relationships that I didn't think would work out. Things changed in fifth grade when I became the subject of gossip. I dressed differently from other girls. I had a big crush on a nerd. That made things worse. This was the first step in God's plan. In Sunday school we had lessons on gossiping. We learned that God did not want us to gossip. I wanted to be trusted by my friends. The girls at school were giving me a taste of my own medicine. It was hard, but by the end of sixth grade I was ready to give it up. I spent the summer almost completely gossip free. When school started back, I thought I was ready for anything. I was wrong. I took a step back and fell into old habits. "The one who reveals secrets is a constant gossip; avoid someone with a big mouth" (Proverbs 20:19). I didn't want my friends to not trust me again. God stood by my side. He gave me the strength to stop. Soon, I was back to not gossiping. Every now and then I would catch myself, but nobody's perfect. I would stop and remind myself this isn't what God would want me to do. I challenge you now. If you gossip, go to God for help. Find out how much gossip is in your life. Gossip was a little sin in my life, but it was a huge problem to get rid of it. That difference made me better and I hope that difference affects you like that too.

**Deanna J. Davis**: 13, Fairchild Air Force Base, WA
Airway Heights Baptist Church, Airway Heights, WA; Medical Lake Middle School, Medical Lake, WA

# To Do or Not to Do

"I pray that your participation in the faith may become effective through knowing every good thing that is in us for the glory of Christ."

—Philemon 6

We see a glimpse of what Jesus thinks about doing as opposed to being in Luke chapter 10. Jesus is visiting the home of Lazarus, Martha, and Mary. The house was packed. Martha was busy in the kitchen, hurrying along the dinner preparations, while Mary was sitting at the feet of Jesus, soaking in His words. Martha gets frustrated with her sister for not helping her with the meal, which wasn't an ordinary meal. This meal was for Jesus, so it was a big deal for Martha, a doer. Luke 10:40–42 says this: "But Martha was distracted by her many tasks, and she came up and asked, 'Lord, don't You care that my sister has left me to serve alone? So tell her to give me a hand.' The Lord answered her, 'Martha, Martha, you are worried and upset about many things, but one thing is necessary. Mary has made the right choice, and it will not be taken away from her.'" Our priority is to spend time simply being with God before we spend all our time doing for Him. Jesus doesn't want us so caught up in constantly doing things for Him that we don't spend time reading His Word, praying, and just soaking in His presence. I am not suggesting that we spend the rest of our lives sitting in a rocking chair reading the Bible. As we spend more and more time with our God, our love for Him grows and we are able to do more for Him than ever before. So as you go about your lives, don't forget to spend time simply being with God, so you can do more for God than ever.

Gabrielle LaCognata: 19, Belleview, FL
Church @ The Springs and College of Central Florida, Ocala, FL

# Achievement

**"Many plans are in a man's heart, but the LORD's decree will prevail."**

—Proverbs 19:21

As teenagers, we are constantly being told to be the best! We are under constant pressure from our families, friends, and mentors to do better, go farther, and achieve more. This pressure seems so demanding because of how subtle and deeply ingrained it is in our lives. It exists both socially and academically, sometimes even religiously. However, with all of these demands on us, there is still only one whose opinion truly matters—God! God created each of us individually, with all of our strengths and weaknesses (Psalm 139:13–14). While we should strive to learn and improve, we should also recognize that He has made us exactly as He wants us. It's perfectly fine to be average; that's the way God made you! Also, it is important to keep in mind that the Lord's opinion of us is more important than the world's. We are told, "Do not be conformed to this age, but be transformed by the renewing of your mind, so that you may discern what is the good, pleasing, and perfect will of God" (Romans 12:2). Our accomplishments in this life should glorify God, not ourselves! My high school résumé may look like a success story, but those things aren't what life is all about. Yes, it is good to do well, but the real focus is God. Jeremiah 29:11 states, "For I know the plans I have for you." We should strive to achieve, but for the glory of God! He has a plan outlined for us, which may be completely different than what others expect. All we have to do is be humble and trust Him, and He will lift us up (James 4:10).

*Kristin Goehl:* 18, Princeton, MA
Bethlehem Bible Church, West Boylston, MA; Princeton University, Princeton, MA

# Our God Is Healer

"But our citizenship is in heaven, from which we also eagerly wait for a Savior, the Lord Jesus Christ. He will transform the body of our humble condition into the likeness of His glorious body." —Philippians 3:20–21

How many carbs are in an apple? Do you even know what carbs are and what they do to your blood sugar? Blood sugar, test strips, insulin, and carbs: What are those things? You may have heard of them in school, but do you understand them? On June 28, 2010, my family had to learn. My brother, Bryce, was diagnosed with Type I Diabetes. For two days my family and I had extensive training on daily, even hourly, requirements to keep Bryce healthy. He has to test his blood sugar by pricking his finger and putting the blood on a test strip in a meter six to ten times a day. His fingers are covered in little scabs now. He has to test before every meal and get a shot of insulin based on how many carbs he is eating at that meal. We all watch him to make sure that he tests at every meal; it requires constant care. We have prayed for him to be healed. One time, while singing "Our God" by Chris Tomlin, the chorus really hit me. "Our God is greater, our God is stronger, and God is higher than any other. Our God is Healer, awesome in power, our God, our God!" Our God is Healer! He could heal Bryce, if that is what is best for him. If that would bring God the most glory, He would heal Bryce. We will continue to trust God and His sovereignty even when we don't understand. And we look forward to heaven when Bryce will be healed and he will have a heavenly body that is complete and healthy, free from disease.

Tyra Ruisinger: 17, Raymore, MO
Summit Woods Baptist Church, Lees Summit, MO; Homeschooled

# If You Don't Have Anything Nice to Say, Don't Say Anything!

**"No foul language is to come from your mouth, but only what is good for building up someone in need, so that it gives grace to those who hear."**

—Ephesians 4:29

We've at least once in our lives heard, "If you don't have anything nice to say, don't say anything." Yet do we really live by it? Sometimes it makes us feel good to put someone down in order to lift ourselves up. However, we also feel degraded, so we plan another attack on someone else. That someone is disgraced due to the harsh comments. Not only are they disgraced, but the cause of so-called harmless, joking words may even lead up to the death of that person. Although that may seem unlikely, the words spoken do cause serious effects. That is why in James 3 we are warned that the tongue is "a restless evil, full of deadly poison." In that regard, it is necessary to tame our tongues and keep them in check. If we ourselves would not want to hear the words we are saying to another person, why would we say them? In Ephesians, Paul urges us to only speak words that lift others up, not words that intentionally or even unintentionally tear them down. Therefore, be on guard! Stop the evil that comes out and turn the hurtfulness into kindness. Not only will that change the people on whom the kind words fall, but it will change you. "Heavenly Father, I seek Your strength in order to let only words of kindness flow from my mouth. I know I have done wrong in speaking cruel things to people around me. Please forgive me and help me to allow the words that come out of my mouth please You and not me. Amen."

*Haley Smith*: 16, Tarpon Springs, FL
Calvary Baptist Church and Calvary Christian High School, Tarpon Springs, FL

# Jumping Hurdles

"Haven't I commanded you: be strong and courageous? Do not be afraid or discouraged, for the Lord your God is with you wherever you go."

—Joshua 1:9

When I was in sixth grade, I joined the track team and fell in love with jumping hurdles. We only had two meets, so I knew I had to give my all. At the first meet, I was ready! I got in my lane, the gun fired, and I bolted! Then bam! My foot caught the first hurdle, and I fell. I got up and ran as the sting of the wind burned my leg. After losing the race, I limped to the first aid station. While looking at the scrapes on my legs, I vowed to never again jump another hurdle. In eleventh grade, my friend Allyson and I joined the track team. The first meet was held at the same school as my first meet in sixth grade! After my event, my friend Annalise told me I should jump hurdles with her. I refused, but then I felt like a coward. I joined Annalise on the field and smiled, but I was so terrified. I prayed hard because I thought I already knew how the story would end. "God, please don't let me fall." The gun fired and I bolted! Then, there was another hurdle to jump, then another, until finally the race was over! I didn't come in first place, but I was breathless and my heart was beating out of my chest. I went into the bathroom and cried because I was so happy! Although He didn't have to, God proved to me that I can rely on Him with struggles both large and small. He kept me from falling and carried me to the end of the race. Maybe there's a race that you're lined up for and the hurdles seem too tall. Put your faith in God and He will not only give you endurance but also keep you from falling.

Kelsey Roberts: 18, Albany, GA
Sherwood Baptist Church and Sherwood Christian Academy, Albany, GA

# Decisions

"Trust in the Lᴏʀᴅ with all your heart, and do not rely
on your own understanding; think about Him in all your ways,
and He will guide you on the right paths." —Proverbs 3:5–6

I am a very busy person. I wake up at 7:00 a.m. or earlier most mornings. There are morning chores, feeding our farm animals, helping my mom around the house, school, and after-school activities including 4-H and church. Often times I don't get home till about 10:00 p.m. Some events overlap others, making decisions about which thing to do difficult because I want to do them all! When I do end up doing all of them, it usually means I don't enjoy the experience and, instead, just end up running around like a chicken with its head cut off! I need to constantly remind myself that God has a plan for my life, and I need to trust in Him that He will take care of me, even when it's something I don't want to do. A lot of times I talk myself into believing that God told me to do something, when really it was my own personal desire. When I end up doing the things I want to do instead of what God wants, I usually come home with a burden on my shoulders because either something went wrong or I ended up doing something wrong. I realize that if I would've just listened to God and done what He asked of me, I wouldn't have done the wrong thing and wouldn't have had to feel bad. I encourage you to pay attention to the verse above. Listen to Him when God tells you to do something. It will save you a lot of trouble in the long run. Trust me!

Nellie Otoupalik: 17, Spokane, WA
Airway Heights Baptist Church, Airway Heights, WA; Homeschooled/Co-op and Spokane Virtual Learning, Spokane, WA

# The Seeds of Faith

**"Consider the sower who went out to sow."** —Matthew 13:3

Think about the biggest, most beautiful tree you've ever seen. That tree didn't start off as you see it. It started off as a tiny seed that had to be watered and nurtured until it was able to grow to what you see now. It's no coincidence that faith is often compared to seeds and trees in the Scriptures. There is something powerful about the metaphor that causes us to really get the message of faith and how it is supposed to grow within us and become something beautiful for the world to see. When I was younger, church was just a place I went on Wednesday and Sunday. I used to sit and marvel at the beautiful trees that were other people's faith, but I had not experienced it for myself. There came a time when the seed was planted by hearing the Word and watered by friends at church and my family members who loved God and shared Him with me. Recently, I had the opportunity to share my faith with a friend and another one of my classmates. I was expecting God to plant the seed and water it just like He did with me, but I was not getting through to them. I was reminded of the parable Jesus told in Matthew 13. The farmer scattered his seeds in different places, but not every seed was rooted in the ground. Some were snatched by birds, some fell on rocky ground, and some were choked by thorny plants. We have to share our faith knowing that everyone will not receive it. Whether it's scattering the gospel seeds or being a beautiful tree that others can admire, God is ultimately pleased with us and will continue to use us as vessels to grow His great kingdom.

*T'Yanna Janai Jackson:* 15, Slidell, LA
Franklin Avenue Baptist Church and Salmen High School, New Orleans, LA

# Commitment

**"Whatever you do, do it enthusiastically as something done for the Lord and not for men."** —Colossians 3:23

Sometimes, we teenagers get tired of our responsibilities, even in small tasks. We worry about others' tasks and lose focus on our own, and then we complain. The Bible clearly says that whatever we do, we should do it as to the Lord. When I came here from Africa, I shared my testimony. One boy from my class wrote a response sharing how some of us complain about going to get a cup of water for our sister. What if you had to walk five miles to get that water? God has given us tasks that we should do as though we are expect nothing in return. We should also set good examples for our younger siblings around us. Just imagine if you were at home and a stranger came and knocked at the door asking for food and water. You should try very hard to provide for him or her. Whatever you do, do it to the glory of God. When you give a stranger food, you are bringing glory to God! Even if it is helping your friend with a math problem, you must do it with all your heart, because that will bring glory to God. I remember one Sunday when I was thirteen years old. It was time for the students to go in front of the church and tell about their lives in the school. My Sunday school teacher pointed to me, but I was reluctant. She reminded me that I should not be shy to speak and, if I was committed to the task, God would be glorified. So whatever you do, do it willingly. We should just be willing to volunteer for whatever work is needed. Maybe some of us are called to mission work. If so, work with all your heart. Our reward is in heaven.

*Lilian Gatheca*: 16, Nanyuki, Kenya (exchange student living in Albany, GA) Sherwood Baptist Church and Sherwood Christian Academy, Albany, GA

# We Need to Know God to Be Able to Show His Love!

"Love the Lord your God with all your heart, with all your soul, and with all your mind. This is the greatest and most important command."

—Matthew 22:37–38

We can learn to love others only after embracing the love that God has for us. I agree that love is the greatest gift God has given us; something so simple, so pure, and it is free! Just think if all people followed these commandments in the verse above. We would not need any other laws, bullying would not exist in our schools, and we would not have mean girls. Evil would not be able to take such a stronghold in our world. It is easy to love our families and friends, but to love our enemies, well, that is something that requires prayer and commitment. Whenever I get mad at someone, I have to remind myself that it could be Jesus in disguise. As long as you do that, it makes you think about how you are treating others. Things in our lives will be so much smoother when we are not intent on fighting with people but learning to love them. The greatest thing is love, so think about receiving God's love and reaching out to others with the love of Christ.

Micki Werner: 16, Gatlinburg, TN
First Baptist Church and Gatlinburg-Pittman High School, Gatlinburg, TN

# Beauty

**"Charm is deceptive and beauty is fleeting, but a woman who fears the Lᴏʀᴅ will be praised."** —Proverbs 31:30

As a teenage girl, I love to feel pretty. I love to wear makeup and many different styles of clothes. But sometimes we, especially teenage girls, can be caught up with our outward appearance and forget about what truly matters: the inside! Beauty is fleeting but our personality, our character is here to stay. What good is a girl who catches everyone's eye yet is unable to be useful—who doesn't know how to cook, let alone care for a family? God made us girls with a motherly instinct, some more than others. We should take this and use this instinct to our advantage. The Bible shows us that, as women, we should all strive to be smart, caring, true ladies. Honestly, no amount of beauty will ever surpass that of a useful, hardworking, God-loving woman. Do you find that you are more interested in the outer appearance and forget that God created in you a beautiful woman that He cherishes? Allow that same woman of God to be cherished for her inner beauty by His choice for you as a husband. God's plans are perfect.

 Holly Kurtz: 16, Holden, MA
Bethlehem Bible Church and Bethlehem Bible Church Homeschooled Co-op, West Boylston, MA

# The Future

"But as it is written: What eye did not see and ear did not hear, and what never entered the human mind—God prepared this for those who love Him." —1 Corinthians 2:9

Life is full of plans: plans of what you're going to do tomorrow, where you're going on vacation this summer, where you're going to college, etc. In a sense, you have to make plans so your life has some sort of order. But you can't forget that there's a bigger plan unfolding and that it's much better than ours. It is so easy to fall into the mind-set that we know what's best for us. When you submit to God's will in your life, it's much easier to go along with His plan, especially when things don't go the way you want. "'For I know the plans I have for you,'—this is the LORD's declaration—'Plans for your welfare, not for disaster, plans to give you a future and a hope'" (Jeremiah 29:11) is one of the most popular verses in the whole Bible. Yet it holds so much truth. The hope is Jesus, and we need to be living for Him. Katie Davis writes in her book *Kisses from Katie*, "There were many moments when the only way I could keep going was to try my best not to look back but to look only forward, relying on God's perfect plan. Like so many other things, this wasn't always easy, but it was the key to conquering the mountains of difficulty that arose on the landscape of my life." And this is my prayer. That when everything seems to be going wrong, that I will look forward and believe that God is in control and rest in that. I hope you will make that your prayer also.

Christa Morgan: 17, Alabaster, AL
Westwood Baptist Church and Thompson High School, Alabaster, AL

# Dealing with Imperfection

## "God is my strong refuge; He makes my way perfect." —2 Samuel 22:33

Everyone wants to be great at something in life; many of us are. When doing whatever it is we are good at we feel awesome, especially if we worked hard to learn the skill. When someone who is also good at the skill comes along and tries to show us something new, we may be uncomfortable and even not as special as we had before. Or when you do a project and you are sure that you got a perfect score. You get your grade back and it's a low B. What? If you're a perfectionist about anything, or everything, then you understand. Sometimes when we are working on something, we get a little carried away. We may be seeking approval, a reward, or the feeling of accomplishment. When we don't receive whatever it was we were reaching for, we may get upset. We are not perfect. We need to get that drilled into our heads. We are human, and teenagers, bound to mess up at some point in life. There is only one who is perfect—Jesus! Whenever I'm dealing with my inner perfectionist because I just messed something up, I immediately pray. God understands. After telling Him what I did that was wrong, it is so much easier to a deal with my imperfection. I find it ironic that the person who has never made a mistake understands our mistakes better than other humans who have made mistakes similar to our own. Let this be a lesson to us. When dealing with the mistakes of others, try to put yourself in their shoes. We all make mistakes; it's how you deal with your own screw ups and the mistakes of others that determine how we get through the tough situations.

*Erin France*: 14, Anchorage, AK
First Baptist Church and Eagle River High School, Anchorage, AK

# Stop Asking That Question!

"'For I know the plans I have for you'–this is the LORD's declaration–'plans for your welfare, not for disaster, to give you a future and a hope.'" —Jeremiah 29:11

Do you ever feel like everyone asks you what you are going to do after you graduate? It feels like a different version of "What do you want to be when you grow up?" Is it OK if I don't desire a career? I want to be a stay-at-home mom. I want to be able to train my kids myself and spend time with them and show them that I love them. Sometimes people don't understand that and give me weird looks when I try to explain it to them. Am I out of my mind? Should I reconsider? The Bible says, "A man's steps are determined by the LORD, so how can anyone understand his own way?" (Proverbs 20:24). The first thing we need to realize is that God is the ultimate planner for our lives. We can have every step lined out, but in the end God's way prevails. Second, we must remember Matthew 6:33, "But seek first the kingdom of God and His righteousness, and all these things will be provided for you." Pray earnestly to Jesus, and ask Him if your plan is His will. Truly seek His will in your life. Think about what your plans are, and ask yourself if you want that for His kingdom or yours. Third, if you honestly feel that it is God's will for you to not have a career, don't have your plan after graduating be to twiddle your thumbs. Have some outline of a plan so you aren't sitting at home with nothing to do until Prince Charming shows up. It is OK if you don't know exactly what your future will hold, because none of us knows for sure. Pray about your future, and ask for God's wisdom and guidance.

Hannah Cooksey: 16, McMinnville, OR
Valley Baptist Church, McMinnville, OR; Homeschooled

# Anger

"You put on the new self, the one created according to God's likeness in righteousness and purity of the truth. Since you put away lying, Speak the truth, each one to his neighbor, because we are members of one another. Be angry and do not sin. Don't let the sun go down on your anger, and don't give the Devil an opportunity." —Ephesians 4:24–27

We all deal with the sin of anger, don't we? Those of us who have siblings know what they are like, yet we get mad at them from time to time. We all need to have self-control, but it's not easy. No matter how mad we get over situations in our lives, we must have self-control. The verses above help us to understand that once we accept Jesus as Lord and Savior, we need to give Him these problem areas, like our lack of self-control. We are to speak truth to everyone because Jesus wants us to. We are told to not be angry and not sin. Don't go to sleep angry, because that gives the devil an opportunity to do something bad in your heart and mind. Even after we are saved we will still get angry, but we have Jesus to help us now. Next time, before you get angry think, *I need to have self-control.* Self-control is a fruit of the Spirit! Have you gotten angry at somebody and said hateful words? Ask for their forgiveness today! Ask God to give you the right words and ask Him to help you have self-control. "Thank You, God, that You love us so much that you want to help us in all areas. Amen."

Beraiah Benavides: 14, Sevierville, TN
Pathways Baptist Church, Sevierville, TN; The King's Academy, Seymour, TN

# My Wedding Day

"For this reason a man will leave his father and mother and be joined to his wife, and the two will become one flesh." —Ephesians 5:31

If you're like me, you've been planning your wedding since you were three. We girls are just that way. We cannot wait to wear a veil and skip down the aisle to take our vows. Sometimes we are not very patient, and we want life to speed up so that we can just get married. God has implemented several points in our lives, so that we can learn patience. He wants us to wait for His perfect timing. It's OK to be excited about marriage, because marriage is God's picture of His love for the church, His bride. There are several things we can do to prepare for marriage. Our role in marriage is to be the helpmeet. Helpmeet means "helper." God created guys with big visions and goals, and we were created to partner with them and help them fulfill those visions. Ephesians 5:24 says, "Now as the church submits to Christ, so wives are to submit to their husbands in everything." Pray for your future spouse when you start dreaming about him. Be careful not to think of a specific person, but pray for whoever God has in mind for you. About the time my mom started praying for her future husband, he became a believer, and she didn't even know him yet! Pray for spiritual protection and growth in your future husband. Also, spend time with God, and grow closer to Him. It is harder to spend lots of time in the Word when you are a busy wife and mother, so now is your chance. God has an amazing plan for each of us, and we will be happiest if we wait for His timing.

Hannah Cooksey: 16, McMinnville, OR
Valley Baptist Church, McMinnville, OR; Homeschooled

# It's Good to Suffer!

"And who will harm you if you are deeply committed to what is good? But even if you should suffer for righteousness, you are blessed. Do not fear what they fear or be disturbed. . . . For it is better to suffer for doing good, if that should be God's will, than for doing evil." —1 Peter 3:13–14, 17

You have probably heard the saying, "If God brings you to it, He will see you through it." In verse 13 of 1 Peter 3, Peter isn't telling us that no one will mess with us if we do what is right. He is saying that when people persecute you for standing up for what is right, they aren't truly getting the benefit, but you are. When you suffer for Christ's sake, He will bless you immensely and be with you no matter what your circumstance. A satisfying eternal reward is far greater than an earthly prize that will last only for a moment. Stay within the will of God and continue to live out your faith, for being outside His will is the most dangerous place you can be. Who wants to be where they cannot be protected when the enemy attacks? When you are constantly being put down for doing good, don't forget that it is you who is blessed. Praise God for loving us enough to promise to stand with us, to cover us with His protection, and to provide for us what we need in every situation. Remember this quote as you take on the daily battle, "Only God can turn a mess into a message, a test into a testimony, a trial into a triumph, and a victim into a victory." Praise God for loving us enough to promise to stand with us, to cover us with His protection, and to provide for us what we need in every situation.

Imani McBean: 14, Leesburg, GA
Mt. Zion Baptist Church and Sherwood Christian Academy, Albany, GA

# Carrying the Load

"But seek first the kingdom of God and His righteousness, and all these things will be provided for you." —Matthew 6:33

Worry! Stress! If you're anything like me, you'll understand exactly what I mean. There are things pulling you in every direction and pressing an impossible weight upon your heart, things that pile up to the point of tears, and things that make you sick with worry and anticipation. Band, sports, homework, school, church, friends, family, and other activities. They all seem to shove you in a million different ways. I know that, for me at least, I put quite a bit of pressure on myself because I want to give things my all. This usually means that I have a lot of really late nights and a lot of really early mornings. I fall into an almost-dead, wracked-with-stress, sleep-deprived state, and I feel as if I'm carrying the weight of the world on my shoulders. What I have come to realize is that things don't have to be that way. I don't have to do it all alone. The Bible tells us that God wants to help. He desires for us to lay down our troubles and our anxiousness before Him, letting Him deal with our problems rather than have us fight through them alone. Don't let life pull you down. Worry and stress? They get us absolutely nowhere. God is there beside us, wanting to help lift the burden from our shoulders. If we're willing to ask for help, then He's always going to be willing to pull us through.

Sarah Ashley Bryant: 15, Springdale, AR
Cross Church and Shiloh Christian School, Springdale, AR

# Family First

"For wherever you go, I will go, and wherever you live, I will live; your people will be my people, and your God will be my God." —Ruth 1:16

One of my favorite characters in the Bible is Ruth, one of the few women in the Bible to have a book written about her. Ruth married an Israelite man, even though she was Moabite. Later, her husband, brother-in-law, and father-in-law all passed away. Her mother-in-law, Naomi, was going to return to Israel since her family was gone. Naomi told Ruth and her sister-in-law, Orpah, not to go with her. Ruth did not want to leave Naomi. "But Ruth replied: 'Do not persuade me to leave you or go back and not follow you'" (Ruth 1:16). Even though Ruth would be an outsider in Israel, she loved Naomi and wanted to take care of her. Ruth had faith that God would take care of her and Naomi as they made their transition into a new life. We should let Ruth be an example in our lives. We should always have faith in God and trust in His plan. By trusting God, Ruth and Naomi were benefited by moving back to Israel. Read the rest of the book of Ruth to see what happens.

*Layne Coleman*: 14, Little Rock, AR
The Church at Rock Creek and Little Rock Christian Academy, Little Rock, AR

# Pink Flamingos

"Your beauty should not consist of outward things like elaborate hairstyles and the wearing of gold ornaments or fine clothes. Instead, it should consist of what is inside the heart with the imperishable quality of a gentle and quiet spirit, which is very valuable in God's eyes." —1 Peter 3:3–4

Have you ever seen those pink plastic flamingos that people put in their front lawns? Those things are kind of tacky, no? You have to wonder what would possess someone to put that thing right on their lawn where everyone can see it. It's not like a piece of art that sends a message; it's just an animal rendered in plastic. Why? I wonder the same thing every time I go to school. I go to a public school that has a dress code, but it's not readily respected. It makes me wonder why girls wear clothes that draw the wrong attention. Why do they do that? I imagine that very few of them do it for their own personal satisfaction at looking their best. Someone once said, "If it's not for sale, don't put it in the window!" But that's not how God says it should be. If you read the verse above, it sounds like we've been wearing "pink flamingos" since the first church. But all we really need is the gentle and quiet spirit. Lots of girls are rolling their eyes at me right now. *What good is a gentle and quiet spirit when no guys are looking at you?* Does that really matter if we're disappointing God? Elsewhere in the Bible our bodies are called temples. Do we want pink flamingos on the lawn of our temple? And if you tell people you're a Christian and then wear clothes that show off too much of your body, will they believe you? Your life is the only Bible some people will ever read. Make it one that proclaims God at all times and in all ways.

Bronte Stallings: 15, Mt. Pleasant, SC
Citadel Square Baptist Church, Charleston, SC; Wando High, Mt. Pleasant, SC

# Don't Forget Yes Ma'ams and Yes Sirs

**"Children, obey your parents in everything, for this pleases the Lord."**

—Colossians 3:20

As teenagers, we realize our parents aren't perfect! We also know that no one is perfect. As teens, we develop attitudes and become easily frustrated with our parents. They may need to ground us from the very thing that we love to do, like telling us that we can't go to a party, or staying after school to be with friends, or maybe we won't be allowed to use our cell phones or watch television. When we are punished, we often become hateful toward our parents, which, as I have learned, never helps the situation! But what if we started obeying our parents wholeheartedly and did everything with good attitudes? Would it end badly? Of course not! Obeying our parents and having a good attitude toward them would cause us to have a better relationship with them. The Bible is full of verses that will help us do what we should, but we need to study the Bible to know what those are and how to apply them. The verse above tells us that it pleases God when we obey and love our parents. I challenge you to do everything that your parents ask, and do it wholeheartedly. See what happens when you do.

*Layne Coleman:* 14, Little Rock, AR
The Church at Rock Creek and Little Rock Christian Academy, Little Rock, AR

# Jealousy

"Do not covet your neighbor's house. Do not covet your neighbor's wife, his male or female slave, his ox or donkey, or anything that belongs to your neighbor." —Exodus 20:17

The Bible is clear that we are not to covet what our neighbors have. We are to be thankful for what God gave us. We are not to be jealous of anyone else. We all have been jealous of someone or something in our lives. I have been through jealous times. I've been jealous for iPod covers, purses, watches, and other things that teens love and want. My guess is that you can relate! There are many people who have nothing. They wish they had a pair of shoes or maybe even a family. Psalm 100:4 tells us to "Enter His gates with thanksgiving and His courts with praise. Give thanks to Him and praise His name." We are to be thankful for all that God blesses us with. We are the richest country in the world and teens have far more than they need. Imagine if you were starving and living on the streets. God promises in the Bible to give us food, shelter, and clothes. We have so much more. Many do not! We can choose to be grateful, or to be greedy and covet what others have. Ask God to forgive you if you have coveted and to help you to be thankful for the things you do have, and thank Him for blessing you the way He does. Thank God for everything.

Beraiah Benavides: 14, Sevierville, TN
Pathways Baptist Church, Sevierville, TN; The King's Academy, Seymour, TN

# Faith, Friendship, and other F Words

"The one who walks with the wise will become wise, but a companion of fools will suffer harm." —Proverbs 13:20

Good friendship equals faith, fellowship, forgiving. Bad friendship equals foolishness, fighting, forbidden. We have all learned the foundations of both a good friend and a bad friend. Though we have learned this, we all have both kinds of friends. I don't enjoy being harmed. I would much prefer being wise. When I was being interviewed to be part of the planning committee for a huge basketball tournament, I was asked who my friends are. My interviewer said she asks this because who you hang out with says a lot about who you are. If you hang out with all the drinkers and smokers you are likely to become one. In youth group once we used the analogy of standing on a chair. It's easier to pull someone off the chair than to pull someone up. It is easier to convince someone to drink than to get someone to stop. I'm not telling you to stay in your Christian bubble, never reaching out to nonbelievers. But 1 Corinthians 15:33 says, "Do not be deceived: 'Bad company corrupts good morals.'" Bad company falls under the three F words of foolish, fighting, and forbidden. It's foolish to hang out with them in their setting; it will lead to lots of fighting, internally and externally. For many teens, it will be forbidden by their parents to go and take part in the acts of some of this bad company. We all want friends with the other F words—faith, fellowship, and forgiveness. Choose your friends wisely. It will affect your life greatly.

Hannah Savage: 16, Dodge City, KS
First Southern Baptist Church and Dodge City High School, Dodge City, KS

# A Bunch of Numbers

"For you are all sons of God through faith in Christ Jesus. For as many of you as have been baptized into Christ have put on Christ like a garment."

—Galatians 3:26–27

One of my life's mottos is, "Don't be a statistic." I really don't remember where it came from, but God has used it in such a big way in my life! A statistic is supposed to define who you are and what you do from your background. For example, my statistics are based off of my parents' divorce when I was a child and growing up without a dad. The statistics say that I am:

- 63 percent more likely to commit suicide
- 71 percent more likely to drop out of high school
- 71 percent more likely to get pregnant as a teen
- 90 percent more likely to runaway or become homeless

But these are just a bunch of numbers some dude good at math decided. I cannot let them define me! God is the only one in whom we should find our identity. According to the verse above, I'm a princess, a daughter of the King of kings! You are a child of the King! Don't let anyone else define you. Don't let your actions define you. Past is past. I challenge you not to be a statistic in life. Don't be the norm. Rise above it and don't be just a bunch of numbers.

*Hannah Thompson:* 15, Leesburg, GA
Sherwood Baptist Church and Sherwood Christian Academy, Albany, GA

# My Biggest Critic

"And if you belong to Christ, then you are Abraham's seed, heirs according to the promise." —Galatians 3:29

I know a girl who lives to make me miserable! She notices every little mistake I make and never lets me forget it. Whenever she sees my face, she finds flaw after flaw after flaw to pick at. My highest grade is still lacking in her eyes, and no matter what I do I just cannot satisfy her. She's my biggest critic. She is me. There is an African proverb that states: "When there is no enemy within, the enemies outside cannot hurt you." There is no person that has more power to make you feel like dirt than yourself. When you have low self-esteem, you are easily influenced by what your peers think of you or how society thinks you should dress or act. It is important that we, as young men and women of God, remember that we are royalty. We are the children of a great, powerful, and immortal King! We have great value in His eyes. Psalm 139:14 says, "I will praise You because I have been fearfully and wonderfully made. Your works are wonderful, and I know this very well." God took great time and detail to design every little thing about you from your voice to your hair, from your personality to your body type. Thank Him for that! We are His masterpieces and should respect ourselves as such. Embrace the things that you think are your flaws or downfalls. They are the only things you have that nobody else does, and God loves them about you. You should too!

Kelsey Roberts: 18, Albany, GA
Sherwood Baptist Church and Sherwood Christian Academy, Albany, GA

# Distractions

"Each one's work will become obvious, for the day will disclose it,
because it will be revealed by fire; the fire will test the quality
of each one's work. If anyone's work that he has built survives,
he will receive a reward. If anyone's work is burned up, it will be lost,
but he will be saved; yet it will be like an escape through fire."

—1 Corinthians 3:13–15

Facebook, Twitter, Instagram, YouTube, blogs, iPods, and cell phones. There are so many things to distract us. There are so many ways to talk with friends without actually speaking to them, ways to follow everything that is going on in the world, and ways to stalk celebrities we will never meet. All of this can be done with a device that fits in your pocket. It may seem like we are doing a lot and accomplishing things while we are plugged into the Internet, but our lives are just getting sucked away. How much time did you spend learning every fact and memorizing each song, or beating each level? How much eternal value do these things have? "But the Day of the Lord will come like a thief; on that day the heavens will pass away with a loud noise, the elements will burn and be dissolved, and the earth and the works on it will be disclosed. Since all these things are to be destroyed in this way, it is clear what sort of people you should be in holy conduct and godliness" (2 Peter 3:10–11). One day Jesus will come back and everything done on the earth will be exposed and things that have no eternal value will be destroyed. Peter tells us to live holy and godly lives, doing things that will have eternal value and glorify God. We really only live here for a breath compared to eternity. Do things with the time you have now that will matter most later.

Tyra Ruisinger: 17, Raymore, MO
Summit Woods Baptist Church, Lees Summit, MO; Homeschooled

# Waffles or Pancakes?

"Love the Lord your God with all your heart,
with all your soul, and with all your mind." —Matthew 22:37

Waffles or pancakes? Which one do you prefer? Made of relatively the same ingredients, these two breakfast foods can be very different. This may sound silly, but God likes pancakes better! God sent His only Son to die for our sins. He loved us that much, and in return He wants us. He wants our lives, but He doesn't just want part of our lives. Waffles have compartments. When you pour syrup over your waffle, it's likely that you will miss a compartment here and there. When you pour syrup over a pancake, it gets everywhere. Not only does the syrup spread over the pancake and soak into it, but it often spills over the sides of the plate and onto your hands and the table. We, like waffles, have separate compartments for school, church, weekend parties, etc. We say, "God, You can have this compartment over here; it's for when I go to church. But that one over there, that's my school compartment, and I kind of want to keep that one. I guess I'll pour your syrup into my Monday night Bible study compartment, but I don't want it in my Friday night party slot." Why do we compartmentalize our lives, choosing certain areas in which we allow God to reside? In some respect, we are all control freaks, not comfortable with someone else being in charge of our lives. So we attempt to maintain control by only giving God certain areas or compartments. We put God in a box, put the lid on, and only take Him out when we need Him. We need to surrender our control to God who can steer us on the proper course. He wants all areas of our lives, covering us and saturating our lives with His love overflowing onto other people. So the question is: What are you? A waffle or a pancake?

Sarah LaCognata: 14, Belleview, FL
Church @ The Springs, Ocala, FL; Homeschooled

# A Laughing Heart

"A joyful heart is good medicine, but a broken spirit dries up the bones."

—Proverbs 17:22

In everything rejoice! There is nothing more important, relaxing, and fun than to laugh. Laughing with others and even laughing at yourself can break down barriers and deepen relationships. Laughing is good for us! Ralph Waldo Emerson said, "For every minute you are angry you lose sixty seconds of happiness." Emerson's quote reminds us of how short life is and how important it is to love and find joy in it. The joy that God brings to my life is indescribable. Knowing that I get to spend eternity in heaven praising Him forever calms my heart, giving me a different way to look at things. I see a glass half full and not half empty. I want to be joyful and thankful for my abundant blessings. I have so many freedoms in this country that are denied to some living in other countries. "But the one who did not know and did things deserving of blows will be beaten lightly. Much will be required of everyone who has been given much. And even more will be expected of the one who has been entrusted with more" (Luke 12:48). I try to use the joy I have in my life and share it with as many people as possible. Since I have been given this amazing life to live, I want to give all the glory to God. He has already blessed me much more than I deserve. God's peace brings a smile to us, and that smile should cause joy to leap from our hearts. God has a clear purpose for your life and mine. Knowing Him is the only way to experience true joy and peace in it.

Micki Werner: 16, Gatlinburg, TN
First Baptist Church and Gatlinburg-Pittman High School, Gatlinburg, TN

# Voices

## "A thief comes only to steal and to kill and to destroy; I have come so that they may have life and have it in abundance." —John 10:10

*You're so fat. You're not pretty or strong enough. Nothing you do or work for matters. You're just a joke to everyone around you. Nothing you will ever do will be worth anything. You're a mistake, and you're invisible to everybody around you. No one cares!* These are all lies that I'm sure we have all told ourselves at some point in our lives. The sad part is that there is someone who puts these lies in your mind and wants you to believe every single one of them. It's normal for us to have these thoughts sometimes, because we are all humans, and we all make mistakes. But what we need to understand is that we have to pick which voice we are going to listen to. It is up to us to determine which voice we listen to. We are God's creation and there is nothing that we can ever do that would make Him love us less. Second Corinthians 10:5 tells us to take every thought captive, to make it obedient to Christ! In other words, if your thoughts go against the Word of God, then it is not truth, which makes it a lie from Satan. Listening to the voice of truth and putting your self-worth in Him is a daily choice we have to make. We need to make an adult decision to choose Christ and His ways. Are you ready to do that?

Hannah McGee: 15, Springdale, AR
Cross Church Springdale Campus, Northwest, AR; Shiloh Christian School, Springdale, AR

# Patience

"Patience is better than power, and controlling one's temper, than capturing a city." —Proverbs 16:32

Don't you just love it when you go to help someone learn something new and you learn something yourself? Recently in children's ministry we had a lesson on one of my least favorite topics: patience. I struggle with having patience. We described it as "Waiting with a happy heart." We talked to our kids about having to wait in line at the store, waiting in the car during a long road trip, or waiting for Mom to get off the phone. I think the scenarios are a bit different for you and me. What about that acceptance letter from the college you are dying to go to? Or the job opportunity you have been praying for? Or that relationship you are waiting for? We see patience paying off in Luke 2. Simeon was an old man whom God had promised would see the Messiah before he died. Simeon waited and waited and waited some more. Then one day, all his waiting paid off. A small baby Jesus came to the temple and Simeon's waiting was over. He took Jesus in his arms and praised the Lord. I have to think Simeon was so happy that he had been patient. What if Simeon had decided not to go to the temple that day? What if he went, but was so busy complaining he missed Jesus? You see, having patience doesn't change the circumstances; it changes how you respond to them. So whether you are waiting for your food at the drive-thru or for an answer to prayer, wait with patience. "Therefore, God's chosen ones, holy and loved, put on heartfelt compassion, kindness, humility, gentleness, and patience" (Colossians 3:12).

Gabrielle LaCognata: 19, Belleview, FL
Church @ The Springs and College of Central Florida, Ocala, FL

# Faithfulness

## "Lord, Your faithful love reaches to heaven, Your faithfulness to the clouds." —Psalm 36:5

Every day we put our faith in something or someone. There's something different, though, when we trust another person. We expect them to honor and respect that trust and to remain faithful to our expectations. However, we are human and we make mistakes. Often faith is broken between people and can cause hurt. We have a God who is perfectly faithful. Psalm 91:4 says, "He will cover you with His feathers; you will take refuge under His wings. His faithfulness will be a protective shield." The Lord protects and cares for us, even when we are unfaithful to Him. Due to our sinful nature, we constantly fall away from God (Romans 3:23). Though God remains faithful in His promise not to allow us to be tempted beyond our ability and to provide a way to escape (1 Corinthians 10:13), we still betray Him repeatedly. Do not be discouraged by failure. "If we confess our sins, He is faithful and righteous to forgive us our sins and to cleanse us from all unrighteousness" (1 John 1:9). While we should repent and feel sorry for sinning against God, we should not let our guilt cripple us. God forgives every single sin of His children. He loves us perfectly, and because of that He is always faithfully guiding us and protecting us, even when we don't realize it. Lamentations 3:22 says, "Because of the Lord's faithful love we do not perish, for His mercies never end." In response to His treatment of us, we should be faithful to Him in our actions. God's love for us is indescribable; we should respond with trust, thankfulness, and praise.

*Kristin Goehl*: 18, Princeton, MA
Bethlehem Bible Church, West Boylston, MA; Princeton University, Princeton, MA

# Going Down a Dark Road toward Suicide (Part 1)

"I call heaven and earth as witnesses against you today
that I have set before you life and death, blessing and curse.
Choose life so that you and your descendants may live."

—Deuteronomy 30:19

Suicide is most common in teenagers. It is the permanent solution normally derived from depression, but taking your life does not overcome problems. God loves us, and once we accept Him as Lord and Savior we are His children! Our lives belong to Him, and we are not to take it or anyone else's. There are ways to overcome depression and suicidal thoughts. If you or anyone you know is considering suicide, you have to seek help. No one truly wants to kill themselves. Everyone just wants to feel loved, important, and better. Suicide is not a joke; it is a serious decision that has an ending you cannot take back. I know what it feels like to be depressed and suicidal. At fifteen, I was depressed from the anger I felt, and my life was in a downward spiral. I was a member of a small church of twenty to twenty-five people and I felt that most of them hated me. It had gotten to the point where lies and horrible rumors were spread about me. I was devastated and so brokenhearted! I wondered what it was about me that was so bad to make them feel the way they did. I started to take my anger out on anyone that said anything to me I didn't like. I became a totally different person. I hated going to church, and when I was there, I acted as if their attitudes toward me did not matter or bother me, but they did. Only God can heal a wounded heart and make good out of bad.

Reagan MiCole Brashears: 17, New Orleans, LA
Franklin Avenue Baptist Church and Eleanor McMain Secondary School, New Orleans, LA

# Going Down a Dark Road toward Suicide (Part 2)

*"I call heaven and earth as witnesses against you today that I have set before you life and death, blessing and curse. Choose life so that you and your descendants may live."*

—Deuteronomy 30:19

If my church family hated me, something had to be wrong with me, so I began to hate myself. It is a bad feeling when your church family treats you the way that they treated me. I just felt as if I was worthless, and I cried myself to sleep every night! As the months went by, I got tired of going through all of that hurt and pain by myself, so I decided to write my family a letter informing them that I was going to kill myself. My mom and dad found it on my dresser, and that was when my life actually started turning around. I was going to kill myself that night. If they had not found that letter while I was at school, I would not be here today. Talk to someone and tell them what you are going through. You have your whole life ahead of you, and it is not worth losing. God loves us, and He would not want anything bad to happen to us. All we have to do is seek Him for help and He will send someone our way. The Bible says that I can call heaven and earth as witnesses against you that I have set before you life and death, blessings and curses. It says I can choose life. Do not choose suicide! Do not take your life away because it is a precious gift from God. Psalm 118:6 says, "The LORD is for me; I will not be afraid. What can man do to me?" With God on our side, we do not have to worry about anything. No man is more powerful than our God! Suicide is not the answer. God is!

**Reagan Mi'Cole Brashears**: 17, New Orleans, LA
Franklin Avenue Baptist Church and Eleanor McMain Secondary School, New Orleans, LA

# Rejoice

"Though the fig tree does not bud and there is no fruit on the vines, though the olive crop fails and the fields produce no food, though there are no sheep in the pen and no cattle in the stalls, yet I will triumph in Yahweh; I will rejoice in the God of my salvation!"

—Habakkuk 3:17–18

In our culture, it is easy to focus on everything going wrong. We get so caught up in all of our problems that we forget to cherish the beautiful things. As Christians, we are commanded by our Lord to rejoice no matter how bad the situation. First Thessalonians 5:16 commands, "Rejoice always!" Philippians 4:4 says, "Rejoice in the Lord always. I will say it again: Rejoice!" *Always* means despite the circumstances. We can trust that the Lord will take care of us. Matthew 6:26 comforts us by saying, "Look at the birds of the sky: They don't sow or reap or gather into barns, yet your heavenly Father feeds them. Aren't you worth more than they?" Though our lives may not be going the way we desire, we have a hope that is eternal. The Bible says in Romans 5:1 that, "Hope does not disappoint, because the love of God has been poured out within our hearts through the Holy Spirit who was given to us." God has given us a reason to rejoice. We get to spend eternity with our Creator because of His sacrifice. Do you only rejoice when things are going good? Whether it is by song, prayer, or something else, rejoice in your heavenly Father always.

Victoria Davidson: 17, Newton, GA
Sherwood Baptist Church and Sherwood Christian Academy, Albany, GA

# You Are Your Father's Favorite Child!

### "But God proves His own love for us in that while we were still sinners, Christ died for us!" —Romans 5:8

You've heard it a million times growing up: Jesus died on the cross for our sins. He did die to pay for our sins; every person who ever lived and who ever will live, He took on their sins. But He also took on all of our worries and anxieties. Have you ever had a time in your life when you just felt alone, and all of the things on your mind weighed you down? I have, and one thing that God showed me was that Jesus felt all these things when He was up there on the cross. Think about how heavy your heart felt, how much weight you felt on your shoulders. Jesus took all that on Himself when He died, plus the rest of the world's anxieties and loneliness. So, when you feel like this, know that Jesus knows what you are going through and how you feel. He can help you get through it all; you just have to let Him. All the pain, loneliness, worries—He took it on Himself so we wouldn't have to. God loved, still loves, and will always love us that much. And it's not like He has favorites. He doesn't have a chart of who He loves more than you. He loves each of us equally, and each of us is His favorite child. That's why, if you were the only person on earth who had sinned, He still would've come and died so you wouldn't have to. That's how loving God is. So, the next time you feel alone, you're worrying about everything, or feel the weight of the world on your shoulders, remember that Jesus knows what you are going through and how you feel, and He can help you through it.

*Hannah Abernathie*: 15, Tulsa, OK
Evergreen Baptist Church, Bixby, OK; Homeschooled and Cornerstone Tutorial Center, Tulsa, OK

# Perfect Christian?

**"And God, who knows the heart, testified to them by giving the Holy Spirit, just as He also did to us."** —Acts 15:8

I know people who seem to be perfect Christians, seemingly doing everything right. They go to church every Sunday, go to youth group, never miss a day of reading the Bible, always say the right thing, and always seem to help others. When I compare myself to others I think are perfect, I feel that I am not good enough. When you are in church and the pastor says you should read your Bible every day and pray all the time, and it seems like everyone else in the room is doing that, you feel like you don't measure up. I have learned God doesn't want us to feel like that. When we are trying, He knows it and He appreciates it. He made us and He knows we are human, with a sinful nature. I'm not saying don't try to be a better Christian, just do it for the right reasons. God doesn't want us to worship Him out of guilt or to look good to others, even the pastor. No one is perfect, and everyone makes mistakes. There is not one person in the world that is always praying and praising God. A perfect Christian doesn't exist, and God knows that. He doesn't expect us to be perfect, He just expects us to try with our whole heart. God knows our hearts and still loves us. Acts 15:8 says, "And God, who knows the heart, testified to them by giving the Holy Spirit, just as He also did to us." If you could see into the life of the person you think is perfect, you would realize they have their own struggles and challenges. We each have a different relationship with God, and that is OK.

**Allison Fisher:** 14, Raleigh, NC
Providence Baptist Church and Leesville Road High School, Raleigh, NC

# My Best Friend

**"I am with you always, to the end of the age."** —Matthew 28:20

My sophomore year was possibly the worst and most terrifying year in high school. My best friend since second grade and I are inseparable, and that year I realized that he had stopped going to church. I knew his secrets, but I kind of blew it off. He was sent away, and my mom hesitated taking me to school because she said I looked like a lost puppy. I felt like I had no one. When he came back, I thought everything would be fine, but it took a lot longer than I imagined. It felt like every time he took a step in the right direction, something would grab his attention and pull him back. It was hard for me to see him like this. Long story short, he basically hit rock bottom. But then God picked him up, brushed him off, and said everything would be OK. One night I invited my friend to church and we were taking notes. The preacher preached on salvation. That night, my best friend asked Christ into his life. Later when I opened my Bible, the notes he took fell out. Written on it was his confession: "I was not truly saved." I still keep that little card in my Bible in the same spot. It reminds me what God can do. God was there when my best friend had to be taken away. He was there when my best friend gave his life to Christ. He has always been there. My friend now attends church and has grown so much in God. He is a totally new person. It's amazing to see what God can do.

*Breanna Smith*: 17, Sharon, SC
Hillcrest Baptist Church and York Comprehensive High School, York, SC

# The Treasures of God, Exhaustless and Free

"Don't collect for yourselves treasures on earth, where moth and rust destroy and where thieves break in and steal. But collect for yourselves treasures in heaven, where neither moth nor rust destroys, and where thieves don't break in and steal." —Matthew 6:19–20

Most people, especially those of us who live in affluent countries, tend to worry about material things on earth and to put all our emphasis on acquiring more things that we think will make us happy. But things are never enough. I am always thinking *want, want, want!* I am always keeping an eye out for the newest iPhone, eReader, or computer. And, of course, don't forget the clothes and shoes! Sometimes I become obsessed with getting the newest device with the latest whistles and bells. I realize that the new device isn't much different than the one I already have, but that thinner version just looks sleeker. Besides, all my friends can tell if I don't have the latest version, and you know what they think is very important! It is our relationship with Jesus that should be more than enough and that never goes out of style. Plus, you will never need a newer or a better version—there is no other God! You will never see a U-Haul following a hearse. Nothing will make you as happy as the love of Jesus.

Micki Werner: 16, Gatlinburg, TN
First Baptist Church and Gatlinburg-Pittman High School, Gatlinburg, TN

# Pressing on with Endurance

"So we must not get tired of doing good, for we will reap
at the proper time if we don't give up." —Galatians 6:9

Being healthy has always been very important to my father. Growing up, I was never allowed to drink sodas like my friends. My dad would always say, "You will understand one day." I grew up taking vitamins and supplements. It was always important to my dad that I exercise. I used to think he was crazy for running and exercising all the time. When I began to play sports, I realized the importance of working on my own to be successful in whatever sport I was playing. My mom and my dad would practice soccer with me, shoot basketball, or sprint with me, to help me with whatever sport I was doing at the time. Lately, my sister and dad have been working out with a trainer. They have been trying to convince me that I should go. At first, I really didn't want to, but I gave it a chance. Working with a trainer is not easy. They push you to the limit, leaving you exhausted and not wanting to do anything else. After a couple days the soreness goes away, just in time to go back. The two hours I spend in the gym each week make me stronger. Every push-up I do, every squat or sprint I accomplish makes me stronger. If I hadn't pushed myself, I wouldn't have gone to the trainer, and I wouldn't be as fast as I am or as strong. Track season is coming up, and I hope to get personal records on my two-hundred-meter race. By training, I have put my goals in sight of success. All of this propelled me to realize that work and effort make me more successful reaping the harvest.

Madison Thomas: 15, Sevierville, TN
First Baptist Church and Gatlinburg-Pittman High School, Gatlinburg, TN

# A Precious Gift

"Draw near to God, and He will draw near to you. Cleanse your hands, sinners, and purify your hearts, double-minded people!"

—James 4:8

"Where is God? I can't feel Him! It's like He's so far away from me!" Have those questions ever rolled through your mind, because I know that they have in mine. It's difficult to keep up your Christian faith when these lies are stopping you at every corner, telling you to give up and not to trust. When we sin, it distances us from God. Have you ever thought that it might not be God that is far from you, but instead that you are far from God? But, how blessed are we that we have a forgiving, loving, and merciful Father, who takes us back despite all our inequities. All it takes is for you to confess your sins and surrender your life to Jesus Christ. He died for all of us, enduring the shame, ridicule, and pain of the cross! Who wouldn't want to accept this precious gift of love? Who wouldn't want to trust a God, the one true God, to be our all every moment of every day?

Emily Pitts: 16, Palm Harbor, FL
Calvary Baptist Church and Calvary Christian High School, Clearwater, FL

# Carry Another's Burdens

## "Carry one another's burdens; in this way you will fulfill the law of Christ." —Galatians 6:2

I am thankful that the Lord watches over me and cares for me. It is a great feeling when someone I know also wants to help me. It shows that they care about me, which is one of the most encouraging and uplifting things on earth. You should never be arrogant and refuse help if you need it; rather, accept it thankfully. There are a few people who help me all the time. My sister-in-law helps me with chores when I'm tired, my oldest brother helps me with school if I'm having trouble, and my friend is always there to cheer me up. Having so many people who care about me encourages me to try my best at everything I do and to be considerate of and help others too. I am thankful that God has provided many people in my life to help me. It is the way the body of Christ is supposed to function. We are gifted with talents and skills that can be used to serve those around us as God leads. Psalm 121:2 tells us that "My help comes from the LORD, the Maker of heaven and earth." Are you being used by God to help others? Just look around, He may have a mission field right next door!

Faith Kurtz: 13, Holden, MA
Bethlehem Bible Church and Bethlehem Bible Church Homeschooled Co-op, West Boylston, MA

# What Am I Going to Wear Today?

**"Women are to dress themselves in modest clothing, with decency and good sense, not with elaborate hairstyles, gold, pearls, or expensive apparel, but with good works, as is proper for women who affirm that they worship God."** —1 Timothy 2:9–10

I like my clothes. I have my fair share of brand-name things—Aeropostale, Hollister, Toms, Converse, Vans, Old Navy, etc. I love to do new things with my hair, and I have fun messing with my makeup. I just need to remember not to make those things an idol over God. It goes through my mind sometimes that if I just had this shirt or those shoes, then I would be called popular. I would be in a higher position than those people who wear second-generation hand-me-downs. How wrong is that? Is it those people in whom God finds favor? First Timothy 2:9–10 explains to us how we should make our appearance be by saying, "Also the women are to dress themselves in modest clothing, with decency and good sense, not with elaborate hairstyles, gold, pearls, or expensive apparel, but with good works, as is proper for women who affirm that they worship God." It's not bad to want to look nice, but it shouldn't be our appearance alone that defines us. It needs to be our attitudes and how we treat and respond to people. We need to remember that we are God's children, and we need to focus not only inwardly, but also outwardly.

Nellie Otoupalik: 17, Spokane, WA
Airway Heights Baptist Church, Airway Heights, WA; Homeschooled/Co-op and Spokane Virtual Learning, Spokane, WA

# Social Media

"I am the LORD your God, who brought you out of the land of Egypt, out of the place of slavery. Do not have other gods besides Me. Do not make an idol for yourself, whether in the shape of anything in the heavens above or on the earth below or in the waters under the earth. You must not bow down to them or worship them; for I, the LORD your God, am a jealous God, punishing the children for the fathers' sin, to the third and fourth generations of those who hate Me, but showing faithful love to a thousand generations of those who love Me and keep My commands."

—Exodus 20:1–6

It was almost summertime, and I was in seventh grade. All of a sudden, I started getting all of these texts saying, "What did I do to you?" and "Why are you acting like this?" I was seriously confused, so I got on MySpace. Someone had hacked my account and sent all of my closest friends really mean and dirty messages. I was petrified and very confused, and all I could do was cry. I got it cleared up with my friends, but I will never forget that night. That is the most negative experience I've had with social media. I think it can be a very positive thing and can bring people together. I've had more positive experiences with it than negative. It's really brought me closer to people I otherwise wouldn't be friends with. One thing about social media, though, is that it can be very addicting, very fast. Technology is so advanced these days and that's great, as long as you don't put it above God and spend more time with it than in the Word. When this happens, it becomes an idol. God despises this, as He expresses in Exodus 20. Remember that you can't take Twitter and Facebook to heaven with you. Your relationship with Him will last eternally.

Christa Morgan: 17, Alabaster, AL
Westwood Baptist Church and Thompson High School, Alabaster, AL

# Loving Family

"Above all, put on love–the perfect bond of unity." —Colossians 3:14

Loving your family can be hard some days. Growing up with three siblings, I can relate to this. There is always someone that seems to enjoy pushing your buttons. Whether it's borrowing your clothes without permission, dumping cold water on you when you're sleeping, nagging you about chores, or embarrassing you in public, our family members have ways to make us crazy. But, I've learned that we need our families. God has placed us with the people in our family for a reason. We don't have to face life's struggles alone. Our families are there to help us. As much as our siblings bother us, they've been through many of life's experiences with us, and they know us better than most people ever will. They can be our only friends sometimes. Our parents may seem annoying, but the reason they don't let us see that movie, or go to that friend's house is because they care about us and want the best for us. They model Jesus for us, and they want us to grow into godly adults. If they let us do whatever we wanted, we wouldn't mature as people or Christians; or learn important life lessons, such as responsibility, self-control, and discipline. The people in our families are the people that will be with us forever. It's our responsibility to love, respect, and honor them, and to be there for them no matter what.

Blair Bodnarchuk: 17, Raleigh, NC
Providence Baptist Church and Wakefield High School, Raleigh, NC

# Self-Control Matters!

"What then are we to say about these things?
If God is for us, who is against us?" —Romans 8:31

During a sports game, it is easy to let the emotion of it all get the best of you. But as a Christian athlete, it is vital to always show self-control. It's important to congratulate the other team after they score, because we are supposed to show respect and to be respectable by showing good sportsmanship. An example of this is helping a player up after they have been knocked off their feet. Another prime example is found in today's verse, where it tells us that no matter who is against us, God is for His children. This verse doesn't mean that as long as you pray before the game that you will come out victorious. We need to remember that the other team's family and friends may also be praying for them to win! One team wins, the other loses, but the team members who show the highest level of professionalism and kindness will be remembered. The team member who emulates Christ will set precedence for players that could result in them coming to know Him as their Lord and Savior. Losing control does nothing but make you and your team look bad, and it is not the way to represent God! I feel this verse is saying that, win or lose, you will be able to handle the outcome, because you have Christ in your life.

Micki Werner: 16, Gatlinburg, TN
First Baptist Church and Gatlinburg-Pittman High School, Gatlinburg, TN

# Control Freak!

### "Stop your fighting–and know that I am God, exalted among the nations, exalted on the earth." —Psalm 46:10

From birth to the present we have, at some point in those years, desired authority. Whether in the form of playing follow-the-leader, bossing a younger sibling, or even getting assigned to be president of your class, we desire control. We believe we are capable of handling anything that comes our way and think that our way of accomplishing things is best. We even try to control our own lives. We plan for the future by hoping to get a job, become rich, get married, and start a family. Do we ever stop to ponder that our lives are not ours to control? We don't need to try to control our lives because God is controlling them! We are not in the driver's seat, but the passenger's seat. God has a big plan for our lives, and although it's reassuring to have everything under control, we don't need to. The heavy burden of trying to be perfect and trying to have everything go according to plan is unnecessary. Let it go, girl! Give it to God, who will gladly accept it. He wants us to lift up our eyes and let Him be in control. It is natural for us to want to control things ourselves, but we must remember that only through our trust in God will we really succeed in whatever we are trying to face. So don't wear yourself out by trying to be the controller. Just sit back and enjoy the ride. All God desires for us to do is to simply pause, breathe, and put into perspective the fact that He is God, He is in control, and He knows the perfect plan for our lives. He needs us to be still and know that He is God.

Haley Smith: 16, Tarpon Springs, FL
Calvary Baptist Church and Calvary Christian High School, Tarpon Springs, FL

# The Search

**"My heart says this about You, 'You are to seek My face.' Lord, I will seek Your face."** —Psalm 27:8

When I surrendered my life to Christ, I gained an intense desire to know who God was; not just facts about Him, but a relationship with Him. Adam and Eve walked and talked with God and their descendants, Enoch and Noah also walked with Him. My heart's desire was to know Him like they did. I spent time in my closet at night searching through Scripture and writing down verses that told how to find what I was looking for: "Keep asking, and it will be given to you. Keep searching, and you will find" (Matthew 7:7). "Draw near to God, and He will draw near to you" (James 4:8). If these verses are promises, why do we sometimes not feel God's presence? The secret is found in Jeremiah 29:13: "You will seek Me and find Me when you search for Me with all your heart." That last portion says "with all of your heart." If we devote ourselves to seeking God's face, then we will find Him. That might require that we limit time spent on distractions: boyfriends, girlfriends, television, video games, cell phones, Internet, etc. Free some time in your day, and replace those old activities searching the Scripture. Try doing devotions both morning and night, so you are giving God the first and last part of your day. All that time I spent in Scripture has provided me with a faith foundation. Ask God to help you seek His face daily, but be warned—this is not a task for the fainthearted.

*Carson Gregors*: 17, Albany, GA
Sherwood Baptist Church and Sherwood Christian Academy, Albany, GA

# Taking the Good with the Bad

"The Spirit Himself testifies together with our spirit that we are God's children, and if children, also heirs—heirs of God and coheirs with Christ—seeing that we suffer with Him so that we may also be glorified with Him." —Romans 8:16–17

Joan of Arc was an incredible person. She was born around 1412 in France, which was not a fun place to be then. France had been involved in the Hundred Years War with England since 1337 and would remain engaged until 1453. Prompted by angels who came and told her what she was to do, Joan of Arc embarked on a mission to bring Charles VII to the throne of France. She weathered many battles and injuries and finally managed to see Charles crowned king of France. She was captured and tried by the British in 1431 and burned at the stake for heresy when she was only nineteen. Why did she fight for Charles when she knew very well the horrific battles she would be facing? Because God told her to! People may debate over whether she actually saw angels, but she certainly thought she did and she was willing to do anything to carry out God's mandate to her. You are probably not going to be burned at a stake for God; but He may ask you to do something unpopular, like sit with the uncool kid, or stand up for what is right even if everyone around you is doing what's wrong. Joan of Arc gave her all for the God that she loved, and we should do the same. The verse above says that we must suffer with Christ so that we can be glorified with Him. And when you do suffer, remember that God works in His own way and His ways are not our ways. When you go through tribulation, remember that God uses everything to shape you into a better person.

Bronte Stallings: 15, Mt. Pleasant, SC
Citadel Square Baptist Church, Charleston, SC; Wando High, Mt. Pleasant, SC

# Loneliness

### "It is the Lᴏʀᴅ your God who goes with you; He will not leave you or forsake you." —Deuteronomy 31:6

At one time or another, everyone will experience the unhappy feeling of loneliness. Loneliness can be magnified through trials and difficulties. Having dealt with much heartbreak, I would often cry myself to sleep. *How can I be comforted?* I would imagine, *How can I rid myself of this lonely feeling?* God is always with you, always. Imagine His arms around you, hugging you close, never letting go. No matter what people may call you or do to you, God will never leave you! "Be strong and courageous; don't be terrified or afraid of them. For it is the Lᴏʀᴅ your God who goes with you; He will not leave you or forsake you" (Deuteronomy 31:6). God made us to want to feel love. God made us to be social creatures and wants us to share this wonderful world with others. First Timothy 6:17 says, "Instruct those who are rich in the present age not to be arrogant or to set their hope on the uncertainty of wealth, put on God, who richly provides us with all things to enjoy." God has given us everything in this world so that we may enjoy it. We can trust God for the comfort of friendship as well as for the provision of our material needs. Make your friends special. Sometimes with loneliness comes the feeling that you are not loved. You are loved. Humans are fickle creatures and change their minds on whims. God is not fickle; He never goes back on His Word, and He loves you as His own child. As John 14:23 says, "My Father will love him, and We will come to him and make Our home with him."

*Holly Kurtz*: 16, Holden, MA
Bethlehem Bible Church and Bethlehem Bible Church Homeschool Co-op, West Boylston, MA

# Watch Your Words!

"I tell you that on the day of judgment people will have to account for every careless word they speak. For by your words you will be acquitted, and by your words you will be condemned." —Matthew 12:36–37

The Bible talks a lot about what we say. We are not to lie or use filthy language (Leviticus 19:11; Colossians 3:8). But how serious are we about our words? Do you ever talk about that weird kid? Do you ever tell your parents you didn't do something that you really did? Do you ever yell at your family when you're having an off day? As Christians, using our mouths in such ways is not acceptable. I know it is hard for me to always say the right thing. In fact, sometimes it feels impossible! However, the Bible makes it clear that control of our mouths is necessary. James 3:2 tells us, "For we all stumble in many ways. If anyone does not stumble in what he says, he is a mature man who is also able to control his whole body." Basically, if we get control of our mouth, we'll be able to control our entire body to the Lord's glory. Sounds great, right? Until we stumble across this verse: "But no man can tame the tongue. It is a restless evil, full of deadly poison" (James 3:8). So now what? We know that we need to control our tongues, and now we know we can't. Are we supposed to just forget about controlling our words? Absolutely not! The key to understanding these verses is that by ourselves we can't control our tongues. Catch that? By ourselves we can't. Philippians 4:13 says, "I am able to do all things through Him who strengthens me." Therefore, through Christ we are able to control our tongues. Pray for Christ's help, and watch that tongue!

Isabella Bako: 14, Anchorage, AK
First Baptist Church, Anchorage, AK; Homeschooled

# Being Shy

**"Do not fear, for I am with you; do not be afraid, for I am your God. I will strengthen you; I will help you; I will hold on to you with My righteous right hand."** —Isaiah 41:10

I've struggled with shyness my whole life. I'm talkative at home, but never anywhere else. I always wanted to be the outgoing and funny person I was with my family, but I was too scared of what people would think. I worried about saying or doing the wrong thing, letting my fears hold me back from opportunities in life. I had few friends at school because I was too scared to talk. Most students didn't even know my name. The summer before my junior year in high school, I went on a mission trip roofing houses for underprivileged families. I knew I would only see the people I was working with for a week, and then we would go back to different cities and states. This made it easier for me to open up and be who I really was on the inside, because I knew if people didn't accept me, I wouldn't have to see them after that week. What I realized was that people did accept me and I made many friends that week. I learned that people will like you for you and if they don't it doesn't matter, because God's opinion is the only one that truly matters. When I went back to school my junior year I was still a little shy, but I started to become more outgoing. Now I feel a lot more confident in myself, and I'm more comfortable talking to people. So, don't hide behind feelings of insecurity. Reach out to those who enjoy the same things you do, then move on to more and more people. You, too, will see that deeper and deeper relationships will develop. God will help you.

*Blair Bodnarchuk*: 17, Raleigh, NC
Providence Baptist Church and Wakefield High School, Raleigh, NC

# Go Back to the Basics

"For God loved the World in this way: He gave His One and Only Son, so that everyone who believes in Him will not perish but have eternal life."

—John 3:16

John 3:16 is the most well-known verse in the entire Bible. It is often the first verse children learn and almost everyone, even many non-Christians, can say it from memory, though many who know the words do not understand the meaning! Many have forgotten that their salvation is not earned but is a free gift from God. Being a Christian today has turned into being the one who doesn't curse, who doesn't drink, who gives the most, or who looks like they have it all together. Sometimes, we may start to feel a little down on ourselves, like we are bad Christians, because we cannot do as much as another. You are not sent to heaven because you are a good person, you are sent to heaven because of the cross! Live your life because of the cross! Do not do things just for attention or to cover up your mess. Do them humbly, for the same reason Jesus died for you: Love! Don't drink because you love Jesus; obey your parents because you love Jesus. Do these things to please Him. The fact that God loved us so much that He sent His Son to die is the reason we need to give our whole hearts to Him. It is not about works, but the grace that is ours. When you feel down on yourself, remember that your Lord died for you because He loved you that much. The cross is absolutely the only way to make it through this dark world into heaven, not your good deeds, not your possessions, not your money: the cross!

Reagan Bell: 17, Tuscaloosa, AL
Valley View Baptist Church and Hillcrest High School, Tuscaloosa, AL

# Hard to Love

"But love your enemies, do what is good, and lend, expecting nothing in return. Then your reward will be great, and you will be sons of the Most High. For He is gracious to the ungrateful and evil." —Luke 6:35

I there anyone in your life who's hard to get along with? Maybe it's a sibling, your parents, someone at school, or even someone at church. Maybe you don't like them because they pick on you or criticize you, or because they spread rumors about you. I have a few people like this in my life. I know God wants us to love them anyway, but sometimes it can be really hard. And sometimes it can be next to impossible. When I'm feeling particularly irritable, I try to remember that Luke 6:35 says to love your enemies, do what is good for them, and to give to them, expecting nothing in return! That comes with a promise: "Then your reward will be great, and you will be sons of the Most High. For He is gracious to the ungrateful and the evil." Isn't it cool that God will reward us for being kind even when it's difficult? These hard-to-get-along-with people are trials that we need in our lives to help us be more like Jesus. Next time someone is driving you crazy, remember that being kind to them will have an eternal reward.

Kaylin Calvert: 18, Medical Lake, WA
Airway Heights Baptist Church, Airway Heights, WA; Homeschooled

# Suicide: Is It a Sin?

"We know that all things work together for the good of those who love God, those who are called according to His purpose."

—Romans 8:28

Suicide is something that many have to deal with. It can be the result of severe depression caused by many factors. Some have had family members die in such a way that it caused them to not want to continue living. We do not need to continue in our suffering through grief. We know Romans 8:28, and we can "call heaven and earth as witnesses . . . that I have set before you life and death, blessing and curse. Choose life so that you and your descendants may live, love the LORD your God" (Deuteronomy 30:19–20). It would be difficult to argue that suicide is not a sin, for it is the taking of a human life or, to put it bluntly, murder. The Bible expresses the sanctity of life in Exodus 20:13. Sometimes with depression, we feel unloved. Paul made it plain that nothing can separate us from God's love: "For I am persuaded that not even death or life, angels or rulers, things present or things to come, hostile powers, height or depth, or any other created thing will have the power to separate us from the love of God that is in Christ Jesus our Lord!" (Romans 8:38–39). Indeed, nothing in all creation will ever be able to separate us from the love of God that is revealed in Christ Jesus our Lord. So, can a sin as grave as suicide destroy one's salvation? The Bible tells us that at the moment of salvation a believer's sins are forgiven (John 3:16; 10:28). When we become a child of God, all of our sins, even those committed after salvation, are no longer held against us.

Holly Kurtz: 16, Holden, MA
Bethlehem Bible Church and Bethlehem Bible Church Homeschool Co-op, West Boylston, MA

# Why Don't I Fit In?

**"Do not be conformed to this age, but be transformed by the renewing of your mind, so that you may discern what is the good, pleasing, and perfect will of God."** —Romans 12:2

My family and I have some different standards than other families we know, even though we get them from the same Bible. Sometimes it is hard because I may feel like I am the only one of my friends who has that conviction, even when there really are others. When I feel like the only one, I am reminded that we should all experience that feeling every now and then. As Romans 12:2 says, "Do not be conformed to this age, but be transformed by the renewing of your mind, so that you may discern what is the good, pleasing, and perfect will of God." We are not to conform to the world's ways, but be transformed by Christ, and He will help us to see what His will is for our lives. He tells each family and person different things, and that makes the body of Christ more unique and special. If we are in submission to our parents, then we know that their standards are God's plan for our lives (unless our parents ask us to sin), and we can rest in that wonderful fact. The next time that I am in a situation where I feel like I am the only one who has a certain standard, I can remember that I am in submission to God if I am under my parents' authority. Job 17:9 says, "Yet the righteous person will hold to his way." Whatever your convictions are, you are not alone, because God is with you. If your standards are in line with the Scripture, you can be reassured that God is pleased.

*Hannah Cooksey*: 16, McMinnville, OR
Valley Baptist Church, McMinnville, OR; Homeschooled

# Family

"God's chosen ones, holy and loved, put on heartfelt compassion, kindness, humility, gentleness, and patience, accepting one another and forgiving one another. . . . Just as the Lord has forgiven you, so you must always forgive. Above all, put on love—the perfect bond of unity."

—Colossians 3:12–14

We all know that family is extremely important, and we are constantly reminded of that from many sources. Not all of us treat our families in the best way though. I know I didn't. Unless it's an abusive situation, everyone in your family deserves respect and your love, even if they aren't the best people in the world. A deadbeat dad or grandparents that are really rude are still family, and that alone deserves respect, because a house functions better all around when there is respect. As we continue to mature, we start think thinking for ourselves more and more, and our friends start having more influence on us. I went through a time where being popular was my top priority. In high school it seems that having friends equals a higher social status, and a higher social status equals power and influence. People tend to want that influence. It's easy to have friends as the most important thing. They're fun and interesting, and they can't ground you. But family is your backbone. No matter what happens, your family will always be your family, either together or far away, by blood or in bond. Specifically think about spending more time with them. Not just, "Hi, how was your day" as you walk in the door, but also bonding time, laughing and crying together. Talking with your family is one of the best things you can do for one another. God gave them to you for a reason. Never take advantage of your family's love.

Leah Harris: 16, Kodiak, AK
Frontier Southern Baptist Church, Kodiak, AK; Homeschooled

# Nothing Can Separate Us

"Why am I so depressed? Why this turmoil within me? Put your hope in God, for I will still praise Him, my Savior and my God."

—Psalm 42:5

Nothing can separate us from His love. How amazing is that? Not anything I do, or say, or go through. Nothing at all can take away God's passionate love for me and for you. I can do all the unholy and unrighteous things in the world, but God will always take me back. His love will never fade; it will remain a burning blue fire—unquenchable. Do not be surprised when you face opposition along the way. Instead, know that God will be right there, walking beside you in your times of trouble. It is when we are closest to God that the devil sees fit to attack us. He will do anything in his power to make us fall away from God's love, but with the Lord's help, we have the power to counteract his attacks and win the battle for our souls. We will stumble. It is inevitable that we will fall. We are sinners by nature and we cannot escape that truth. God knows we will never be perfect and He doesn't want us to be. All He asks is that we strive toward Him and become more like Jesus everyday. It matters not how many times we fall away from Him. It is completely irrelevant how far we run. His arms will always be outstretched toward us, ready for us to embrace Him. There is comfort and joy in knowing that He will never leave us; He will never forsake us. God's love for us is like the sands on the shore of the sea. You cannot count their multitude, as you cannot measure His love. And nothing in this world, or in the heavenly realms above, can separate us from that love. "Nothing can separate, even if I ran away. 'Cause your love never fails" (Jesus Culture's "Your Love Never Fails").

Sarah LaCognata: 14, Belleview, FL
Church @ the Springs and Lighthouse Academy, Belleview, FL

# Self-Worth

## "I will praise You because I have been remarkably and wonderfully made."
### —Psalm 139:14

Being a girl is difficult! Society tells you how to dress and how to fix your hair. One of society's biggest measures of your worth is if you have a boyfriend. This is a sensitive topic for most girls, me included. I am seventeen and have never had a boyfriend. Until recently this has been difficult for me to discuss. I thought not having a boyfriend means you are not worthy, which made me feel unwanted. I was confused, because my family would tell me I'm beautiful, but no one else would. I would look at myself and think, *Who would want me?* I am broken and bruised. Who could possibly want me? God does. He wants your brokenness because He is the only one who can fix it. I can't tell you the moment that I regained my self-esteem, but I can say that it was all thanks to God. He told me that I was beautiful and I was worthy. My newfound self-esteem doesn't mean I walk through the halls yelling about my beauty, but I am much more confident. I used to resent God for the few hopefuls I had in the past. It felt as if He was taunting me, but now I know it was preparation. God used those experiences to save me. My first temptation with a guy came shortly after my junior year. A boy I barely knew attempted to make a move. It was completely unexpected, but I stepped away. Looking back, I'm glad that I did. I'm not ending this story as a fairy tale. I'm still single and have not found my Prince Charming. My advice is to look to your fathers for your worth, and if you don't have a father figure in your life look to your heavenly Father. He never disappoints.

*Taylor Dillon*: 17, Stafford, VA
Grace Life Community Church, Bristow, VA; Emmanuel Christian High School, Manassas, VA

# As You Are Going

"Go therefore and make disciples of all nations, baptizing them in the name of the Father and of the Son and of the Holy Spirit."

—Matthew 28:19

This is one of those verses that most Christians know backward and forward. We can recite it from memory and have most likely heard multiple sermons on it. As a child, I was taught that this verse was referring to foreign missions. I remember the picture that was in my kids' Bible next to this passage. It showed a family on a boat sailing into the wide open sea. As I have grown up, I have found myself continuing to associate that image with this verse. I am sure that I am not the only one who has thought that. Instead of thinking of this verse as a call to a mission field, meaning that we have to go, we should see it as our call to missions. The call to missions is placed on the life of every Christian at the point of salvation. There is no way around it, and we have no outs. If you are a Christian, you are a missionary, plain and simple! Now, we are not all called to spend our lives on the foreign mission field, but every single one of us is called to spread the good news to the people around us. So today, think about who you will see that doesn't know Jesus. Is it someone in your family? Someone at school? Maybe even the cashier at Starbucks? Who can you take the good news to? Because "Go therefore" doesn't mean pack all of your stuff and leave the country. It means as you are going in your day-to-day life, be a witness for Jesus Christ!

*Annalise Clem*: 17, Albany, GA
Sherwood Baptist Church and Sherwood Christian Academy, Albany, GA

# Contentment

"Your life should be free from the love of money. Be satisfied with what you have, for He Himself has said, I will never leave you or forsake you."

—Hebrew 19:5

I would like us to be the people who are satisfied with whatever we have, wherever we are. Many teens in Africa starve. One day in eighth grade, I asked my mother why we did not have new Christmas clothes. My mother was disappointed by the question. She asked me whether we needed food or new clothes. She told us to be content with whatever she gives us and that we should be thankful and trust the Lord. I have since realized that God's ways are always the best. We should not desire what our parents cannot afford. God's promises are always the best! Many of us have houses where you can sleep, while there are many people somewhere sleeping in cold nights, homeless. They don't even have beds to sleep in or places to lay their weary heads. You should be thankful for whatever you have been blessed with and whatever you have achieved. Many of us want to be the best in certain areas, like in education or sports. Be satisfied and be grateful in every situation. God created us with different abilities and talents so that we can serve Him with them. Some of your parents may not get the car or provide the clothes you really want, but we should learn to be happy with whatever the Lord provides through whatever your parents can give you. Always be thankful for whatever you have!

*Lilian Gatheca:* 16, Nanyuki, Kenya (exchange student living in Albany, GA) Sherwood Baptist Church and Sherwood Christian Academy, Albany, GA

# Being Willing

"Then I heard the voice of the Lord, saying, Who should I send? Who will go for Us? I said; "Here I am. Send me!" —Isaiah 6:8

We are all called to something. We are all passionate about something. We all have a personality and characteristics that make up that personality. God uses those passions and characteristics for His glory. The trick is that in order for God to use us, we have to be willing. Isaiah was willing to do whatever the Lord called him to. The beautiful thing about Isaiah's answer is that he didn't even have to think twice about it. Living in this generation we have so many comforts. As teenagers, we get too used to routines and the ways of life, and we forget the true point of why we are on this earth. If we are to let God use us, we have to die to those comforts and routines on a daily basis. God desires nothing more than to have our whole hearts. He wants to be able to use us in ways that we cannot imagine. All we have to do is be willing to let God take and do with us whatever needs to be done. It is not promised to be an easy task, and not everyone will stay true to it. But even if it's just you and God, with God on your side, you can change the world.

*Taylor Glow*: 17, Albany, GA
Sherwood Baptist Church and Sherwood Christian Academy, Albany, GA

# For Shaniah

"For the Lord will not reject us forever. Even if He causes suffering, He will show compassion according to His abundant, faithful love. For He does not enjoy bringing affliction or suffering on mankind."

—Lamentations 3:31–33

I have experienced loss. Every day someone reaches the end of his or her life. Three years ago, the seventh and eighth graders were called together and told some very painful news. A fellow seventh grader named Shaniah had died in a car crash on her way to Texas. I took this news hard. Shaniah and I played volleyball and basketball together, and we were starting to get to know each other. Then she was gone. I was overwhelmed with guilt because I didn't try to talk to her about Christ, and there was a chance she wasn't with Him. This guilt followed me for two years. I can only hope that one day when I go to heaven, I will meet her there. Some say death is a part of life. But I don't believe it was ever intended to be. In the beginning, we were meant to live by His side for all eternity. Death was never supposed to be a factor. God doesn't want to give us grief through death. I believe He wants us to realize that grief is a result of the poor choice made a long time ago by Adam and Eve. Their decision brought sin into the world, and so began the struggle between good and evil until the end of time. We have hope in Jesus, but we must make the choice to follow Him. As Christians, we are supposed to grieve. In fact, God actually encourages it. But we can't be stopped by grief. We remember the loss, the person, but we must move on. My memory of Shaniah will always be a fond one, dear to my heart.

*Hannah Arrington*: 15, Borger, TX
First Baptist Church and Texas Virtual Academy, Borger, TX

# Pray, Pray a Lot

"The door is already locked, and my children and I have gone to bed. I can't get up to give you anything.' I tell you, even though he won't get up and give him anything because he is his friend, yet because of his friend's persistence, he will get up and give him as much as he needs. So I say to you, keep asking, and it will be given to you. Keep searching, and you will find. Keep knocking, and the door will be opened to you." —Luke 11:7–9

One of my favorite parables is found in Luke 11:5–9. In this parable, we find Jesus teaching the disciples how to pray. The parable begins as a man goes to his friend's house at midnight to ask a favor of him. Although the friend had already closed his door for the night, the man began to knock on the door and ask for bread. The friend asked him to go away and explained both he and his children were already in bed. But the man kept knocking and asking through the door for the bread. He needed the bread and he was not going to take no for an answer. Finally, the friend gave up, got up out of bed, and gave the man as much bread as he wanted. The man making the request was annoying. He simply would not give up. Jesus is telling us this is how we should pray, without stopping. We should be in constant prayer and conversation with the Lord throughout the day. We have tried to practice this in our own home. My family has a habit of posting notes around the house as reminders for us to pray for certain things. And we have seen results. When it comes to praying, we believe in repetition. Pray. Pray a lot. Seriously, pray a lot.

Mallory McClearn: 16, Leesburg, GA
Sherwood Baptist Church and Sherwood Christian Academy, Albany, GA

# Don't Worry! Just Trust God! His Plan Is Always Best

## "Trust in the LORD and do what is good; dwell in the land and live securely." —Psalm 37:3

When I found out in tenth grade that I would be moving and switching churches, I was a little nervous about it. I went straight to worrying how long it would take to find the right church, how I was going to continue learning about God, how I was going to learn how to disciple others. Psalm 37:3 says, "Trust in the Lord and do what is good." Such an easy instruction, yet how often we forget that God has a perfect plan for us. "'For I know the plans I have for you'—this is the LORD's declaration—'plans for your welfare, not for disaster, to give you a future and a hope'" (Jeremiah 29:11). In some ways, it was hard to not be rooted in a specific church. But in other ways I almost liked the absence of routine. Not to mention that God taught me that He is enough no matter what. He taught me to trust Him and not to be worried about anything! In Matthew 6:25–34, Jesus went into details of what not to worry about and why. He concluded with, "Therefore don't worry about tomorrow, because tomorrow will worry about itself. Each day has enough trouble of its own." Don't worry. Simply trust God with your future, because He has a perfect plan for all of us and has our best interests in mind! After searching for months, countless family discussions, and all too many disagreements, I ended up becoming a part of First Baptist Church of St. Charles. While I have been at that church, I have been given the opportunity to go through a discipleship training class. Praise God, for He is faithful and trustworthy. His plan for our lives may be hard but it's always the best and perfect way!

Sara E. DuBois: 16, St. Peters, MO
First Baptist of St. Charles, St. Charles, MO; Fort Zumwalt East High School, St. Peters, MO

# Focus Failure

**"You will seek Me and find Me when you search for Me with all your heart."** —Jeremiah 29:13

Social media and electronics have become a large part of our culture. Watching television while eating meals, listening to music while riding in the car, and playing on Facebook while doing homework are considered normal activities. It's as if entertainment has taken over our generation. We wake up to the news channel and fall asleep to music. Is there something wrong with doing this? Although these acts may seem harmless, spending ample amounts of time absorbed in them can be destructive. No, I'm not against modern technology, I love my Netflix account. It has provided a way to watch television whenever I want and view episodes back-to-back, nonstop. Once hooked on a series, I watch it as soon as I get home from school and into the evening. Once these shows have my attention, the outcome is always the same—my relationship with God takes a backseat. When we fall victim to the world's enticing offers, our Christian walks suffer. Our minds are similar to a camera only focusing on one thing at a time. For example, if a photographer wants to capture a picture in which one item is far away and a second is up close, one of the objects will be blurry and the other clear. When something draws our attention away from God, we lose focus on His voice and it becomes distorted. Media has a talent for capturing our attention because it's a form of escape. We spend hours watching people live their lives while wasting our own. Finding the balance between time spent on media and time spent in Scripture can be challenging, but it's the only way to maintain focus on what truly matters.

Carson Gregors: 17, Albany, GA
Sherwood Baptist Church and Sherwood Christian Academy, Albany, GA

# Heigh-Ho, Heigh-Ho, It's Off to Work We Go!

### "Serve with a good attitude, as to the Lord and not to men."

—Ephesians 6:7

Picture it: Beautiful summer day in Sioux Fall, South Dakota. The past few days have been used to serve God and grow relationships with amazing local kids. Then the opportunity comes to work in a homeless recovery shelter. The whole trip to the shelter is filled with dreams of big important jobs to save the lives of hobos. When assigned tasks, you get cutting strings off of towels. Yep, I had that job! I had to cut every little string off of these rags. Others were packing lunches, working in the garden, cleaning the shelter; I was cutting strings off of rags. The first half of this little endeavor was spent mulling over the job at hand. "Why do I have to do this job? Why can't they just buy new towels?" I asked myself. "I would rather do anything else." All of a sudden, God stopped me in my tracks, and this verse came to mind: "Serve with a good attitude, as to the Lord and not to men." I was definitely knocked off of my pedestal with that one. I was here, a girl who had all that was needed, in a place for those who have nothing. I couldn't believe how stuck-up and arrogant I was. The least I could do for these poor people was clean up their rags a bit. After that epiphany, I cut every little strand off of the cloths. I made sure every piece of string was even and nice. When I had to cut a towel into a rag, I made sure it was the straightest line they had ever seen. I was humbled that day. Now, whenever I have to do a job I don't enjoy, like stacking chairs or vacuuming the upstairs after a potluck at church, I remind myself of that verse. I say over and over, "I'm serving God, not men. I'm serving God, not men." That makes every little task so much more important.

*Hannah Savage*: 16, Tarpon Springs, FL
Calvary Baptist Church and Calvary Christian High School, Tarpon Springs, FL

# Grieving

**"Those who mourn are blessed, for they will be comforted."**

—Matthew 5:4

I lost my grandmother two years ago. When she passed away just a week before Easter, it was the strangest feeling I had ever known. I felt a sense of emptiness. She had been in the hospital for a few weeks, and we knew she wasn't going to get any better. So it was only a matter of time, right? Well, I don't know if you have ever lost a loved one, but if you have, you will know that death is not something one can prepare for. When they are gone, they are gone. Forever! That's the worst part of it, and it's the hardest part to cope with. I will say that it was a dark time in my life. Things went downhill from the moment she passed, because I decided not to rely on God in the situation. If I had given up matters to God, things would have turned out much better. Romans 8:28 became my favorite verse: "We know that all things work together for the good of those who love God: those who are called according to His purpose." Although I didn't apply the verse at that time, this verse speaks to me today in every situation. If you allow God to take over your grieving, He will help you! He will pick you up and help you realize good will come out of it. God doesn't mind us grieving. Grieving is completely normal. It is simply how long you grieve and how you handle that grieving. My challenge to you: don't be like me and shut God out. If you've lost a loved one, I am so sorry for your loss. I know it's not easy. God will bring you through it; you just have to let Him.

*Angela Stanley*: 17, Woodbridge, VA
Dale City Baptist Church, Woodbridge, VA; Emmanuel Christian School, Manassas, VA

# Speak Life or Death!

"Life and death are in the power of the tongue,
and those who love it will eat its fruit." —Proverbs 18:21

Someone once told me that I had a big nose. Before that I had never really thought much about my nose. Since then, every time I look in the mirror I see it. I see my big nose. That quick remark about my nose left a lasting impact on me. Then there was another time that my mom told me she was really proud of me and so thankful that I was her daughter. I have never forgotten those words, and that brief remark has had a long and lasting impact on my life. Words are powerful. They can breathe life or bring death. They can build others up, or they can tear others down. Words sometimes hurt, but words also heal. Just as easily as you can speak death with your words, you can also speak life with them. As Christians, a lot of the time we focus on not saying the bad things. We try not to curse, say rude things to people, or talk back to our parents. It's hard enough to not do those things. It's difficult to control your tongue. It is important that we focus on not speaking "death," but it is equally important that we focus on speaking "life." Encouraging, loving, and blessing others with our words is not always easy. Either we don't want to bless the other person with kind words, or we honestly forget. Our goal should be to encourage others. Speaking encouragement to others takes work. It is not always what comes naturally, but it is what we are called to do. We can make a difference in the lives of others with our words. We have the chance to impact them in a good way, or in a bad way. Life and death are in the power of the tongue. Which will choose to speak?

McKenzie Sutton: 17, Waverly Hall, GA
Cornerstone Baptist Church, Ellerslie, GA; Homeschooled

# Man, O Man

"Just as sin entered the world through one man, and death through sin, in this way death spread to all men, because all sinned. . . . For just as through one man's disobedience the many were made sinners, so also through the one man's obedience the many will be made righteous."

—Romans 5:12, 19

"How bad can I be? I'm just doing what comes naturally. . . . I'm just following my destiny. How bad can I possibly be?" (From the television movie, Dr. Suess' *The Lorax: How Bad Can It Be?* Performed by Ed Helms, produced by DePatie-Freleng Enterprises, 1972.) This is the chorus of a catchy little song from a movie that I watched with my family. The lyrics lingered and I thought, *Well you can be really bad, man is terribly sinful.* Then when another tragedy happened in the U.S., and we all wondered how someone could do such a thing, I realized that the world would agree with that song. They believe that man is good. Is man naturally good or naturally evil? Is man born good or is it his environment that makes him evil? If man is good, why would we need Jesus to save us? The world would say that man is good and capable of doing well by himself, but that his environment and circumstances may influence him and make him do evil. I believe this is why so many people think that they don't need Jesus and ignore us when we share the gospel with them. They think they are just fine. The Bible says that man is born sinful because of Adam's sin and that all men are terrible sinners, all are capable of doing evil. "There is no one righteous, not even one. . . . There is no one who does what is good, not even one" (Romans 3:10, 12). Man is not good and cannot be good apart from Christ. It is important for us to understand this so we can help others see that they, too, have sinned and need Jesus to save them.

Tyra Ruisinger: 17, Raymore, MO
Summit Woods Baptist Church, Lees Summit, MO; Homeschooled

# A Tree

"He is like a tree planted by streams of water,
which yields its fruit in season and whose leaf does not wither.
Whatever he does prospers." —Psalm 1:3

Imagine you are in a forest surrounded by a multitude of weak, thin, and scrawny trees. You find yourself wondering if there are any big trees around. You keep walking through the forest. After a while, you reach the end of the forest and walk into an open field. You see the most beautiful tree you have ever beheld. This tree looks energized, mighty, and powerful. It stands proud and tall as if no one can defeat it. This tree has an abundance of beautiful fruit on it. Its large roots travel down to the edge of the river, taking in water it uses to grow. Looking up at this tree, you believe that this tree will never wither away, but prosper till the very end of time. In David's opening psalm, this mighty tree you have imagined is the believer—a believer who takes in God's Word to grow in faith and to produce the fruit of the wisdom they have taken in. David adds that this tree will not wither, but prosper. How awesome it is to be compared to a tree! In order to stand tall like this tree David describes, we must read the Word, and soak up what it tells us in order to produce actions and attitudes that glorify God. Don't feel as though you are not worthy to become mighty like a tree because, guess what? You already are! God sees you as this beautiful tree; you just have to believe that to be true. He has mighty plans for us, but we have to get ourselves out of the forest of scrawny trees and instead take up our position as a mighty tree where we will not wither, but prosper by the strength of our God.

Haley Smith: 16, Tarpon Springs, FL
Calvary Baptist Church and Calvary Christian High School, Tarpon Springs, FL

# Help! Help!

"Two are better than one because they have a good reward for their efforts. For it either falls, his companion can lift him up; but pity the one who falls without another to lift him up. And if someone overpowers one person, two can resist him. A cord of three strands is not easily broken."

—Ecclesiastes 4:9–10, 12

Have you ever needed help? In your entire life, have you had a moment when you needed a hand? Maybe you don't understand your trigonometry homework. Or you could be like me, short, and you just can't reach that thing you need on the top shelf. We all need help sometimes. But how many times have you rejected help? How many times have you been stubborn about it, not wanting to accept the fact that you could use a hand? I get caught in this all the time. Someone asks me if I need help and my response is, "I can do it myself!" Suddenly I feel like I have to prove myself to them. There are times when asking for help feels a lot like admitting defeat. I recently taught a lesson on this very thing in the children's ministry of my church, and I have a feeling I got more out of it than they did. We looked at the story of Naaman, the commander of an army. Naaman was suffering from leprosy and couldn't find a cure. Naaman needed some major help. You can read the whole story in 2 Kings 5, but Naaman ends up getting help from four or five different people (plus God, of course) before he was healed. One thing I know is that people are willing to help you. The people who ask to help really do care! So why not let them give you a hand? And why not give them a hand in return when they need help?

Gabrielle LaCognata: 19, Belleview, FL
Church @ The Springs and College of Central Florida, Ocala, FL

# The Mold

**"I set you apart before you were born."** —Jeremiah 1:5

Being a Christian teen can be tough, especially for girls. We often determine our value by our appearance, popularity, athletic abilities, and academic success. We struggle with desiring approval, which causes us to measure ourselves against the world's idea of worth. I attend our family's annual reunions, and someone always asks if I have a boyfriend. Society considers it normal for teens to have a special someone, so when you're the only niece without one, eyebrows raise. Maybe it's because there aren't many girls willing to challenge the teenage mold. Without the expected boyfriend, it seems we aren't considered valuable in the eyes of the world. Our desirability becomes even more complicated when our peers gets involved. We begin to wonder about our social status; the last thing anyone wants is to be labeled a loner. Due to insecurities, we dress and act differently in order to fit in. And if we fail to have the same body shape as the more popular girls, we'll exercise and diet like crazy to get it. All because we want to be accepted! When we conform to this teen mold, we lose ourselves. Girls throw away their innocence to feel cool around others; but when they're alone, they feel empty. There is only one way we can find acceptance and value—abiding in God. So, let go of your desire to fit in and run into His arms. Only there will you find contentment. When you decide to make this change, know that God may call you to cut ties with old friends and lifestyles. God values holy, pure, and blameless hearts, and He can restore yours if you let go of your past and start a new journey alongside Him.

*Carson Gregors*: 17, Albany, GA
Sherwood Baptist Church and Sherwood Christian Academy, Albany, GA

# Listen Up

## "Children, obey your parents in everything, for this pleases the Lord."

—Colossians 3:20

"Do this," "Do that," "Will you get this for me?" "Will you change the baby's diaper?" Have you heard commands like these before? My parents have said things like this, and I don't always appreciate being told to do something for them, especially when I'm in the middle of doing something for myself. It doesn't matter that I don't want to do certain things; I need to do them to please my parents and, ultimately, God. Parents are wiser and we need to respect their teachings and corrections. Our parents don't boss us around just for sheer joy of it! They do it to teach us something new, to help us adapt good behaviors and habits, and to be willing to help with a grateful heart. We learn how to listen to and obey God by listening to and obeying our parents. We need to listen to God. He won't tell us to do something that can harm us. He is perfect! He knows everything, where we'll succeed and where we'll fail. God wants us to listen to correction. When we do, we have favor with God. Do what you do with a grateful heart. When you do these things with a grateful heart, God will bless you. He will be proud of you, and I'm sure your parents will be too.

Nellie Otoupalik: 17, Spokane, WA
Airway Heights Baptist Church, Airway Heights, WA; Homeschooled/Co-op and Spokane Virtual Learning, Spokane, WA

# Be-YOU-ti-ful

## "I praise You because I am fearfully and wonderfully made."
—Psalm 139:14

Have you ever felt like you were not pretty enough? I have, many times. I came to believe that no one would ever like me because I wasn't pretty like all the other girls. For a long time I was stuck in that belief. I heard someone say that God doesn't make mistakes. He makes us the way He sees fit and then says, "It is good." But I would look at myself and then look at another person and think, *No, I'm not good.* Yet God worked through me and taught me that if I had come to hate myself I also hated His creation. I thought to myself, *Whoa, hold your horses, isn't that jumping the gun just a little?* I didn't hate God's creation. I finally saw the connection. Everywhere I went God's beautiful creation took my breath away. As I got lost in it, I found His affection for me. I saw with every sunrise and sunset, with every star that sparkled, and with every bird that chirped that it was all to show me how much God loved me. The beauty I found in all these things was the beauty that God saw when He looked at me. He will always love me. And now, every morning when I see the sun rising, I hear God's voice whispering, "Good morning, beautiful. I made this for you because I love you." When we come to realize that we are God's creation and we are beautiful, then we can allow ourselves to believe that we are beautiful. That is why David praises the Lord, because he discovered that he was fearfully and wonderfully made. Once you make that realization, you, too, will be able to praise the Lord because you have found the beauty within you. So be you—and be beautiful!

Haley Smith: 16, Tarpon Springs, FL
Calvary Baptist Church and Calvary Christian High School, Tarpon Springs, FL

# Nationalities

"In every province and in every city, wherever the edict of the king's command and his law reached joy and rejoicing took place among the Jews. There was a celebration and a holiday. Any many people of the ethnic groups of the land professed themselves to be Jews because fear of the Jews had overcome them." —Esther 8:17

I go to school with a lot of people from different countries. In today's society, just turning on the television can reveal what it's like to live in other places. One of my all-time favorite shows, *House Hunters International,* shows me how people in different countries lay out their homes and what is considered a roomy kitchen. I believe this is a good thing. It shows my peers and me what it is like to live somewhere else and how blessed we are to live in a country where we have our freedom. I have some really great friends at school who are from China, and they are such nice people. Personally, I feel that being able to be friends with teens from other nations shows that though we look different and speak different languages, we are basically the same. I am a very big YouTube fan, and a lot of YouTubers are from different countries. By watching their videos, I really gain an understanding of their culture. God has blessed us with the ability to know and learn from people who are different from us. We can't take that for granted, because it shows us how others live and that we find children of God in every nation. He would want you to treat everyone equally, so make it a point to! You never know, that foreign exchange student with the accent may just turn out to be your new best friend.

Clara Davis: 14, Little Rock, AR
The Church at Rock Creek and LISA Academy, Little Rock, AR

# Somebody Smells Good

"For we are to God the aroma of Christ among those who are being saved and those who are perishing." —2 Corinthians 2:15

You have probably heard people say, "Oooh, somebody smells good!" If it happens to be your lucky day, that person they smell is you. You then get to reply by saying, "It's me!" Somehow, just that small interaction gives us confidence. We like the fact that we smell so good that people notice. We want to be sweet smelling, but we want more for people to recognize the sweet aroma of Christ. In 2 Corinthians, Paul tells us that we are the scent of Christ. Are we making sure that the smell that is given off is good? Do people recognize the smell of Christ on us? As believers, we were given the greatest gifts of all: salvation and the Holy Spirit. The gift we have was not meant to be hidden. If we truly have this gift, we should not cover up the scent of Christ but, instead, let it flow out of us. Having Christ living inside of us allows for Him to naturally flow out of us. Sin blocks the scent of Christ, so let go of that sin in order that the aroma of Christ is recognized. When God looks down and gives a big sniff, what does He smell? Sin or Christ? How sad must it be for Him to smell sin on us rather than Christ! If you know there is something that is blocking your scent, work to get rid of it. Give it over to Christ in order that when He gives a big sniff He says, "Ooooh, she smells good!"

Haley Smith: 16, Tarpon Springs, FL
Calvary Baptist Church and Calvary Christian High School, Tarpon Springs, FL

# Discipleship

"Go, therefore, and make disciples of all nations, baptizing them in the name of the Father and of the Son and of the Holy Spirit, teaching them to observe everything I have commanded you. And remember, I am with you always, to the end of the age." —Matthew 28:19–20

When I was in junior high, and to an extent still today, I wanted to have an older girl to love and accept me, care enough to break the cliques, invest in me, and share who she was with me. I realized recently that I am now the older girl. I am the age that the younger girls look up to. I have seen that I am not being the influence in their lives that I craved at that age. As I have come to this conclusion, I have endeavored to figure out why I can't seem to bring myself to be a friend to the younger girls. I tell myself, "When I can drive, then I'll go and choose a seventh or eighth grade girl to disciple." What I think it comes down to is this: I have become comfortable with my friends, I am not in the same stage of life as the younger girls, and so it would take extra effort to bring myself into their circles. I have decided to challenge myself to have a quality conversation with a junior-high girl when I am at church next. I can't wait to see what God will do. If you are an older teen, I encourage you to take this challenge. You have more influence than you realize. Why not use this influence to build up others? If you are younger, you still have influence. It is important for all of us, no matter how young or old we are, to pass on what we know in order to help others through the struggles that come with life regardless of age.

Rebekah Byrd: 16, Tulsa, OK
Evergreen Baptist Church, Bixby, OK; Homeschooled

# Trusting in Him

*"'For I know the plans I have for you,'-this is the L*ORD*'s
declaration-'plans for your welfare, not for disaster,
to give you a future and a hope.'"* —Jeremiah 29:11

We live in such a fast-paced world. Everything around us, even our own lives, are constantly moving. I guess that explains why we so often we become impatient with God. When I want something from Him, I want it then and there, exactly how and when I want it. It's hard to wait and trust in God's will and timing. We're human; we don't understand. All we see is what's going on in the now. We forget that God is all-knowing, which means that He knows exactly what's to happen and exactly what we need to face it. Often, His decisions don't make sense. I didn't understand why He had my family leave Little Rock. I was angry with Him. Why would He take me away from all my friends, my church, and my school? In hindsight, I see that I'm able to attend a Christian school, which has affected my walk with Him in a huge way. My best friend, Hannah, and her family didn't understand when her mother was diagnosed with leukemia. But you know what? I can't even count how many hundreds of people have been touched and affected by their testimony. We don't always understand why or when God causes things to happen, but His plan, His perfect plan, is so much more amazing than ours. All we need to do is put our trust and faith in Him, not ourselves, and He'll make our journey more incredible than we could ever imagine.

*Sarah Ashley Bryant:* 15, Springdale, AR
Cross Church and Shiloh Christian School, Springdale, AR

# #foreveralone: Finding Your Match

"Do not be mismatched with unbelievers. For what partnership
is there between righteousness and lawlessness?
Or what fellowship does light have with darkness?" —2 Corinthians 6:14

In today's world, technology and social networking sites are a big deal. Personally, I don't care for technology—except for my phone, Twitter, and Pinterest. Instead of fasting from food, I have to fast from those three things. I love Twitter too much. When my best friend and I text each other, we'll sometimes text in tweet, complete with hash tags and all. One we both use frequently is #foreveralone. An example would be, "Just ate a whole thing of *Chunky Monkey* Ben & Jerry's ice cream while watching *The Notebook*. . . . #foreveralone." Even though at times like those it seems like I'll be alone forever, I know God has my own Prince Charming planned for me. Everyone knows that one guy that is so sweet, funny, and cute, you can't imagine passing up the opportunity to date him. Then you find out he isn't a Christian. The question is: Do you still date him, or do you pass him up? According to 2 Corinthians, a pass is required. It's easier to pull someone away from their faith than bring someone into faith. Even if the guy doesn't smoke, drink or party, loves his mom, and is fine with you being a Christian, he still isn't a good choice. Even if he isn't bringing you down, he isn't building you up either. A good match is someone who can encourage you in your faith and challenges you to be a better person. Don't settle! In high school and college years, standards should be so high, very few fit the mold. With so much life ahead, there is no need to settle for an OK person. Always strive to be the best and find the best.

Hannah Savage: 16, Tarpon Springs, FL
Calvary Baptist Church and Calvary Christian High School, Tarpon Springs, FL

# Life Happens

"Do not be anxious about anything, but in everything, by prayer and petition with Thanksgiving, present your request to God."

—Philippians 4:6

Do you ever stop to think about what you have to be thankful for or what your true joy is? It is so easy to get caught up in daily activities or just life. I know you have heard the expression "life happened." Maybe you had big dreams of being a writer or a doctor, but then something happened and you had to put your dreams on hold. Did you ever stop to think that the something is what God had in mind for you the whole time? The secret is to find the joy in everything that comes your way. Remember God doesn't make mistakes. God has placed you in every circumstance of your life, either because of your obedience or lack thereof. Life is much easier to take when you thank God for everything, even the detours. He wants to give you the desires of your heart. You just need to ask and then wait on Him to pour out His blessings like He promises He will.

Brianna Carter: 19, Sharon, SC
Hillcrest Baptist Church and York Technical, York, SC

# Background

## "He must increase, but I must decrease." —John 3:30

In the Bible there are so many great examples of those who made God a big deal in their life. There was Abraham, who was willing to sacrifice his son to please God; John the Baptist, who paved the way for Jesus and didn't even feel worthy to baptize Him; Paul, who went from persecuting Christians to being enslaved for being a Christ follower; and so many more. What this generation needs to realize is that having God as #1 isn't just for biblical characters. A popular song *Background* from the album "Rehab" by Lacrae, produced by Rehab sums up this verse well: ". . . if you need me I'll be stage right. . . . when I follow my obsessions I end up confessing. That I'm not that impressive, matter of fact, I'm who I are; A trail of star dust . . ." The artist understands that if he is center stage, the whole point of giving your life to God is lost. When someone is a born-again Christian, they give their life to God. Not just the bits and pieces that are easy to give up—all of it! Lecrae is trying to get the point across that if we, being mere humans, decide to make us the focus, God won't be able to do all that He is capable of doing. We limit Him when we step up and take control. If we stay in the back, waiting for His command, then He can do so much more through us and for us. When we focus on God, and keep Him #1 in our lives, everything else will fall into place for us. If we live to show His glory at school, work, on the court or the field, we will be rewarded for it. Just continue to play the background and let God do what He does best.

*Haley Smith*: 16, Tarpon Springs, FL
Calvary Baptist Church and Calvary Christian High School, Tarpon Springs, FL

# Looking at the Heart

### "Endurance produces proven character, and proven character produces hope." —Romans 5:4

There is always that popular girl or guy who seem to have it all. They have the perfect family, house, car, hair, looks, etc. We as people, and by human nature, look at the worldly items a person has, or their physical appearance, and decide what kind of person they are. The Bible tells us in many instances that good hair and owning a convertible are pointless. "Who can find a capable wife? She is far more precious than jewels. . . . Strength and honor are her clothing, and she can laugh at the time to come. She opens her mouth with wisdom and loving instruction is on her tongue. . . . Charm is deceptive and beauty is fleeting, but a woman who fears the Lord will be praised" (Proverbs 31:10, 25–26, 31). "Endurance produces proven character, and proven character produces hope" (Romans 5:4). "But the Lord said to Samuel, 'Do not look at his appearance or his stature, because I have rejected him. Man does not see what the Lord sees, for man sees what is visible, but the Lord sees the heart'" (1 Samuel 16:7). All of these verses reveal God's outlook on physical appearance and worldly items. Ladies, God calls us to be wise and loving and to fear the Lord. Men, look for a woman whose character is like that found in Proverbs 31. God also tells us that He looks at the heart. We should not be concerned by what brand our clothes are or if we have the latest iPhone. As you go about these next few days, view people by how they treat others and their character. You may be surprised what you find.

Layne Coleman: 14, Little Rock, AR
The Church at Rock Creek and Little Rock Christian Academy, Little Rock, AR

# How to Be a Froot Loop

"Love must be without hypocrisy. Detest evil, cling to what is good. Show family affection to one another with brotherly love. Outdo one another in showing honor. Do not lack diligence; be fervent in spirit, serve the Lord. Rejoice in hope; be patient in affliction, be persistent in prayer. Share with the saints in their needs, pursue hospitality. Bless those who persecute you, bless and do not curse. Rejoice with those who rejoice, weep with those who weep. Be in agreement with one another. Do not be proud, instead, associate with the humble. Do not be wise in your own estimation. Do not repay anyone evil for evil. Try to do what is honorable in everyone's eyes." —Romans 12:9–17

In the eighth grade I was a member of Student Council. I joined because I had passed around a petition to change the uniform policy, and the Student Council leader pressured me into it. Toward the end of the year, it came time for the seventh graders to make their speeches for president of Student Council. The most memorable one was a girl who talked about being a Froot Loop. Her speech was about a breakfast cereal. As crazy at that sounds, it is the one speech we all remember to this day. She said, "My brother always told me to be a Froot Loop in a bowl full of Cheerios." To be different, go against the flow, be you, be bold, and all the other sayings we hear all the time. Love sincerely, be nice, serve God, serve others. Instead of trying to be better than someone at basketball, try and do more good things than them, be humble, and let God handle the payback. Froot Loops are hard to find, hard to be, and even harder to not look up to.

Haley Smith: 16, Tarpon Springs, FL
Calvary Baptist Church and Calvary Christian High School, Tarpon Springs, FL

# You Get What You Get

**"Enter His gates with thanksgiving and His courts with praise.
Give thanks to Him and praise His name."** —Psalm 100:4

Thanksgiving is filled with traditions, whether you eat at the table, pray and thank God, or fill your plates and crowd around the television for the Macy's Thanksgiving Day Parade and a football game. Usually there's a turkey, stuffing, potatoes, cranberry sauce, and by the end of the day you're so full of food you can't move. We often forget what Thanksgiving is actually about. We think turkey, family, and football, forgetting to thank God for what we've been given. With only two drumsticks on a turkey, my brothers and I end up competing for them. I claim that I'm the oldest and, therefore, I should get the drumstick. Malachi claims he's the second oldest and he should get the other drumstick. Tyler is the youngest, which gives him an advantage. He can convince Mom or Dad to give him the drumstick due to his cuteness. Traditionally, when we wake up on Thanksgiving morning, the first one to call a drumstick gets one. There's no calling the day before. You have to be quick, and there has to be at least three witnesses, otherwise no one will believe that you called dibs. Anyone complaining about not having a drumstick usually gets told the same thing: "You get what you get and don't throw a fit." We tend to forget that Thanksgiving is not about the turkey leg or which football team wins. The Pilgrims were thankful for the new land God provided them, and God has blessed us with so much. We are blessed, so let's pray for others that they may receive God's blessings too.

*Hannah Arrington*: 15, Borger, TX
First Baptist Church and Texas Virtual Academy, Borger, TX

# Where It All Begins

## "For from the heart come evil thoughts, murders, adulteries, sexual immoralities, thefts, false testimonies, blasphemies. These are the things that defile a man." —Matthew 15:19–20

If what comes out of the heart defiles us, why does everyone keep telling us to follow our hearts? The world has embraced the idea of abandoning your thoughts and reason and letting your emotions rule over you—something we, as Christians, cannot do. Ephesians 4:22–24 says, "You took off your former way of life, the old self that is corrupted by deceitful desires; you are being renewed in the spirit of your minds; you put on the new self, the one created according to God's likeness in righteousness and purity of the truth." We're supposed to live in righteousness and purity of the truth. How do we keep our thoughts pure and fight temptation—not only physically, but mentally? The hardest time to keep my thoughts pure is at night, when I'm lying in bed trying to sleep. Reviewing Bible verses and praying for people helps a lot. My sister thinks of a Bible verse and then goes through each word in her mind, imagining each individual letter being highlighted. By the time she's done, she's usually asleep. When I'm bothered with ungodly thoughts during the day, I review memorized Scripture. Memorize verses that remind you of what God has done for you and who you are in Christ. Sharing your struggles with someone will help keep you accountable. Our actions reflect our thoughts and what's inside our hearts, and when we're dwelling on Christ and His Word, or serving others and not thinking about ourselves, we'll be able to stand strong against temptation when it comes.

Tara Greene: 16, Fort Belvoir, VA
Guilford Baptist Church, Sterling, VA; Homeschooled

# Christian Joy

"Why am I so depressed? Why this turmoil within me?
Put your hope in God, for I will still praise Him, my Savior and my God."

—Psalm 42:5

Teenage girls are known for mood swings, and we try to cover up feelings of sadness or "the blues." It's easy to feel alone when you're trapped in a pattern of unhappiness, especially if you don't understand why. As Christians, we are called to live in joy (1 Thessalonians 5:16), but it can be so difficult when caught up in the troubles of this world. Jesus says in John 16:33, "I have told you these things so that in Me you may have peace. You will have suffering in this world. Be courageous! I have conquered the world." We will be discouraged by life's trials; yet God reminds us that we are victorious in Him. Feelings of depression result from leading a "Me-focused" life. Focusing on self causes us to lose sight of Christ's great sacrifice. Our lives are important however their importance is in God's plan for them. Jeremiah 29:11 says "For I know the plans I have for you . . . to give you a future and a hope." Focus on God's will for your life, and you will find the cares of the world starting to slip away. We have been given the greatest gift that could ever be given—our salvation! We should rejoice for who we are in Christ, heirs to His kingdom! This gift can never be taken away! "For I am persuaded that not even death or life . . . or any other created thing will have the power to separate us from the love of God that is in Christ Jesus our Lord!" (Romans 8:38–39). Whatever we face in life or think of ourselves, God is greater and loves us unconditionally! Rejoice!

*Kristin Goehl:* 18, Princeton, MA
Bethlehem Bible Church, West Boylston, MA; Princeton University, Princeton, MA

# Be the Example

"All bitterness, anger and wrath, shouting and slander must be removed from you, along with all malice. And be kind and compassionate to one another, forgiving one another, just as God also forgave you in Christ."

—Ephesians 4:31–32

Do you have younger siblings? I do. Do you have older siblings? I do too. Have your siblings ever taken something of yours that they didn't ask for? Mine have. You know that feeling that you get inside, like all you want to do is get back at them, even in a small way. I get that feeling sometimes. We need to remember that we cannot hold anger inside of ourselves because God tells us not to. Instead of being angry at our siblings we need to be compassionate and understanding. Perhaps your younger sibling took something from you because they wanted to pretend to be like you. Or maybe they borrowed something of yours because they wanted to look as cool as you. Thinking like that sometimes gets rid of the anger, and you start to be forgiving. The verse above tells us that we are to be kind and compassionate, so I'm not making it up when I say that we have to understand and be compassionate toward those who do us wrong. Even though we don't like to admit it, we've done something wrong to either them or someone else. Now imagine how it feels, or would've felt, if that person you wronged held a grudge over your head for the rest of your life and never forgave you. It wouldn't feel too good, would it? We need to be imitators of Christ.

*Hannah Abernathie:* 15, Tulsa, OK
Evergreen Baptist Church, Bixby, OK; Homeschooled and Cornerstone Tutorial Center, Tulsa, OK

# Depression

### "He surrounded him, cared for him, and protected him as the pupil of His eye." —Deuteronomy 32:10

Depression is common among teens. We are in between stages, as they call it. We have a greater desire to get out and do things, yet we are not yet able. Sometimes we feel weak, questioning *Why? Why do I feel like this?* You are not weak. Even the greatest can be plagued by depression; this sinful world, full of hate, makes sure of that. With depression, we sometimes feel as if our world has become colorless, things we once found enjoyable lose their call. Get out and breathe some fresh air. Even if you'd rather not, look around and try to appreciate everything around you. "Count your blessings, name them one by one, and you'll be surprised what the Lord has done." When caught in a rut of self-pity, try your best to do things for others. Smile! Even if you don't want to, smile and remember God is always with you. Remember, everything should be done for Him. Good times come and go, as well as bad times. If you are always thinking about others, praying and asking God for help, you won't even have time to worry and fuss about yourself. Sometimes I feel like I can't go on, that everything is too much, and I just can't do it anymore. If you have ever felt like this, remember most of all that God loves you like His child and will never give you trials you are unable to bear. We can rest in Him with the knowledge that every difficulty He puts in your path is His way to draw you closer to Him, to depend on Him, and put your trust in Him. Once we have done this—you will be amazed—those huge difficulties turn out to be tiny. With God's help, we can overcome anything, including depression.

*Holly Kurtz*: 16, Holden, MA
Bethlehem Bible Church and Bethlehem Bible Church Homeschooled Co-op, West Boylston, MA

# Great I AM

> "God replied to Moses, 'I AM WHO I AM. This is what you are to say to the Israelites: I AM has sent me to you.'" —Exodus 3:14

Moses asked God who he should say had sent him to Pharaoh. God replied with "I AM WHO I AM . . . I AM has sent you." God's way of telling Moses His name has always fascinated me. Just the fact that He can call Himself "I AM." Just that He is. We live because He lives. He created everything on this earth. Look around, whether outside, in your room, or somewhere else, God created it and everything in it. Think about what that means. He deserves all the praise on earth. None other than Him is worthy of our praise. He can raise the dead and demons tremble and flee just at His name. There is no greater power than our God. Throughout the New Testament, Jesus uses I AM in many ways. "I AM the way, the truth and the life" (John 14:6). "Who do you say that I AM?" (Luke 9:20). "I AM . . . and all of you will see the Son of Man seated at the right hand of the Power and coming with the clouds of heaven" (Mark 14:62). "Before Abraham was, I AM" (John 8:58). He uses it continually to describe Himself. With these two little words, Jesus professed His being God. God is eternal, He has no beginning and no end; He is the Alpha and Omega. God does exist and will always exist because He is God. There is a song by New Life Worship that describes this. It is an amazing song and I encourage you to look it up and listen to it. It is called "Great I AM." So when you are worshiping God, remember those two little words, "I AM." Remember who God is and how worthy He is, and give Him the praise He deserves.

*Hannah Abernathie*: 15, Tulsa, OK
Evergreen Baptist Church, Bixby, OK; Homeschooled and Cornerstone Tutorial Center, Tulsa, OK

# Adorned in Splendor

"Therefore don't worry about tomorrow, because tomorrow will worry about itself. Each day has enough trouble of its own." —Matthew 6:34

We get caught up in worldly things and worry, but worrying distracts us from God and puts the focus on us. Each day is hard enough without worrying about tomorrow. I sometimes find myself worrying about things like school deadlines. Matthew 6:26–33 says, "Look at the birds of the sky: They don't sow or reap or gather into barns, yet your heavenly Father feeds them. Aren't you worth more than they? . . . And why do you worry about clothes? Learn how the wildflowers of the field grow: they don't labor or spin thread. Yet I tell you that not even Solomon in all his splendor was adorned like one of these! If that's how God clothes the grass of the field, . . . won't He do much more for you? . . . But seek first the kingdom of God and His righteousness, and all these things will be provided for you." You can trust God to deal with not only big things but even the tiny details. Nothing is too small for God to help you with. Matthew 10:31 commands us: "So don't be afraid therefore; you are worth more than many sparrows." Whatever happens, God is sovereign. The Bible assures us that if we love Him, everything will work out for the best. We should take each day as it comes, focusing not on our own problems, but trusting in the Lord to care for us as we serve others to the best of our ability.

Holly Kurtz: 16, Holden, MA
Bethlehem Bible Church and Bethlehem Bible Church Homeschooled Co-op, West Boylston, MA

# Modesty

"Women are to dress themselves in modest clothing, with decency and good sense, . . . but with good works, as is proper for women who affirm that they worship God." —1 Timothy 2:9–10

Why is it important for women to dress modestly? Shouldn't we be able to wear whatever we wish to wear? One of the most important reasons we are to dress modestly is so that we do not aid in causing men to sin. Jesus said, "But I tell you, everyone who looks at a woman to lust for her has already committed adultery with her in his heart" (Matthew 5:28). It is not our responsibility to make sure men are not sinning, but if Jesus was telling someone to not lust I would not want my name in the sentence. How do we dress in a way that does not cause wrong thoughts to enter into guys' heads? First of all, we are representatives of Jesus, because He is in us. First Corinthians 6:19–20 says, "Don't you know that your body is a sanctuary of the Holy Spirit who is in you, whom you have from God? . . . Therefore glorify God in your body." We are to glorify Christ, not ourselves in our body. Drawing attention to our bodies is glorifying our flesh, not our inside beauty. "Your beauty should not consist of outward things. . . . Instead, it should consist of what is inside the heart" (1 Peter 3:3–4). "For man sees what is visible, but the Lord sees the heart" (1 Samuel 16:7). Instead of drawing attention to our bodies, we should draw attention to our faces, because they reflect the light of Christ inside of us. Every family has their own modesty standards, so ask your father or brothers what they believe is a God-honoring way to dress.

Hannah Cooksey: 16, McMinnville, OR
Valley Baptist Church, McMinnville, OR; Homeschooled

# Don't Forget Your Neighbors

"For this reason also, since the day we heard this, we haven't stopped praying for you. We are asking that you may be filled with the knowledge of His will in all wisdom and spiritual understanding." —Colossians 1:9

As believers in the good Lord Jesus Christ, it should be our desire to pray for one another. In times of confusion and indecision, we should go to Him in prayer. But, sometimes we forget and when we do it is important that we make it right immediately. We should also pray for our fellow believers, that they will follow God's will in every aspect of their lives. I must admit that sometimes in my prayer life, I've become self-absorbed. At times I get caught up and focus on making sure that God gives me strength for the day, wisdom to guide my actions, and the things that I need. Yes, those are important, but it is also important that I pray for my classmates, my friends and family, neighbors, and the salvation of this fallen world. God answers prayer, and we must never forget that the spiritual lives of our brothers and sisters in Christ, including pastors and those in service on the mission field, mean as much to Him as our own. I don't know about you, but I love knowing that someone has been praying for me. It just gives me a warm fuzzy feeling. Encouragement is one of the best things you can give someone. Set aside a time each day to pray for your fellow believers in Christ. You never know what God may do in answer to your prayers. Prayer changes things, and so can you through prayer.

*Imani McBean:* 14, Leesburg, GA
Mt. Zion Baptist Church and Sherwood Christian Academy, Albany, GA

# God Cannot Leave Us

"For I am persuaded that not even death or life, angels or rulers, things present or things to come, hostile powers, height or depth, or any other created thing will have the power to separate us from the love of God that is in Christ Jesus our Lord!" —Romans 8:38–39

Nothing can separate us from His love. How amazing is that? Not anything I do, or say, or go through. Nothing at all can take away God's passionate love for me and for you. I can do all the unholy and unrighteous things in the world, but God will always take me back. His love will never fade; it will remain a burning blue fire, unquenchable. Do not be surprised when you face opposition along the way. Instead, know that God will be right there, walking beside you in your times of trouble. It is when we are closest to God that the devil sees fit to attack us. He will do anything in his power to make us fall away from God's love, but with the Lord's help, we have the power to counter his attacks and win the battle for our souls. We will stumble. It is inevitable that we will fall. We are sinners by nature, and we cannot escape that truth. God knows we will never be perfect, and He doesn't want us to be. All He asks is that we strive toward Him and become more like Jesus every day. It matters not how many times we fall away from Him. It is completely irrelevant how far we run. His arms will always be outstretched toward us, ready for us to embrace Him. There is comfort and joy in knowing that He will never leave nor forsake us. God's love for us is like the sands on the shore of the sea. "Nothing can separate, even if I ran away. 'Cause your love never fails" (Jesus Culture's "Your Love Never Fails," Bethel/Integrity Label, 2010).

Sarah LaCognata: 14, Belleview, FL
Church @ The Springs, Ocala, FL; Homeschooled

# There's Power in the Word of God

"For the word of God is living and effective and sharper than any double-edged sword, penetrating as far as the separation of soul and spirit, joints and marrow. It is able to judge the ideas and thoughts of the heart." —Hebrews 4:12

God's Word is so powerful. It is the only thing in this world, besides our souls, that is eternal. It stands forever. Since it is so important, it is no wonder we are told to hide it in our hearts. The Word of God is many things to us, but it is described in Ephesians 6:17 as being our sword. And in Hebrews it tells us that it is sharper than any double-edged sword. So we have not only a sword, but the sharpest sword we can get. We have access to the greatest defense weapon against the enemy. David, a warrior for the Lord, treasured God's Word in his heart. In fact, he writes in Psalm 119 about the Bible and the importance of God's Word, precepts, and commands in our lives. I am pretty sure David knew what he was talking about when he wrote that psalm. He wasn't just making all that up. He, a man after God's own heart, had hidden God's Word in his heart, and it was the most important thing to him. David lays out the key to being a girl after God's own heart, a valiant warrior for Him—His Word. It is our sword. We can't do battle without it.

McKenzie Sutton: 17, Waverly Hall, GA
Cornerstone Baptist Church, Ellerslie, GA; Homeschooled

# I Wish I Was Fill in the Blank . . .

"Do not be conformed to this age, but be transformed
by the renewing of your mind, so that you may discern
what is the good, pleasing, and perfect will of God." —Romans 12:2

There are always those people who have the fancy clothes, the cool mom, the expensive car, the latest iPhone, or even the person who is allowed to do whatever they want. Have you ever wanted to be like that person? I have. More than once! Many times I find myself getting jealous of them, and that is where I always go wrong. I know this family that moved to a smaller house. It took almost a month to move out. It was painful to get rid of the majority of their possessions. After five trips to the local Goodwill donation station and three to the dump, the mom was nearly in tears. She told me that, "All these years, I held on to all that junk because I thought it would serve some purpose later on in my life. All it ended up doing was coming between me and my husband and my kids. It is so overwhelming to see all of these worldly things I was holding onto, and how much I truly wasn't focusing on God." It's not a sin to have things, but if we idolize them over God, it becomes sin. God tells us to not be conformed, but to be transformed by the renewing of our minds so that we will have discernment to know His will. We need reminding that what we have is much better than what the world offers. Christ is the only one who can fill our empty hearts and provide all that we need.

Nellie Otoupalik: 17, Spokane, WA
Airway Heights Baptist Church, Airway Heights, WA; Homeschooled/Co-op and Spokane Virtual Learning, Spokane, WA

# Cliques

**"Pride comes before destruction and an arrogant spirit before a fall."**
—Proverbs 16:18

Having friends is a great thing, but choosing the right ones is important. A lot of people want to hang around with the popular kids. Just think about it for a second: How would that friendship work out? How do they treat each other as a group? I doubt they treat each other with respect and love. Would they care about your feelings? The groups of popular people have the tendency to treat others badly and bring others down emotionally. They have the tendency to use you to get stuff that they cannot. Please choose your friends wisely. Good friends are the ones who are always there for you. They won't judge you in what you do, how you act, or what you believe. They will love you for you and not for what you can do for them. They won't put you in bad situations, but they will get you out of them. It never hurts to have a friend who will tell you when you are doing wrong or will help you through situations. Honestly, I love having a friend like that in my life. But most of all, God is the best friend you could ever ask for. He will love you no matter what. He will encourage you in everything. He won't always help you out of situations, but He will fight for you and carry you to somewhere safe. He will get jealous if you don't spend time with Him. He knows that you must in order to grow as a Christian. Be careful how you choose your friends. You want to emulate Christ and not them!

*Dianah Edwards*: 16, West Monroe, LA
First West Monroe Baptist Church and Northeast Baptist School, West Monroe, LA

# Forgiveness

*"For if you forgive people their wrong doing, your heavenly Father will forgive you as well. But if you don't forgive people, your Father will not forgive your wrongdoing."* —Matthew 6:14–15

A lot of us have witnessed bullying at school. Maybe that group of mean girls thinks you're heavier than they are, so they have a right to make you feel bad. Sometimes guys will make fun of one another because one is skinnier, shorter, or weaker than the others. I've seen all types of bullying. One mentally challenged boy in a public school music class was yelled at and taunted just so his tormentors could be entertained by his reactions. Another boy in a different class was teased because he dressed weirdly. He was different, but did he deserve that? I've been a victim of bullying. I still don't know why, but a group of girls I didn't know followed me in the hall saying mean, racist things to me. It was scary, because I was in a new town and new to public school. It didn't last very long, yet it was long enough for me to realize how bad it must be for people who get bullied daily. If you are one of the many people subjected to bullying, it may feel that everyone is out to get you. Most of the time, the tormentors don't know your life, your story, or why you made the choices you have. We are wounded people looking for things to make ourselves feel better. That's why God puts such an importance on forgiveness. Without forgiveness, we wouldn't be able to make free choices. God is the King of forgiving. God gives battles to everyone. Overcoming them is the challenge. With Him all things are possible.

**Leah Harris:** 16, Kodiak, AK
Frontier Southern Baptist, Kodiak, AK; Homeschooled

# We Have a Choice!

**"Don't envy a violent man or choose any of his ways."** —Proverbs 3:31

Sometimes the world looks like so much fun—those popular girls at school who seem to have a party to go to every weekend, or that girl with the boyfriend. It can seem that what they have is so much better than what we have. They spend their days hanging out with the populars, while all you ever do is homework and chores and an occasional sleepover with your best friend. I have found myself guilty of envying them, wanting to have plans, parties, and popular people to hang out with. Though those things aren't necessarily bad, and though those people might not be violent, they just aren't on the best path in life—and the Bible tells us not to envy them, not to crave what they have. Even though it might look great and fun and marvelous, the truth is it won't last. Those people who we sometimes spend so much of our time desiring to be like are focused on temporal things. And we are not to choose that way. We are to choose the way of the Lord. Our way may be lonely because instead of giving ourselves to the first guy who calls us pretty, we have to choose to stay home from the party, because you know there might be some not-so-great things there. Many times the Christian life doesn't look so glorious if you look at it in a physical sense. I mean taking up your cross, denying yourself, giving up your desires for Christ's isn't always the most fun thing. The world's way looks more fun, but that is not true. The world is temporal, but we are living for something that is eternal. Don't ever envy the world. Why would you? People normally envy something they think is better than what they already have. But nothing is better than Jesus!

*McKenzie Sutton:* 17, Waverly Hall, GA
Cornerstone Baptist Church, Ellerslie, GA; Homeschooled

# Be a Friend

"Say these things, and encourage and rebuke with all authority. Let no one disregard you." —Titus 2:15

There are always people who are hurting and just need a good friend to stand up for them. People may make fun of you for being their friend, but it is always worth it in the end. When people start to discourage that person, stand up for her, ask the people to stop. They will see in you a kind and caring heart. We can all think of a time when someone was being picked on and we did nothing. We just let the other person get hurt emotionally or physically. Keep a look out for those who are hurting. I promise there are a lot of them, and a friend is just what they might need at that moment in time. You never know, it could end up as a great relationship. You could grow strong together in many ways. Just take that first step. Ask God to give you the strength to stand up for the downtrodden and wounded, and He will shine through you. He will be at your side at all times. If you get nervous about helping someone, just turn to God. You may be thinking, *I'm not strong enough for this, I'm only thirteen, fourteen, fifteen,* or so on. The Bible says that Gideon told the angel of the Lord that he was weak, he was the youngest in his family, and his tribe was the lowest. But God still used him, the weakest, to drive out the enemy (Judges 6). Remember that God can use you in many ways—ways that you thought impossible. A minister once said, "This day has not been lived before, nor will it be lived again." So make the most of your relationships with new friends, family, and God.

Dianah Edwards: 16, West Monroe, LA
First West Monroe Baptist Church and Northeast Baptist School, West Monroe, LA

# A Courtroom

**"Christ has liberated us to be free. Stand firm then and don't submit again to a yoke of slavery."** —Galatians 5:1

Picture this with me. A courtroom. There are only two people in it: It's just you and the Judge. There is no jury, for none is needed. The Judge is the best you will ever see. He is kind, but He knows that justice must be served. He knows you are wrong, and you do too. You are trembling, dreading the moment He raises His gavel and says the word that strikes fear into your heart: "Guilty!" As the Judge brings His gavel up, you cringe, on the brink of tears, then suddenly you hear the door open. You look back and see a shining figure walking confidently down the hall. He comes to the front, bows respectfully, and says, "Father, You and I both know that this man is guilty, but I paid the price for his sin. You can let him go." The Judge smiles at who you now know to be His Son, then He turns to you and says, "My Son paid your penalty. You are forgiven. You have been given life, now go and live." You smile through your tears and walk out of the room. You are thankful, but you don't understand. Why would the Son of the Judge pay your penalty? This picture is exactly how it is with us and God. We are guilty, and we know it. Justice must be served, and the penalty is death. But Jesus, God's only Son, came so we wouldn't have to pay the price. His death means our freedom. The question is: What will you do with this freedom?

*Gabrielle LaCognata:* 19, Belleview, FL
Church @ The Springs and College of Central Florida, Ocala, FL

# Carry Another's Burdens!

"Carry one another's burdens, in this way you will fulfill the law of Christ." —Galatians 6:2

Ever had a really bad day or had something bad happen to you? You go to unload on your friend about it, and the whole time she looks annoyed. The look on her face is saying "hurry up already." As soon as you are done she begins to tell you about how she was walking today and one of the heels on her favorite pair of shoes fell off. Uncaring, selfish, not a really great friend—these are some words that might describe that person. If you are a Christian and these types of words or situations describe you, you are not fulfilling the law of Christ. His law is to love our neighbors as ourselves. We fulfill that law when we carry one another's burdens. I looked up the word carry in Webster's dictionary, and it has over twenty-five definitions. The very first is "to hold or support while moving." As Christ followers, lovers of Jesus, whatever you want to call us, we are commanded to hold or support each other. When one of our brothers or sisters in Christ is going through a difficult time, it is our job to be the hands and feet of Jesus to them, to love them and to walk (move) with them through it. Living for Jesus is loving others. What better way to love them than to be there for them? Throughout Scripture, the church is called to love, be there, support, and encourage one another in the faith. We need one another. Be a caring friend who is always ready to carry someone else's burdens. Be the friend who always listens to the other person before going on about what's happening in your life. By doing this you will be imitating Christ, who put us first and carried our burdens all the way to the cross!

McKenzie Sutton: 17, Waverly Hall, GA
Cornerstone Baptist Church, Ellerslie, GA; Homeschooled

# Hurt and Forgiveness

"Do not be conquered by evil, but conquer evil with good."

—Romans 12:21

"I'm sorry." How much do these words mean for you now? This phrase is repeated so often each day, so casually, that one may wonder if it holds any meaning anymore. It's possible you have been hurt by someone deeply—someone who uses those words repeatedly but never means them. There is Someone though, who always cares. He always understands. "Now the God of all grace, who called you to His eternal glory in Christ Jesus, will personally restore, establish, strengthen, and support you after you have suffered a little" (1 Peter 5:10). In this world suffering will affect us. The people of this world will fail and hurt us, even (and often especially) those closest to us. The Lord is not like them; He is perfect. He will build you up from your grief. However, in order for His work to be completed in you, you have to submit to Him. God calls us to "be kind and compassionate to one another, forgiving one another, just as God also forgave you in Christ" (Ephesians 4:32). If we remember the tremendous gift we've been given in Christ, it is easier to forgive others around us. Remember, they are only human and will fail. Love them through your forgiveness. They may not acknowledge or accept your forgiveness, but in your actions you imitate Christ who will lift you up because of it. No hurt is so deep that Christ and His love cannot heal it. By His example, we can learn to forgive others. Think of the wounds we caused Him. If He can forgive us, how much more can we forgive the hurts others cause us? "Love your enemies, do what is good, and lend, expecting nothing in return. Then your reward will be great, and you will be sons of the Most High. For He is gracious to the ungrateful and evil" (Luke 6:35).

Kristin Goehl: 18, Princeton, MA
Bethlehem Bible Church, West Boylston, MA; Princeton University, Princeton, MA

# Enough

"Know the Messiah's love that surpasses knowledge, so you may be filled with all the fullness of God." —Ephesians 3:19

Is God enough for you? Think about your answer for a moment. You're saying, "Of course He is." But is that really what you believe? Look at how you're living your life right now. Are you stressed out about something? What are your goals for the future? I'm not saying that it's bad to have goals or to make plans, but look at your motivations. In Philippians 3:7 Paul writes, "But everything that was a gain to me, I have considered to be a loss because of Christ." Our ambitions, our plans, they all pale in comparison to Christ's gift of salvation. We all recognize that we are weak as humans, which is part of the reason we strive so earnestly for things that will make our lives better. However, we should rejoice in our weakness, because Christ works through weak people (2 Corinthians 12:9)! I understand how difficult this is. Our human nature drives us to try to find things or people to replace God. But none of these will ever fill you completely or provide the happiness you think they will. There will always be some discontentment there, which can only be resolved by God. God is the one person in your life who will be constantly faithful, who always understands. A boyfriend won't meet your expectations. You may be rejected by your first-choice college. Your friend may take the job you wanted. If you focus on this world, you will be disappointed. "Happy are the people who know the joyful shout; Yahweh, they walk in the light of Your presence. They rejoice in Your name all day long, and they are exalted by Your righteousness" (Psalm 89:15–16). We can find joy and fulfillment in Christ alone. The things of the world should no longer be our concern and focus. The Lord is enough!

Kristin Goehl: 18, Princeton, MA
Bethlehem Bible Church, West Boylston, MA; Princeton University, Princeton, MA

# Stand Up

> "Without guidance, people fall, but with many counselors there is deliverance." —Proverbs 11:14

Do you lead or follow? I'm one of those people who are in between. I'm perfectly fine being the leader, and I'm good at being a follower. God made us so unique that He gave us the will to be leaders and/or followers. There are people who can lead a nation with their eyes closed, while others sit back and wait for someone to take charge. Both are OK. We need to be sure that we are proving to others that we are standing up for what is right—the ways of Christ. We can't be led by evil, and we cannot lead others into evil. We, as believers in Christ, need to make sure that we are of one nation. We need to be the leaders who can lead the right way. And if you're a follower, be sure that you are following the right people for the right reasons. Temptations are great, so stand firm and walk away from them. We need to be stronger, and to help us be stronger we need to have accountability. And that can come from having strong faithful leaders.

*Nellie Otoupalik*: 17, Spokane, WA
Airway Heights Baptist Church, Airway Heights, WA; Homeschooled/Co-op and Spokane Virtual Learning, Spokane, WA

# How Do I Not Judge?

## "Do not judge, so that you won't be judged." —Matthew 7:1

Many times I find myself listening to people talk about their lives and I catch myself thinking about how much they need to get right with God. When I think like this, I'm focusing on how much worse their sin is than mine. Even if each sin were categorized by how bad it is, no one would be worse off than anyone else. What is the worst sin? Some people say sex before marriage, others say murder, and the list goes on. My take is that breaking the most important command of God is the worst sin. What is that command? "Love the Lord your God with all your heart, with all your soul, with all your mind, and with all your strength" (Mark 12:30). Haven't we all broken this command; are we not breaking it most of the time? How then can we judge others for their faults when we are just as guilty as they are? I often forget this truth and find myself judging people I know because of what they have done compared with what I have. The problem with the comparison of sins is that we can always find someone we think is worse off than we are. We even lie to make ourselves look better. Instead of condemning people, we should pray that God will give us His love for them. When we judge people, we're not loving them as Christ would. Jesus died for them. The Bible says, "There is no one righteous, not even one" (Romans 3:10). That would set limits on God's power. Do you struggle with judgment? Ask God to give you His love for the lost world that He has called you to be His witness to. Pray for the eyes of Christ to make you aware of those around you who need to know Him.

Nellie Otoupalik: 17, Spokane, WA
Airway Heights Baptist Church, Airway Heights, WA; Homeschooled/Co-op and Spokane Virtual Learning, Spokane, WA

# David's Anointing

"But Saul replied, 'You can't go fight this Philistine. You're just a youth, and he's been a warrior since he was young.'" —1 Samuel 17:33

First Samuel 17 tells the story of David and Goliath, a well-known, iconic story to anyone who knows a bit of the Bible. But instead of telling the story most of us know, I want to tell a little of the back story. First Samuel 16 tells the story of Samuel anointing David as king. From the beginning of David's life, he was the runt of the family, the smallest of his brothers, and the least likely to be a king. But God chose David because of his heart, not his height. "Man does not see what the LORD sees, for man sees what is visible, but the LORD sees the heart" (1 Samuel 16:7). This is what the Lord said to Samuel when he questioned which brother to anoint. But this is also what the Lord says to us. Not only does this tell us not to be worried about how we look on the outside, but it also says that the outside is all we see, and that's not enough to truly know a person. This passage also tells us that the smallest of people can make the biggest difference. David was no big deal; just a kid, a little shepherd boy. But God saw his heart and knew he was just the man for the job. So what does David's story have to do with us? Well, I'll tell you. Everything. We are young and can often feel incapable of changing anything. But the example set for us by David's and Samuel's trust in the Lord can inspire us to believe that, through Christ, we can truly do anything. "I am able to do all things through Him who strengthens me" (Philippians 4:13).

Sarah LaCognata: 14, Belleview, FL
Church @ The Springs, Ocala, FL; Homeschooled

# God Has a Plan

"You planned evil against me; God planned it for good to bring about the present result—the survival of many people." —Genesis 50:20

Ever felt the bad things in your life make no sense? Ever feel like it was never a part of God's plan for you to go through those things? As a younger girl, I went through a lot of things that most people shouldn't and haven't gone through. I had a pretty rough past. My biological parents neglected me by not providing proper care that a child needs. My biological sister's dad abused me. My actual biological dad would smoke drugs right in front of me. I could say that God had me experience those things because I was a bad child, but that wouldn't be true. God had me go through those life experiences because He wanted me to take them and help those who are going through similar situations and help them find Jesus. I can use my past to further God's kingdom. I can use all those things that happened to me, things that no child should have to go through, to bring someone else to Christ. The verse above tells us that we go through bad things because God has a purpose for them—for good! God will not give you something you cannot use as a testimony. The next time you are going through something difficult, just remember that God is actually blessing you. He's going to want you to use your struggles to help someone else in need. God is the most loving person in the universe, and He would not let trouble pass your way if it wasn't for a better purpose.

Nellie Otoupalik: 17, Spokane, WA
Airway Heights Baptist Church, Airway Heights, WA; Homeschooled/Co-op and Spokane Virtual Learning, Spokane, WA

# Biographies

**Hannah Abernathie:** 15, Tulsa, OK; Evergreen Baptist Church, Bixby, OK; Homeschooled and Cornerstone Tutorial Center, Tulsa, OK; Parents: Mike/Angi Abernathie; two brothers (one deceased); likes to read, doodle with Sharpies and markers, enjoys writing stories; absolutely loves to cook and bake; on the yearbook staff at Cornerstone Tutorial Center; active in youth group; wants to be a chef and hopes to own restaurant or bakery, maybe both; favorite verse is Psalm 16:5–6.

**Hannah Arrington:** 15, Borger, TX; First Baptist Church and Texas Virtual Academy, Borger, TX; Parents: Pastor Joel/Ronnie Arrington; two brothers and a sister; active in youth group and Sunday school; occasionally helps in the nursery or Children's Worship; serves on short-term missions; has a passion for writing; likes to draw, play video games, play piano, watch movies, and goof around with siblings; hopes to pursue a career in journalism after college, possibly writing for a magazine; favorite verse is Joshua 24:15.

**Isabella Bako:** 14, Anchorage, AK; First Baptist Church, Anchorage, AK; Homeschooled; Parents: Ed/Ruth Bako; one sibling; active in Acteens. Wants to complete school and follow where God leads; favorite verse is John 14:1.

**Reagan Bell:** 17, Tuscaloosa, AL; Valley View Baptist Church and Hillcrest High School, Tuscaloosa, AL; Parents: Jimmy/Cathy Bell; likes to travel, bake, twirl baton, shop, serve on short-term mission teams and Royal Family Kids Camp/Club; wants to pursue degrees in Spanish and psychology, intending to work with abused children with continued involvement in mission trips; favorite verse is Ephesians 3:16–19.

**Beraiah Benavides:** 14, Sevierville, TN; Pathways Baptist Church, Sevierville, TN; The King's Academy, Seymour, TN; Parents: Moses/Zinamong Benavides; one brother; likes to sing; enjoys "LARP" (Live Action Role Playing); plays Upward basketball; currently in a musical; wants to be many things: a lawyer, basketball player, a family physician, and a missionary like her dad; favorite verse is Revelation 22:13.

**Blair Bodnarchuk:** 17, Raleigh, NC; Providence Baptist Church and Wakefield High School, Raleigh, NC; Tim/Robin Bodnarchuk; two older brothers and one older sister; enjoys spending time with family, loves photography, drawing, reading, and volunteers for numerous activities; desires to be a graphic designer; favorite verse is Lamentations 3:22.

**Reagan MiCole Brashears**: 17, New Orleans, LA; Franklin Avenue Baptist Church and Eleanor McMain Secondary School, New Orleans, LA; Parents: Ricky/Sybil Brashears; two older brothers; enjoys reading, texting, cooking, helping others, and researching information; former member of the flag team; currently a part of the robotics team and culture club; a student leader at church; looking forward to miming; plans to go to college to become a successful dermatologist and writer; favorite verse is 1 Timothy 4:12.

**Sarah Ashley Bryant**: 15, Springdale, AR; Cross Church and Shiloh Christian School, Springdale, AR; Parents: Pastor Heath/Shelli Bryant; four siblings; describes her life as crazy; a drum major in school band; wants to be an author, but would also like to continue her musical studies; favorite verse is Philippians 4:6.

**Rebekah Byrd**: 16, Tulsa, OK; Evergreen Baptist Church, Bixby, OK; Homeschooled; Parents: Rick/Kathleen Byrd; three brothers; likes to read, dance, volunteer at a deaf day care and hang out with friends; wants to major in graphic design and minor in deaf education; plans to be a foreign missionary; favorite verse is Matthew 11:28–29.

**Kaylin Calvert**: 18, Medical Lake, WA; Airway Heights Baptist Church, Airway Heights, WA; Homeschooled; Parents: Shannon/Lanette Calvert; two brothers, one sister-in-law; loves reading, gaming, writing, and playing piano; participates in AWANA as a student and a helper; wants to have a career as an editor; favorite verse is Psalm 121.

**Jessie Cardin**: 16, Sutton, MA; Bethlehem Bible Church, West Boylston, MA; Sutton Memorial High School, Sutton, MA; Parents: Brian/Joanie Cardin; two brothers and one sister; ran as a member of the varsity cross-country and outdoor track teams; runs 5K for cross-country, two-mile, and other distance events for track; voted "Runner of the Year" by the local newspaper; interested in archery, art, creative writing, singing, playing the piano, and quoting famous movie lines; involved in drama club; favorite verse is 1 Corinthians 16:13.

**Brianna Carter**: 19, Sharon, SC; Hillcrest Baptist Church and York Technical, York, SC; graduate of York Comprehensive High School, York, SC; Parent: Tammy Carter; currently working on a Bachelor's Degree in neonatal nursing; loves spending time with family, hanging with friends, and being an active witness for the Lord; plans to be God's hands and feet now and in the future to not only save lives, but also to spread the gospel of Jesus Christ; favorite verse is Philippians 4:13.

**Alaina Clem**: 14, Albany, GA; Sherwood Baptist Church and Sherwood Christian Academy, Albany, GA; Parents: Ted/Stacey Clem; one brother and one sister; likes to play sports, travel, read, and spend time with friends and family; participates in volleyball, soccer, National Honor Society, Student Council, and GPS (a student-led service ministry at school); VP of Freshman Class; actively involved in youth group, Sunday school, Relevate student worship team, prayer meetings, Bible studies, and Drey Line ministry to the homeless; plans for college and to do what God calls her to do; favorite verse is Philippians 3:7–8.

**Annalise Clem:** 17, Albany, GA; Sherwood Baptist Church and Sherwood Christian Academy, Albany, GA; Parents: Ted/Stacey Clem; one brother and one sister; loves to read, do mission work, play volleyball, and spend time with family; participates in musical theatre, Student Council, National Honor Society, and GPS student-led ministry at school; also participates in youth group, Sunday school, student leadership team, Relevate student worship team, and Drey Line ministry to homeless; been on trips to inner-city Baltimore and twice to Uganda; plans on a bachelor's degree in nursing and to obey God in His calling; favorite verse is Acts 20:24.

**Layne Coleman:** 14, Little Rock, AR; The Church at Rock Creek and Little Rock Christian Academy, Little Rock, AR; Parents: Karen Whatley, Robert Coleman, and Trey Whatley; two older stepsisters and one younger half-brother; loves to run, read, write, sing, laugh, travel, and to be creative; participates in school's cross-country and track team, is involved in youth group, and volunteers in the children's ministry; plans to become a family psychologist; favorite verse is 2 Corinthians 4:16–18.

**Hannah Cooksey:** 16, McMinnville, OR; Valley Baptist Church, McMinnville, OR; Homeschooled; Parents: Pastor Ronny/Kathy Cooksey; seven siblings; would like to homeschool her own children someday; desires to be IMB missionary once married; open to whatever God has for her life; plays violin in instrumental ensemble; likes to play games; plays piano for nursing home ministry; likes to cook, read, play violin and piano, and spend time with family; favorite verse is Psalm 27:1.

**Hailey Culberson:** 17, Tulsa, OK; Evergreen Baptist Church, Bixby, OK; Homeschooled; Parents: Nathan/Tracy Culberson; siblings: two sisters, one brother; likes to play basketball, tennis, volunteer at Happy Hands (deaf day care), and read; member of the yearbook club; wants to be a nationally certified deaf interpreter; favorite verse is Proverbs 3:3–6.

**Victoria Davidson:** 17, Newton, GA; Sherwood Baptist Church and Sherwood Christian Academy, Albany, GA; Parents: Wesley/Cindy Davidson; two siblings; enjoys traveling, working with children, laughing and making others laugh, and anything that is sports related; plays varsity basketball and soccer; helps with middle school girls' discipling; involved in youth group,

Sunday school, and volunteers in children's programs; plans to get her degree in medicine and serve in medical missions; favorite verse is Galatians 6:9.

**Clara Davis:** 14, Little Rock, AR; The Church at Rock Creek and LISA Academy, Little Rock, AR; Parents: Mark/Lissa Davis; an older sister and an older brother; has a passion for drawing; would love to work in animation for Disney, Pixar, or DreamWorks; favorite verse is Psalm 46:10.

**Deanna N. Davis:** 13, Fairchild Air Force Base, WA; Airway Heights Baptist Church, Airway Heights, WA; Medical Lake Middle School, Medical Lake, WA; Parents: Ron/Jenni Davis; one brother and two sisters; loves to read and write; plays flute in band and jazz band; member of the choir and Science reporters; serves as helper to Cubbies and helps with children's church; on youth praise team that leads worship every Thursday; plans to be a professional fashion designer and a well-known author; favorite verses are 1 John 4:10 and Exodus 15:11.

**Taylor Dillon:** 17, Stafford, VA; Grace Life Community Church, Bristow, VA; Emmanuel Christian High School, Manassas, VA; Parents: Russell/Genoa Dillon: two older sisters; participates in after-school sports; serves in VBS; loves to read, write, and to hang out with friends; plans to attend NOVA for two years then transfer to UVA; wants to become a radiology technician and go wherever God leads; favorite verse is Philippians 4:13.

**Sara E. DuBois:** 16, St. Peters, MO; First Baptist Church of St. Charles, St. Charles, MO; Fort Zumwalt East High School, St. Peters, MO; Parents: Paul/Rebecca DuBois; four siblings; enjoys physical activities such as rock climbing, lacrosse, football, and tennis; likes to be with friends and family, to help people with their problems, to write (sometimes lyrics), and loves music and singing; member of National Honor Society and Hazelwood West Varsity Lacrosse team; considering being a personal trainer, but perhaps a missionary; favorite verse is Ephesians 2:8–9.

**Dianah Edwards:** 16, West Monroe, LA; First West Monroe Baptist Church and Northeast Baptist School, West Monroe, LA; adopted at age four; Parents: Bob/Donna Edwards; served on mission trips and worked in Kids Camps; likes to cheer, dance, paint, sing, and run track; a cheerleader, in a science club at school, plays soccer; wants to do what God calls her to do after high school; favorite verse is John 15:15.

**Allison Fisher:** 14, Raleigh, NC; Providence Baptist Church and Leesville Road High School, Raleigh, NC; Parents: Christopher/Cynthia Fisher-Hernandez; four brothers, two sisters; loves to sing, dance, and play the guitar; ninth grade student council VP, in Key Club, runs track, member of Fellowship of Christian Athletes and school chorus; plans to attend college; interested in singing, teaching chorus, or being a worship leader; favorite verse is Philippians 4:13.

*Abby Fortner:* 15, Gatlinburg, TN; First Baptist Church and Gatlinburg-Pittman High School, Gatlinburg, TN; Parents: Bryon/Lori Fortner; one brother; member of high school soccer and track teams; plays piano; after graduation from college would like to serve in missions; favorite verse is Romans 12:2.

*Erin France:* 14, Anchorage, AK; First Baptist Church and Eagle River High School, Anchorage, AK; Parents: Derek/Amanda France; two sisters; enjoys reading, writing, dancing, soccer, and spending time with family and friends; participates in productions at school; active in youth group and hopes to be playing her saxophone in the praise band soon; desires to be an interior designer while still writing, directing, and dancing; favorite verse is Psalm 62:8.

*Lilian Gatheca:* 16, Nanyuki, Kenya (exchange student living in Albany, GA); Sherwood Baptist Church and Sherwood Christian Academy, Albany, GA; American parents: Mark/Debbie Glow; three siblings in Africa; loves to sing, go to school, read, and go to church; member of Growing in Christ, Positive Leadership, and Service (GPS); active in youth group and Relevate student worship team; desires to be a surgeon in Africa to help people from poor families, the way people helped her; wants to be a positive influence and share the love of Christ with those who don't know Him; favorite verse is Psalm 84:10.

*Kristin Goehl:* 18, Princeton, MA; Bethlehem Bible Church, West Boylston, MA; Princeton University, Princeton, MA; Parents: Mark/Melissa Goehl; one brother; enjoys reading, singing, writing, contra dancing, hiking, and playing piccolo in the university band; Princeton Evangelical Fellowship; College Major: Mechanical Engineering/Engineering Management; favorite verse is Isaiah 40:31.

*Taylor Glow:* 17, Albany, GA; Sherwood Baptist Church and Sherwood Christian Academy, Albany, GA; Parents: Mark/Debbie Glow; exchange student lives with family, most recently a girl from Kenya; loves to read, perform in musicals; plays volleyball; on student council, is in positive leadership and service group called GPS (Grooming in Christ) at church; active in youth group and Relevate worship group; would like to travel the world and live in New York City; favorite verse is Psalm 27:1

*Tara Greene:* 16, Fort Belvoir, VA; Guilford Baptist Church, Sterling, VA; Homeschooled; Parents: Christopher/Corrine Greene; six siblings; enjoys piano, writing, ultimate Frisbee, and swimming; would like to perform piano and write after college; favorite verse is Ephesians 4:7.

*Carson Gregors:* 17, Albany, GA; Sherwood Baptist Church and Sherwood Christian Academy, Albany, GA; Parents: Joe/Tammy Gregors; one sister; enjoys reading and rock climbing; serves as tour guide at Flint River Aquarium; varsity cheerleader captain for football and basketball; president of Junior class and on Prom Planning Committee; member National Honor Society; involved in youth group; plans to attend Ellerslie in Colorado, then on to college to be in youth ministry and counseling; favorite verse is Ephesians 4:1–2.

*Leah Harris:* 16, Kodiak, AK; Frontier Southern Baptist Church, Kodiak, AK; Homeschooled; Parents: Rich/Voni Harris, who adopted Leah as an infant; two birth brothers and one birth sister; loves to play and teach violin, make crafts, and watch movies; plans to go into nursing; favorite verse is Isaiah 41:10.

*J'Yanna Janai Jackson:* 15, Slidell, LA; Franklin Avenue Baptist Church and Salmen High School, New Orleans, LA; Parents: Raymond, Sr./Juanette Allen Jackson; three brothers; likes to read, listen to music, dance, cheer, and just hang out with friends; varsity cheerleader; student leader at church and participates in mentoring ministry; plans to attend four-year university and medical school to become an oncologist; favorite verse is 1 Timothy 4:12.

*Sarah King:* 18, Gainesville; VA; Emmanuel Baptist Church and Emmanuel Christian School, Manassas, VA; Parents: Wendell/Debbie King; four siblings; likes to read, write, swim, and play basketball, and participate in church plays; active in girls' Bible study in school; after receiving a BA in journalism or English wants to be an editor for a major publishing company; favorite verse is Isaiah 41:10.

*Faith Kurtz:* 13, Holden, MA; Bethlehem Bible Church and Bethlehem Bible Church Homeschooled Co-op, West Boylston, MA; Parents: Jack/Denise Kurtz; four siblings; enjoys hanging out with friends, swimming, jumping on the trampoline, listening to music, playing piano, board and card games, video games, movies, drawing, and reading (especially manga); active in Sunday school, AWANA; favorite verse is Matthew 10:16.

*Holly Kurtz:* 16, Holden, MA; Bethlehem Bible Church and Bethlehem Bible Church Homeschooled Co-op, West Boylston, MA; Parents: Jack/Denise Kurtz; four siblings; loves to draw and cook; enjoys sports like rock climbing and paintball; loves video games, movies and animes; active in youth group and helps at AWANA; upon graduation plans to go into cake decorating or something within the culinary arts, or be a designer artist for video games; favorite verse is Psalm 31:1–18.

*Gabrielle LaCognata*: 19, Belleview, FL; Church @ The Springs; College of Central Florida, Ocala, FL; Parents: Joe/Kim LaCognata; four siblings; enjoys writing, reading Jane Austen novels, and crafting; currently serving in Source (the youth group of the Springs) and in Springsville (the elementary ministry); College Major: Early Childhood Education; after graduation plans to become a kindergarten teacher and actively serve in her local church, while serving on short-term missions; favorite verse is 1 Corinthians 15:58.

*Sarah LaCognata*: 14, Belleview, FL; Church @ The Springs, Ocala, FL; Homeschooled; Parents: Joe/Kim LaCognata; four siblings; enjoys reading any book possible—from sci-fi to fantasy to poetry, photography, and baking; volunteers in church preschool ministry; favorite verse is Joshua 1:9.

*Emily Matlock*: 15, Springdale, AR; Cross Church Springdale Campus and Shiloh Christian School, Springdale, AR; Parents: Larry/Donna Matlock; three older siblings; enjoys reading, sleeping, watching anime; would like to attend a local college and study music, Japanese, and some form of graphic design or computer engineering; favorite verse is Revelation 21:3–4.

*Imani McBean*: 14, Leesburg, GA; Mt. Zion Baptist Church and Sherwood Christian Academy, Albany, GA; Parent: Sandra Satchell; one sibling; likes to bake, draw, play guitar, and photography; member of Student Council, ninth grade chaplain, active in GPS; plays basketball, volleyball, soccer; wants to study theatrical production at NYC performing arts school; favorite verse is Joshua 1:9.

*Mallory McClearn*: 16, Leesburg, GA; Sherwood Baptist Church and Sherwood Christian Academy, Albany, GA; Parents: J. K./Ashley McClearn; loves Jesus, music, food, the sun, the beach, and the city; plays guitar, some piano, and sings; loves to play volleyball; favorite verse is Hebrews 12:1–2.

*Hannah McGee*: 15, Springdale, AR; Cross Church Springdale Campus, Northwest, AR; Shiloh Christian School, Springdale, AR; Parents: David/Debbie McGee; plays trumpet in marching band; actively involved in serving her church; plans to become a teacher to elementary students; favorite verse is Revelation 3:8.

*Megan Medford*: 14, Bryant, AR; The Church at Rock Creek and Bryant High School, Little Rock, AR; Parents: Grant/Jennifer Medford; one sister; avid softball player, loves to read and draw; teaches four-year-old Sunday school and volunteers for numerous activities; plays softball at school, and active in Christian club, Youth Alive; desires to be a fashion designer or an architect; favorite verse is Proverbs 3:5.

**Amy Meeks:** 16, Tulsa, OK; Evergreen Baptist Church, Bixby, OK; Mingo Valley Christian School, Tulsa, OK; Parents: Scott/Martha Meeks; four sibling; likes to swim, run, hang out with friends, and play the flute/listen to music; part of the Key Club and National Honor Society; plans to be either a nurse practitioner or a physician's assistant; favorite verse is Romans 8:16–17.

**Christa Morgan:** 17, Alabaster, AL; Westwood Baptist Church and Thompson High School, Alabaster, AL; Parents: Allan/Janet Morgan; active in youth group, enjoys helping with the middle school events such as D-Now and core groups as a mentor to middle school girls; plays clarinet in the band; leads devotions before every football game; enjoys spending time with family and friends and just loving life; plans to attend Jefferson State Community College, majoring in nursing and to work in the ER; favorite verse is Acts 20:24.

**Nellie Otoupalik:** 17, Spokane, WA; Airway Heights Baptist Church, Airway Heights, WA; Homeschooled/Co-op and Spokane Virtual Learning, Spokane, WA; Adopted Parents: Sean/Kristen Otoupalik; with a foster parent with foster siblings; loves to read, rides her own horse and competes through 4H, swimming; volunteers in AWANA, plays violin for church worship team; wants to be a Christian counselor; favorite verse is Genesis 50:20.

**Emily Pitts:** 16, Palm Harbor, FL; Calvary Baptist Church and Calvary Christian High School, Clearwater, FL; Parents: James/Catherine Pitts; one sister and one brother; loves youth group and music; enjoys singing, acting, dancing, playing the guitar, reading, hanging out with friends, and traveling the world; dreams of being a worship leader, a missionary, or an actress on Broadway; favorite verse is Acts 20:24.

**Danielle Quesinberry:** 15, Knoxville, TN; Valley Grove Baptist Church Youth Group, Knoxville, TN; The Kings Academy, Seymour, TN; Parents: Robin/Lisa Quesinberry; one sister and one brother; member of Phoenix Rising Volleyball Club; enjoys Live Action Role Playing; wants to be a long-term missionary; favorite verse is Romans 6:4.

**Michaela Reed:** 15, Albany, GA; Institutional First Baptist Church and Sherwood Christian Academy, Albany, GA; Parents: Dr. William/Shelia Reed; likes to read and draw; enjoys writing stories and playing piano; in young adult choir, National Honor Society; participates in musical theater; wants to study veterinary medicine or astronomy; favorite verse is Matthew 25:14–30.

**Kelsey Roberts:** 18, Albany, GA; Sherwood Baptist Church and Sherwood Christian Academy, Albany, GA; Parents: Chuck Roberts/Cynthia Turner; enjoys dancing, singing, acting, and writing—anything that stimulates creativity; participates in musical theater, show choir, a student-led ministry called GPS (acronym for Growing in Christ, Positive Leadership, and

Service); served in praise youth choir and dance team; plans to attend college in Georgia to become a pharmacist, get married, start a family, and strive to follow Christ; favorite verse is 2 Corinthians 4:7–10.

**Laura Roggenbaum:** 17, Palm Harbor, FL; Calvary Baptist Church and Calvary Christian High School, Clearwater, FL; Parents: Doug/Jayanne Roggenbaum; one brother; likes to sing, play piano, spend time with friends, and read; studying voice, participates in student government, the praise team, track, the play, drama club, culinary arts club, and film society at school; active in youth group and community groups; wants to do something in either music or psychology; favorite verse is Philippians 1:21.

**Tyra Ruisinger:** 17, Raymore, MO; Summit Woods Baptist Church, Lees Summit, MO; Homeschooled; Parents: Rick/Heather Ruisinger; two younger brothers; loves teaching three-year-old Sunday school class and working in the children's ministry; enjoys Bible quizzing, playing the piano and harp, and running; favorite verse is Psalm 121:7–8.

**Anna Sapone:** 15, Medical Lake, WA; Airway Heights Baptist Church, Airway Heights, WA; Medical Lake High School, Medical Lake, WA; Parents: Rick/Sheri Sapone; one older sister; loves to travel, play sports through school and on leagues; plays fall soccer, winter basketball, spring tennis, summer basketball, and indoor soccer; active in youth group, would like to be a doctor serving God overseas; favorite verse is Proverbs 17:22.

**Hannah Savage:** 16, Dodge City, KS; First Southern Baptist Church and Dodge City High School, Dodge City, KS; Parents: Pastor Greg/Heidi Savage; two brothers and a sister-in-law; participates in softball, student council, Tournament of Champions Committee, and Fellowship of Christian Athletes; active in youth group, serves in the nursery, various mission trips; worked in an inner-city youth center in Des Moines, IA; on steering committee for a state girls weekend called S.H.I.N.E; plans to attend Oklahoma Baptist University to become a Pediatric Nurse Practitioner and serve in an orphanage in Africa and in medical missions; favorite verse is John 3:30.

**Emily Sherrod:** 17, Mobile, AL; Christ Fellowship Baptist Church and Stanford University Online High School, Mobile, AL; Parents: John/Julie Anna Sherrod; four siblings; hopes to study biology after graduating from high school; favorite verse is Romans 8:38–39.

**Breanna Smith:** 17, Sharon, SC; Hillcrest Baptist Church and York Comprehensive High School, York, SC; Parents: Travis/Lisa Smith; one sister; loves anything with music or art; member of marching band, brass captain; member of HOSA; plans to go to York Technical College to become a nurse; favorite verse is Psalm 12:1–2.

*Haley Smith*: 16, Tarpon Springs, FL; Calvary Baptist Church and Calvary Christian High School, Tarpon Springs, FL; Parents: Steve/Jean Smith; two siblings; active in church's youth group and programs; enjoys reading, cooking, baking, hanging out with friends and family, going to the beach, and fishing; member NHS and involved in community service in the area; participates in cheerleading, track and field, and is involved in school plays; coleads a Bible study and is a mentor; favorite verse is Psalm 62:5–8.

*Callie Spencer*: 14, Broken Arrow, OK; Evergreen Baptist Church, Bixby, OK; South Intermediate High School, Broken Arrow, OK; Parents: Darren/Lorna Spencer; one sibling; likes to write, sing, play flute, games, Internet, music; wants to be a vet, journalist, or TV anchor; favorite verse is Isaiah 41:13.

*Bronte Stallings*: 15, Mt. Pleasant, SC; Citadel Square Baptist Church, Charleston, SC; Wando High School, Mt. Pleasant, SC; Parents: Jody/Stephanie Stallings; one brother; loves to read, especially historical fiction books about the monarchy of medieval England, and to knit; plays cello in school orchestra; plans to attend college and earn a degree in education to teach high school history; favorite verse is John 16:33.

*Angela Stanley*: 17, Woodbridge, VA; Dale City Baptist Church, Woodbridge, VA; Emmanuel Christian School, Manassas, VA; Parents: Gary/Gena Stanley; three siblings; likes to spend time with family, read, take long car rides, and do cheerleading; member of National Honor Society and a main star in the upcoming spring play; involved with youth group and helps with children's class as needed; wants to be either a social worker or an interior designer; favorite verse is Romans 8:28.

*Brenna R. Strain*: 15, Spokane, WA; Airway Heights Baptist Church, Airway Heights, WA; Medical Lake High School, Medical Lake, WA; Parents: Leroy/Francee Strain; one brother; likes reading, singing, playing basketball, and watching football; sings for church youth worship team; in youth group, Sunday school, and AWANA; desires to study photography in college; favorite verse is Hebrews 13:5.

*McKenzie Sutton*: 17, Waverly Hall, GA; Cornerstone Baptist Church; Ellerslie, GA; Homeschooled; Parents: Ray/Angela Sutton; two sisters; active in youth group; serves on short-term mission trips; helps with sixth-grade girls' Bible study; enjoys dancing, singing, guitar, hanging out with friends; plans to serve at Orphanage Emmanuel in Honduras before college to major in biblical studies and Spanish; favorite verse is Jeremiah 29:13.

**Madison Thomas:** 15, Sevierville, TN; First Baptist Church and Gatlinburg-Pittman High School, Gatlinburg, TN; Parents: Davy/Nina Thomas; one sister; plays competitive and high school soccer; competitive and high school track; plays violin; FBC Gatlinburg short-term mission trip to Washington, DC; desires to be a athletic trainer; favorite verse is Philippians 4:13.

**Makenzie Thomas:** 16, Sevierville, TN; First Baptist Church and Gatlinburg-Pittman High School, Gatlinburg, TN; Parents: Davy/Nina Thomas; one sister; competitive and high school soccer; plays violin; FBC Gatlinburg short-term mission trip to Washington, DC; desires to be a trauma physician; favorite verse is Psalm 55:16–17.

**Hannah Thompson:** 15, Leesburg, GA; Sherwood Baptist Church and Sherwood Christian Academy, Albany, GA; Parents: Michael/Cheryl Thompson; two siblings; loves to read, write, hang out with friends, play soccer, and travel; plays volleyball and is the goalkeeper for school's varsity team; while in college, desires to serve on several short-term mission trips to Africa, become a biblical counselor or work for a mission ministry; favorite verse is Acts 1:8.

**Micki Werner:** 16, Gatlinburg, TN; First Baptist Church and Gatlinburg-Pittman High School, Gatlinburg, TN; Parents: Mike/Cindy Werner; four sisters and two brothers; enjoys hanging out with friends; plays high school soccer, basketball, and track; active in youth group; desires to be a dermatologist; favorite verse is Matthew 6:34.

**Hanna Wilbourn:** 14, Seymour, TN; First Baptist Church and The Kings Academy, Seymour, TN; Parents: Rick/Polly Wilbourn; one brother; TKA Basketball; likes to read and spend time with family; wants to be a panda scientist at Wolong Society; favorite verse is Ecclesiastes 12:13–14.

**Hannah Zimmerman:** 16, Greencastle, PA; Greencastle Baptist Church and Greencastle-Antrim High School, Greencastle, PA; Parents: Marty/Marcie Zimmerman; two older brothers; likes to draw; spend time with friends and family; plays basketball; in youth group at church, noonday sun; would love to go to college for interior design and create own company; favorite verse is Psalm 37:5.

I pray that the God of our Lord Jesus Christ, the glorious Father, would give you a spirit of wisdom and revelation in the knowledge of Him. I pray that the perception of your mind may be enlightened so you may know what is the hope of His calling, what are the glorious riches of His inheritance among the saints, and what is the immeasurable greatness of His power to us who believe, according to the working of His vast strength. —Ephesians 1:17–19

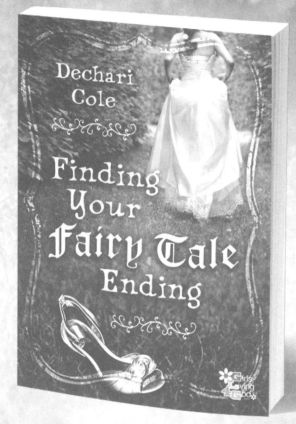